IDW PUBLISHING presents

Written by **Chris Ryall**

KAMPF Art by **Menton³**

MASQUES Art by **Paul McCaffrey**

ZUVEMBIE VS. ROBOTS Art by **Gabriel Hernandez**

Lettering by **Robbie Robbins**

Collection Edits by **Justin Eisinger** and **Mariah Huehner**

Collection Design by **Shawn Lee**

Logo Design and Cover by **Ashley Wood** for 7174 Pty, Ltd.

ZOMBIES VS. ROBOTS created by **Ash and Ryall**

www.**IDWPUBLISHING**.com   ISBN: 978-1-60010-717-7   13 12 11 10   1 2 3 4

Operations: Ted Adams, Chief Executive Officer • Greg Goldstein, Chief Operating Officer • Matthew Ruzicka, CPA, Chief Financial Officer • Alan Payne, VP of Sales • Lorelei Bunjes, Dir. of Digital Services • AnnaMaria White, Marketing & PR Manager • Marci Hubbard, Executive Assistant • Alonzo Simon, Shipping Manager • Angela Loggins, Staff Accountant • Cherrie Go, Assistant Web Designer • Editorial: Chris Ryall, Publisher/Editor-in-Chief • Scott Dunbier, Editor, Special Projects • Andy Schmidt, Senior Editor • Bob Schreck, Senior Editor • Justin Eisinger, Editor • Kris Oprisko, Editor/Foreign Lic. • Denton J. Tipton, Editor • Tom Waltz, Editor • Mariah Huehner, Associate Editor • Carlos Guzman, Editorial Assistant • Design: Robbie Robbins, EVP/Sr. Graphic Artist • Neil Uyetake, Art Director • Chris Mowry, Graphic Artist • Amauri Osorio, Graphic Artist • Gilberto Lazcano, Production Assistant • Shawn Lee, Production Assistant

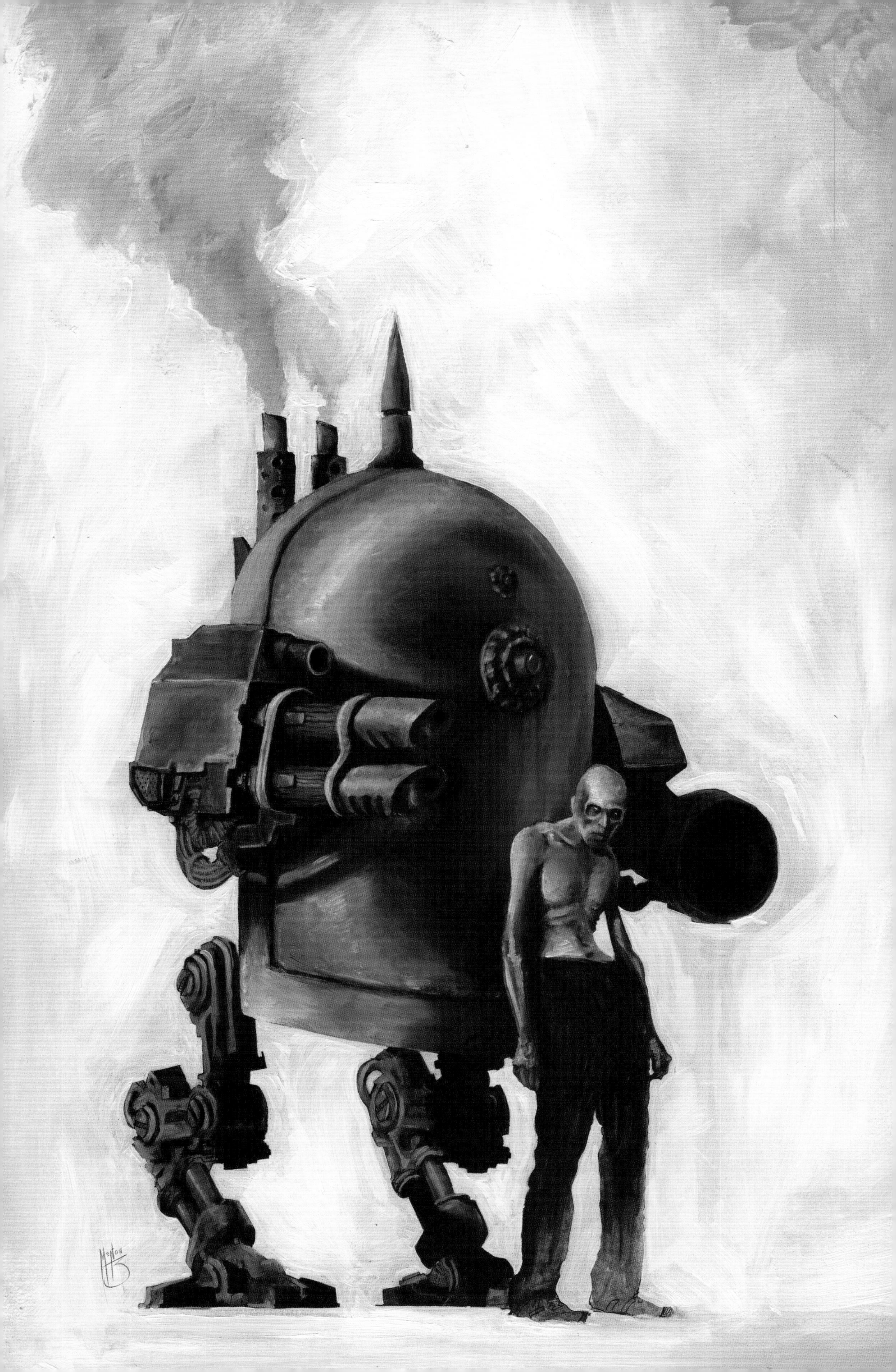

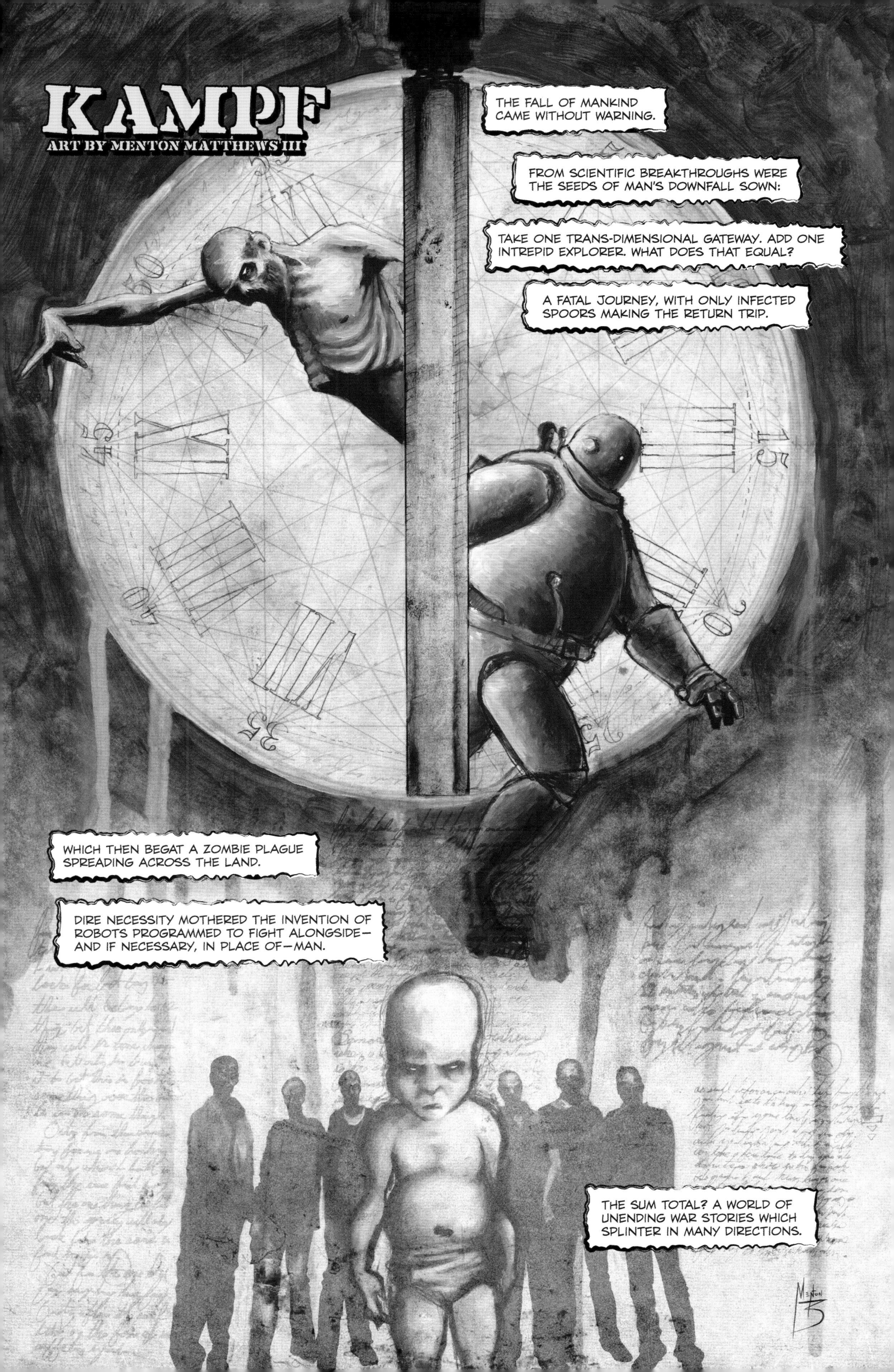
KAMPF
ART BY MENTON MATTHEWS III
THE FALL OF MANKIND CAME WITHOUT WARNING.
FROM SCIENTIFIC BREAKTHROUGHS WERE THE SEEDS OF MAN'S DOWNFALL SOWN:
TAKE ONE TRANS-DIMENSIONAL GATEWAY. ADD ONE INTREPID EXPLORER. WHAT DOES THAT EQUAL?
A FATAL JOURNEY, WITH ONLY INFECTED SPOORS MAKING THE RETURN TRIP.
WHICH THEN BEGAT A ZOMBIE PLAGUE SPREADING ACROSS THE LAND.
DIRE NECESSITY MOTHERED THE INVENTION OF ROBOTS PROGRAMMED TO FIGHT ALONGSIDE— AND IF NECESSARY, IN PLACE OF—MAN.
THE SUM TOTAL? A WORLD OF UNENDING WAR STORIES WHICH SPLINTER IN MANY DIRECTIONS.

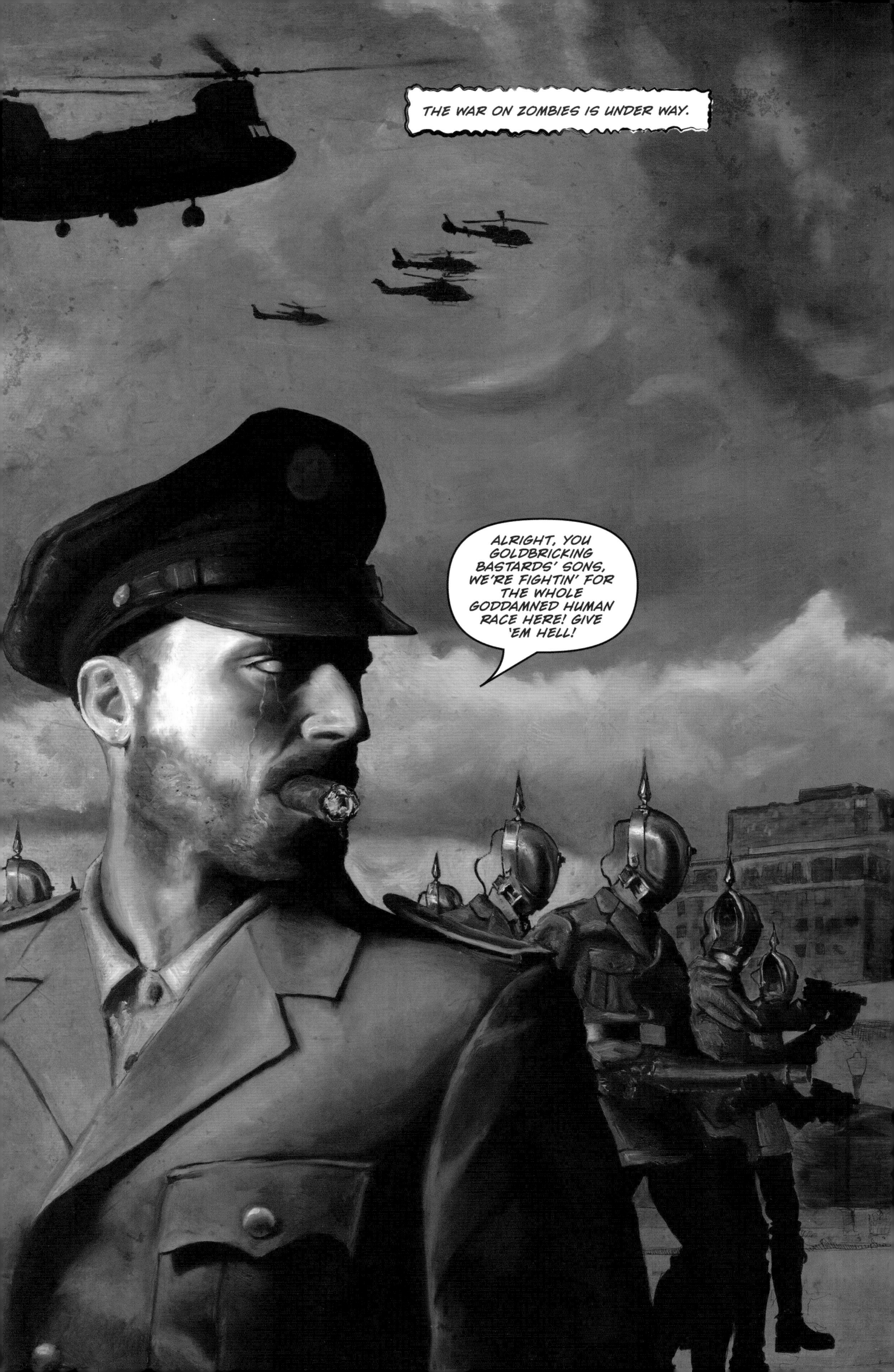
THE WAR ON ZOMBIES IS UNDER WAY.
ALRIGHT, YOU GOLDBRICKING BASTARDS' SONS, WE'RE FIGHTIN' FOR THE WHOLE GODDAMNED HUMAN RACE HERE! GIVE 'EM HELL!

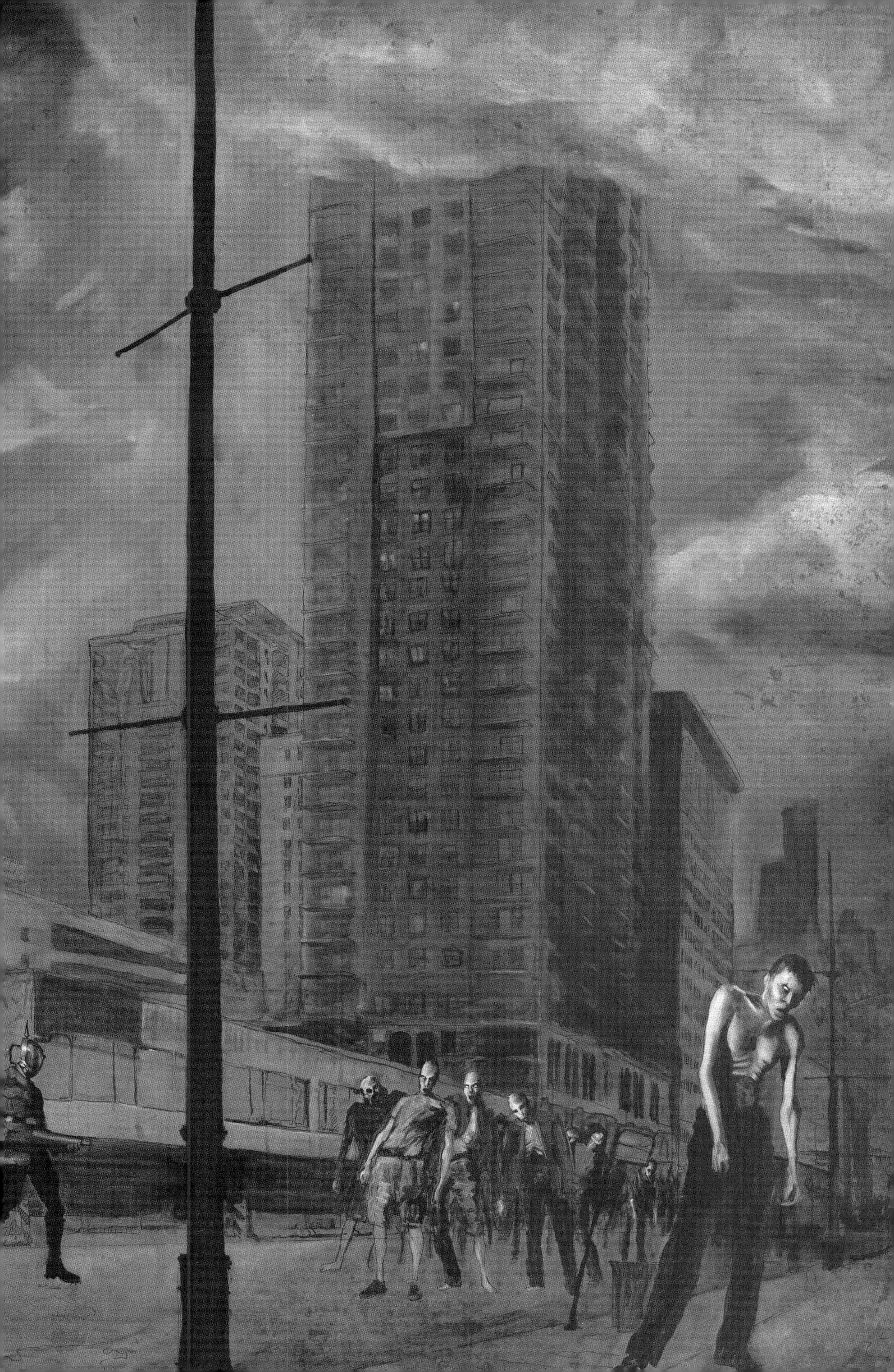

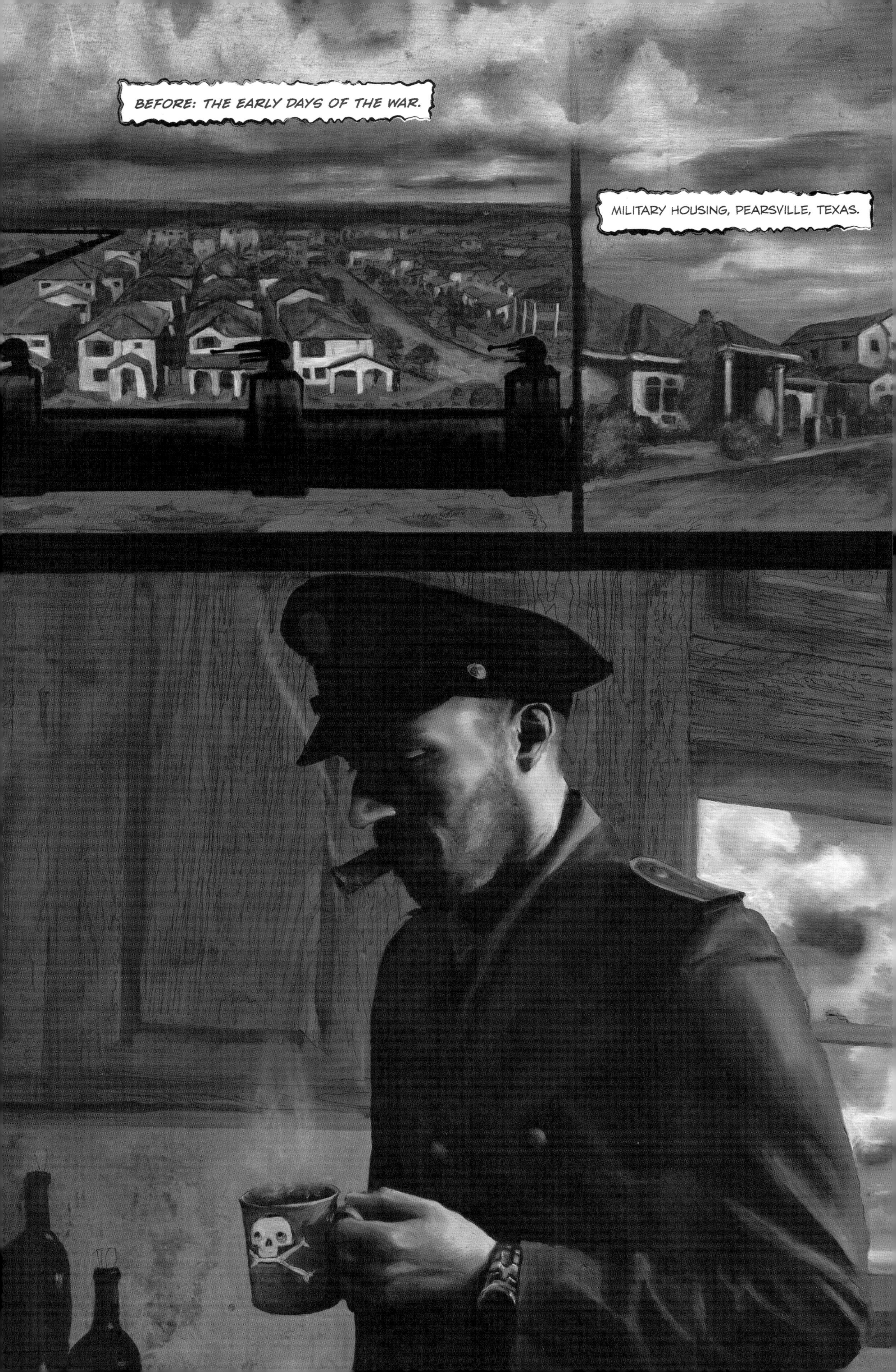
BEFORE: THE EARLY DAYS OF THE WAR.
MILITARY HOUSING, PEARSVILLE, TEXAS.

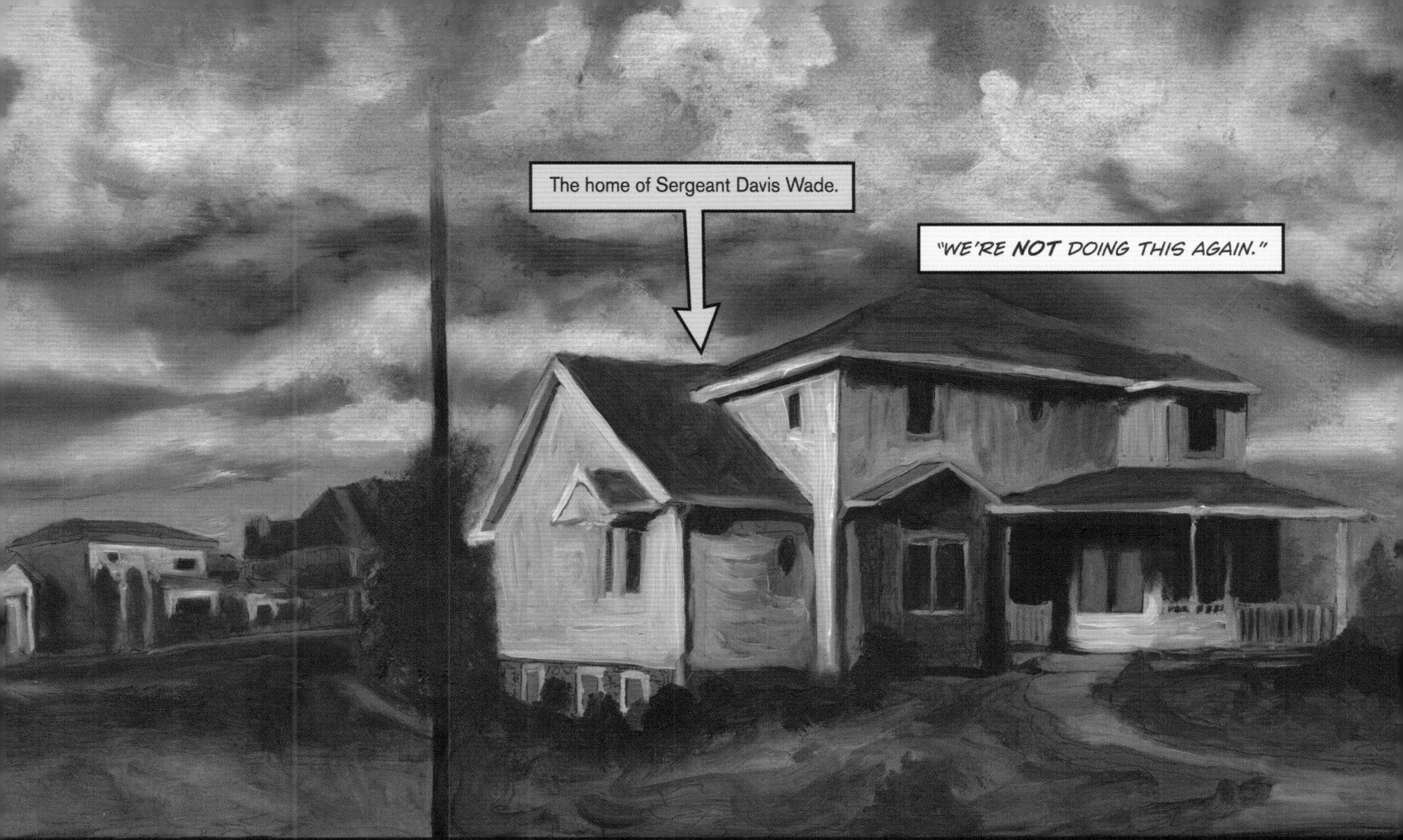
The home of Sergeant Davis Wade.
"WE'RE NOT DOING THIS AGAIN."

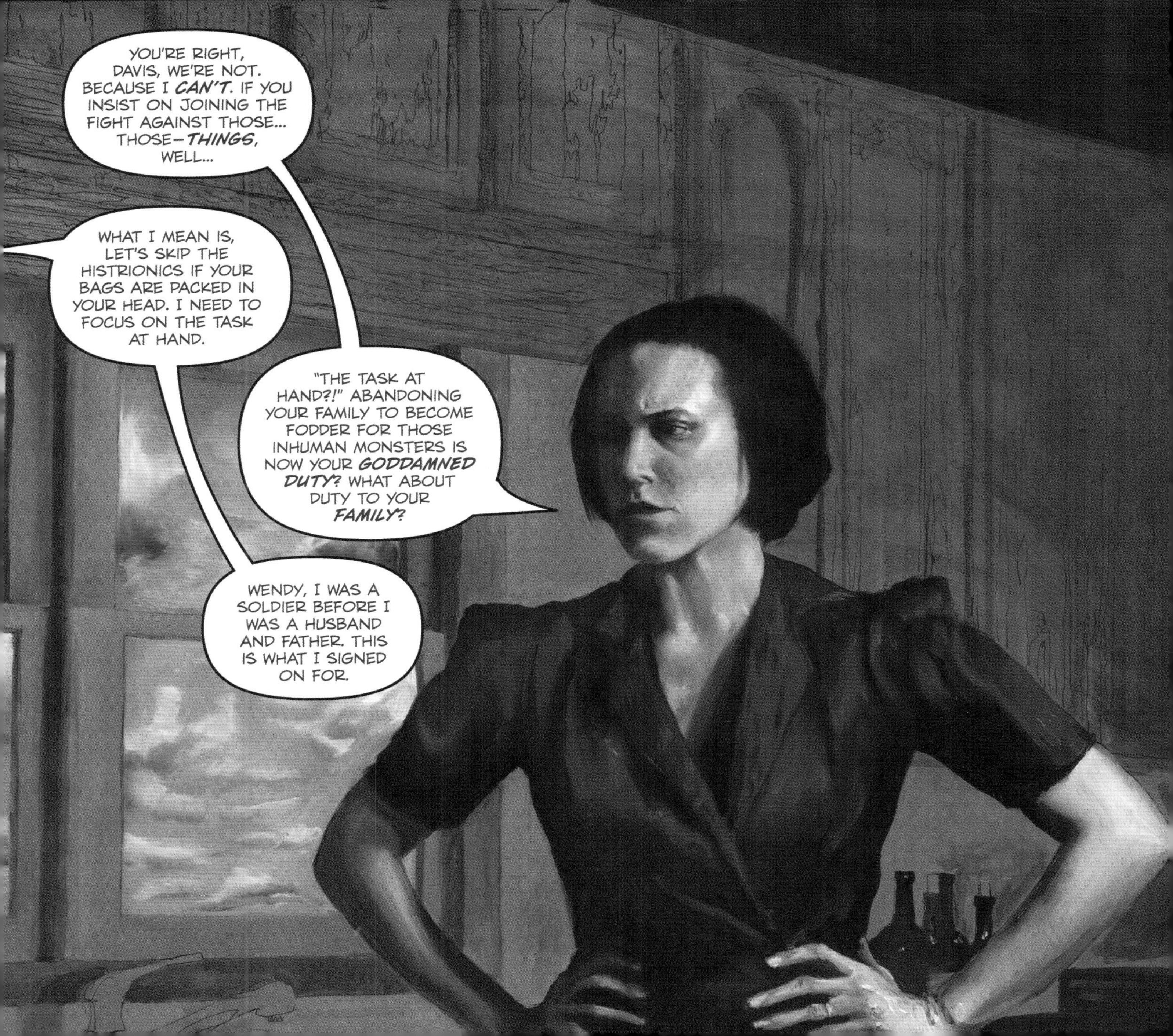
YOU'RE RIGHT, DAVIS, WE'RE NOT. BECAUSE I CAN'T. IF YOU INSIST ON JOINING THE FIGHT AGAINST THOSE... THOSE—THINGS, WELL...
WHAT I MEAN IS, LET'S SKIP THE HISTRIONICS IF YOUR BAGS ARE PACKED IN YOUR HEAD. I NEED TO FOCUS ON THE TASK AT HAND.
"THE TASK AT HAND?!" ABANDONING YOUR FAMILY TO BECOME FODDER FOR THOSE INHUMAN MONSTERS IS NOW YOUR GODDAMNED DUTY? WHAT ABOUT DUTY TO YOUR FAMILY?
WENDY, I WAS A SOLDIER BEFORE I WAS A HUSBAND AND FATHER. THIS IS WHAT I SIGNED ON FOR.

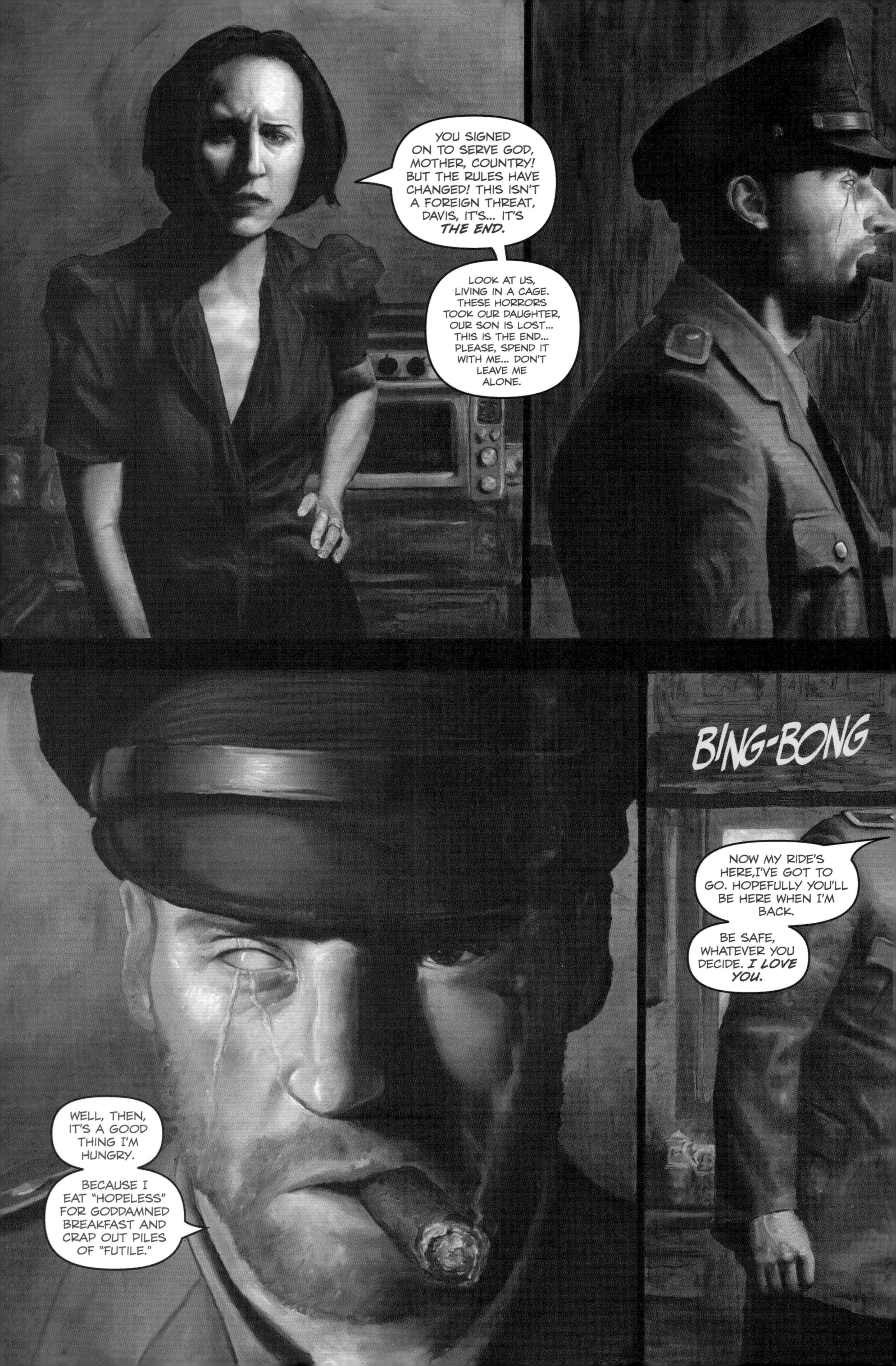
YOU SIGNED ON TO SERVE GOD, MOTHER, COUNTRY! BUT THE RULES HAVE CHANGED! THIS ISN'T A FOREIGN THREAT, DAVIS, IT'S... IT'S *THE END.*
LOOK AT US, LIVING IN A CAGE. THESE HORRORS TOOK OUR DAUGHTER, OUR SON IS LOST... THIS IS THE END... PLEASE, SPEND IT WITH ME... DON'T LEAVE ME ALONE.
WELL, THEN, IT'S A GOOD THING I'M HUNGRY.
BECAUSE I EAT "HOPELESS" FOR GODDAMNED BREAKFAST AND CRAP OUT PILES OF "FUTILE."
BING-BONG
NOW MY RIDE'S HERE,I'VE GOT TO GO. HOPEFULLY YOU'LL BE HERE WHEN I'M BACK.
BE SAFE, WHATEVER YOU DECIDE. *I LOVE YOU.*

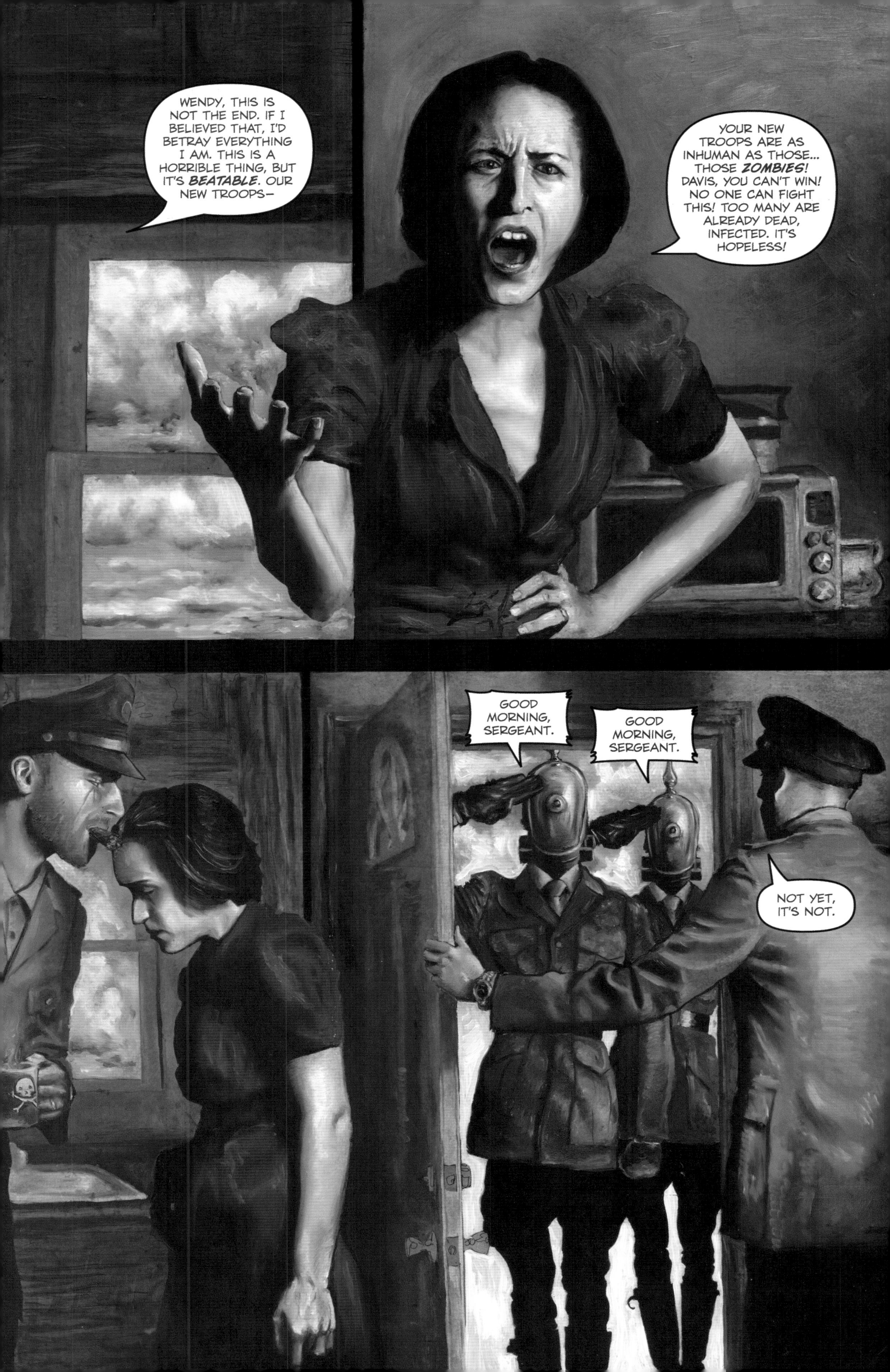
WENDY, THIS IS NOT THE END. IF I BELIEVED THAT, I'D BETRAY EVERYTHING I AM. THIS IS A HORRIBLE THING, BUT IT'S ***BEATABLE***. OUR NEW TROOPS–
YOUR NEW TROOPS ARE AS INHUMAN AS THOSE... THOSE ***ZOMBIES***! DAVIS, YOU CAN'T WIN! NO ONE CAN FIGHT THIS! TOO MANY ARE ALREADY DEAD, INFECTED. IT'S HOPELESS!
GOOD MORNING, SERGEANT.
GOOD MORNING, SERGEANT.
NOT YET, IT'S NOT.

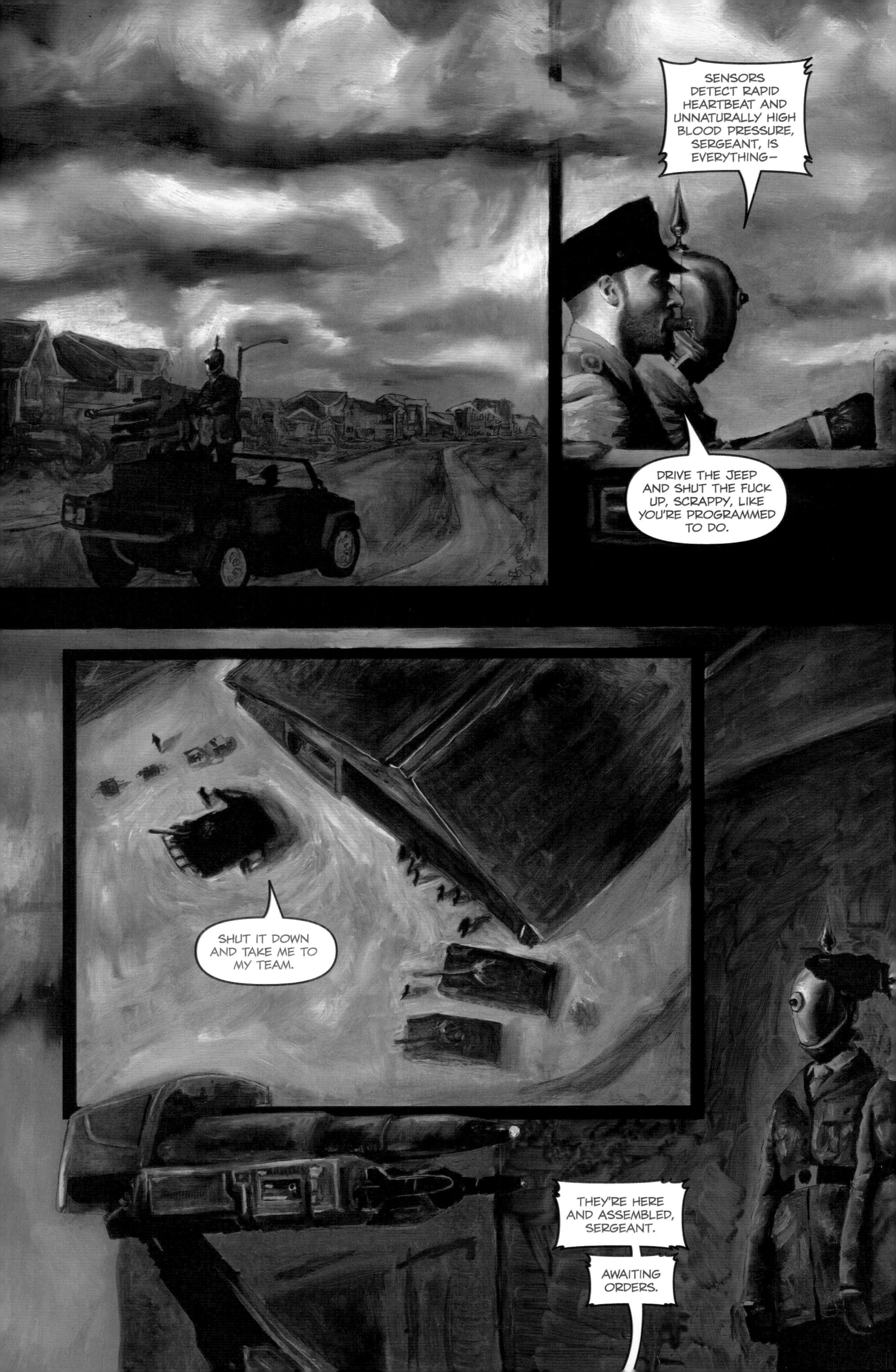
SENSORS DETECT RAPID HEARTBEAT AND UNNATURALLY HIGH BLOOD PRESSURE, SERGEANT, IS EVERYTHING–
DRIVE THE JEEP AND SHUT THE FUCK UP, SCRAPPY, LIKE YOU'RE PROGRAMMED TO DO.
SHUT IT DOWN AND TAKE ME TO MY TEAM.
THEY'RE HERE AND ASSEMBLED, SERGEANT.
AWAITING ORDERS.

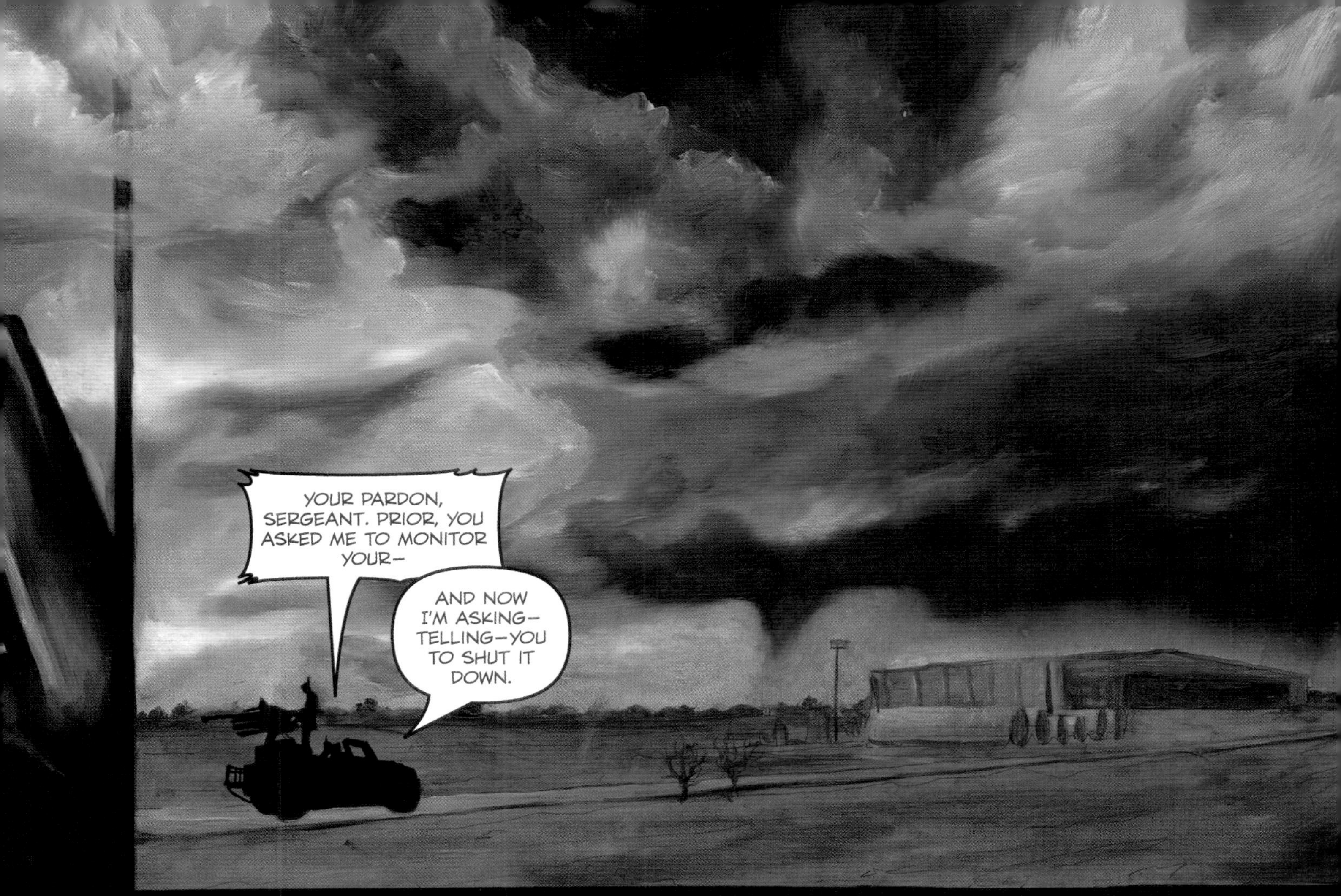
YOUR PARDON, SERGEANT. PRIOR, YOU ASKED ME TO MONITOR YOUR–
AND NOW I'M ASKING–TELLING–YOU TO SHUT IT DOWN.

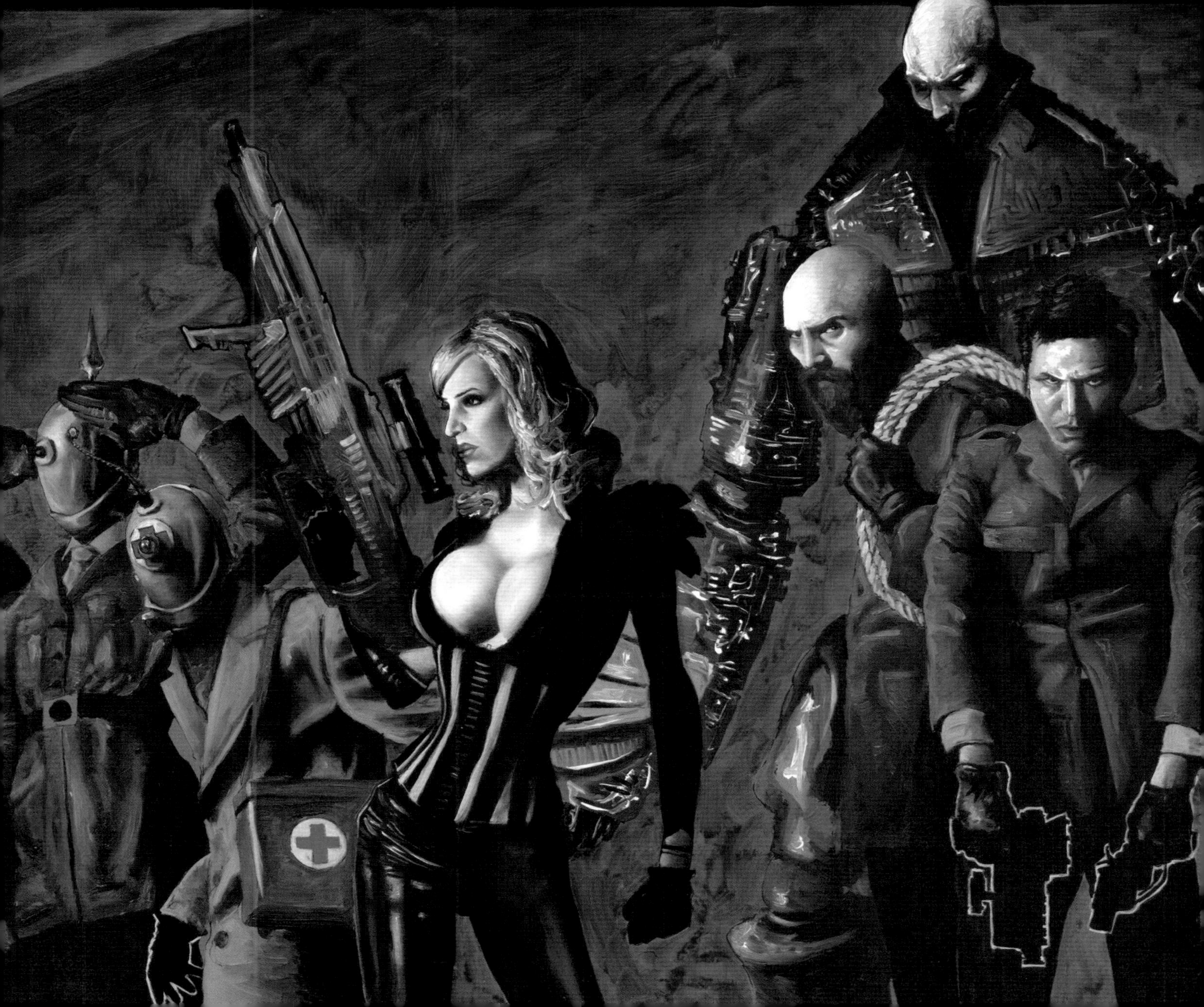

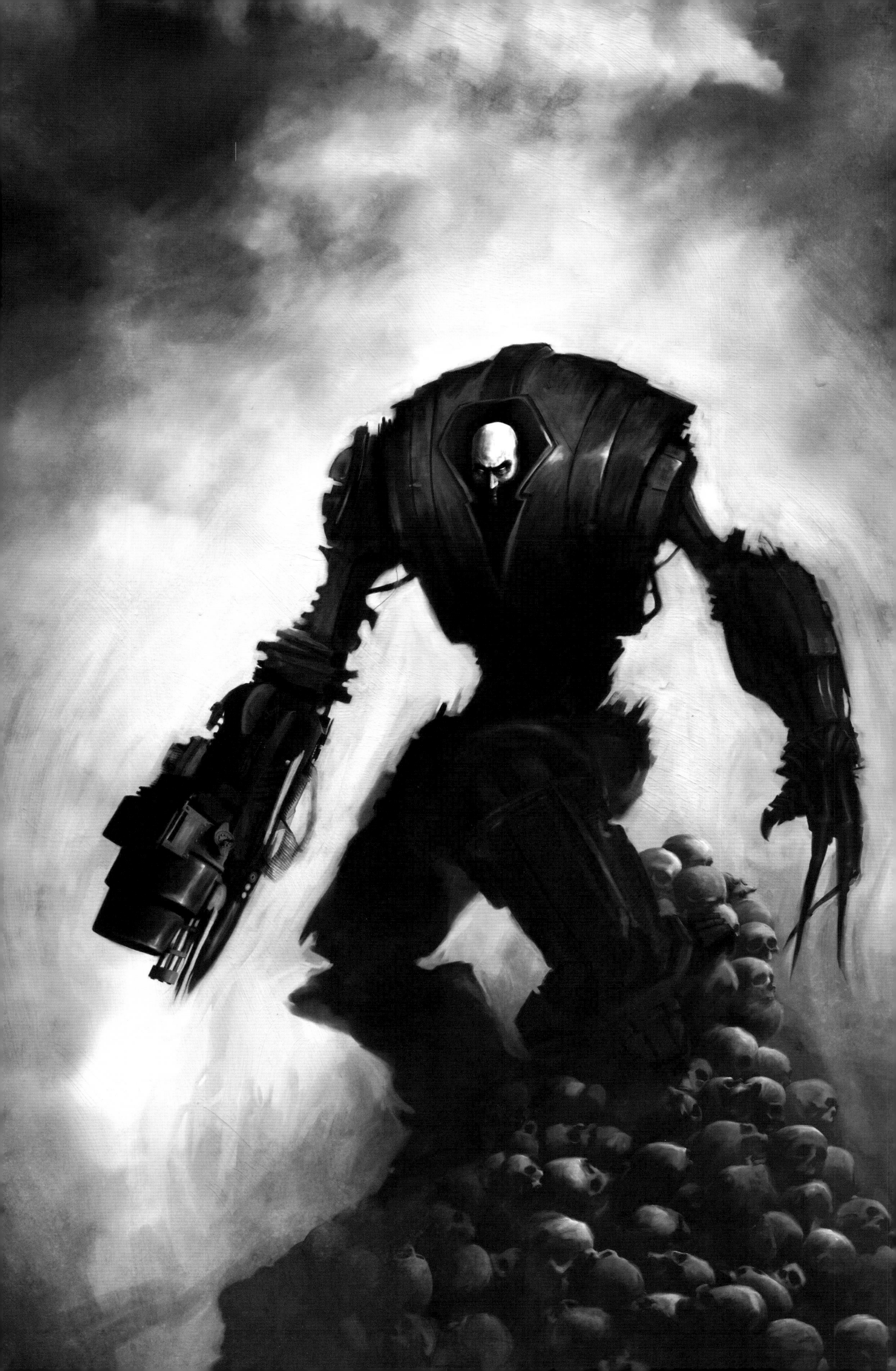

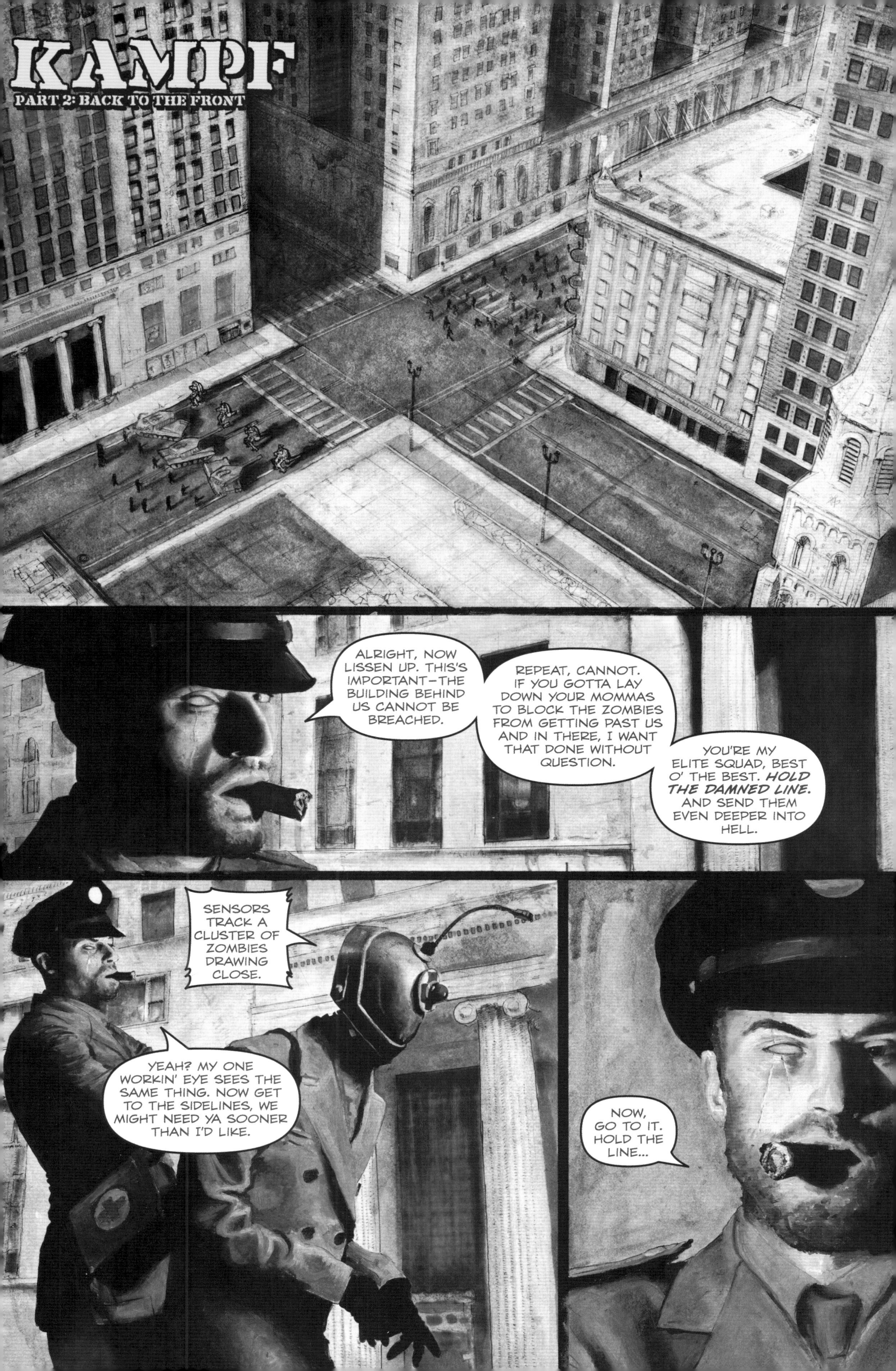
KAMPF
PART 2: BACK TO THE FRONT
ALRIGHT, NOW LISSEN UP. THIS'S IMPORTANT—THE BUILDING BEHIND US CANNOT BE BREACHED.
REPEAT, CANNOT. IF YOU GOTTA LAY DOWN YOUR MOMMAS TO BLOCK THE ZOMBIES FROM GETTING PAST US AND IN THERE, I WANT THAT DONE WITHOUT QUESTION.
YOU'RE MY ELITE SQUAD, BEST O' THE BEST. HOLD THE DAMNED LINE. AND SEND THEM EVEN DEEPER INTO HELL.
SENSORS TRACK A CLUSTER OF ZOMBIES DRAWING CLOSE.
YEAH? MY ONE WORKIN' EYE SEES THE SAME THING. NOW GET TO THE SIDELINES, WE MIGHT NEED YA SOONER THAN I'D LIKE.
NOW, GO TO IT. HOLD THE LINE...

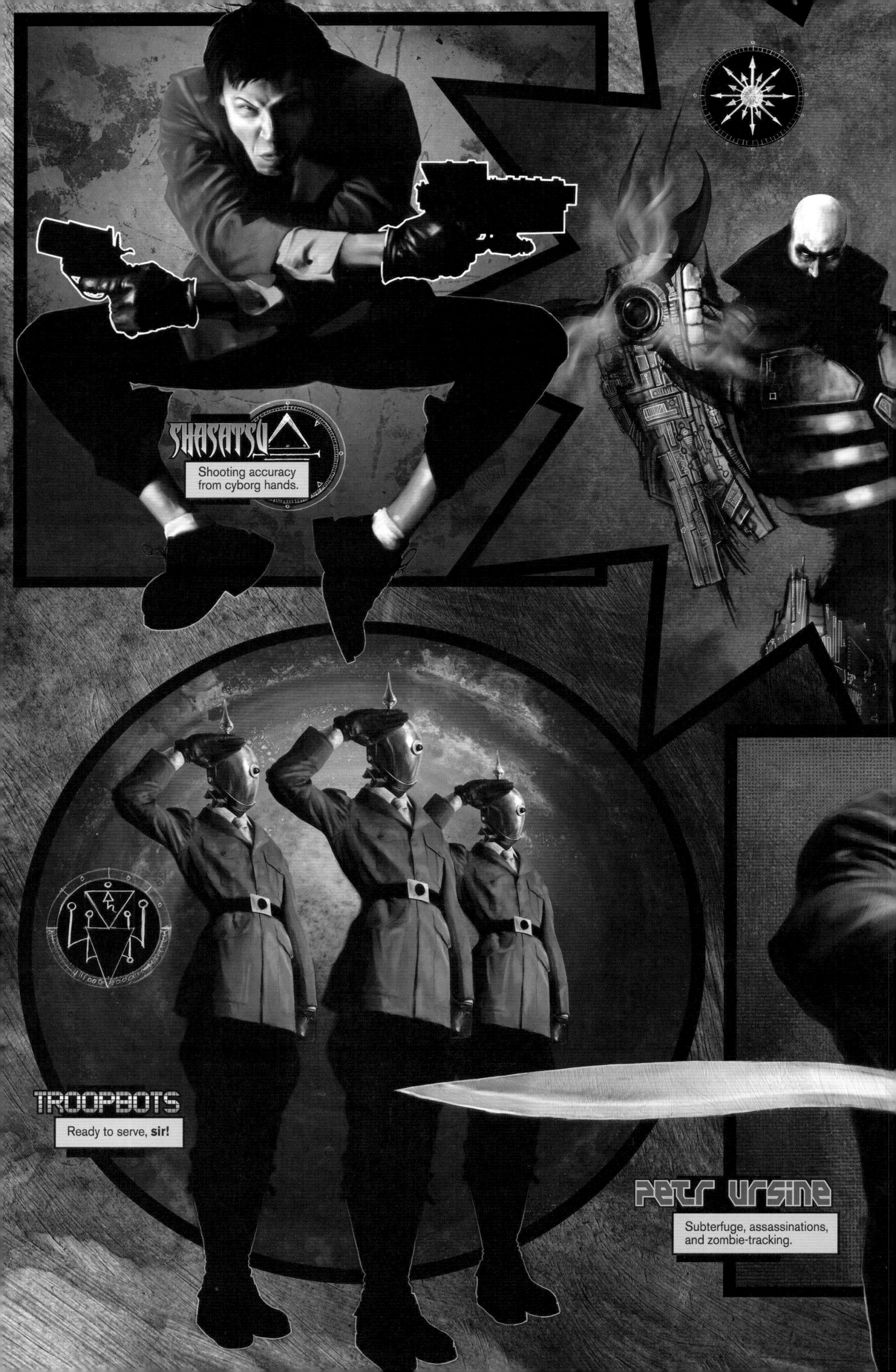
SHASATSU
Shooting accuracy from cyborg hands.
TROOPBOTS
Ready to serve, sir!
PETR URSINE
Subterfuge, assassinations, and zombie-tracking.

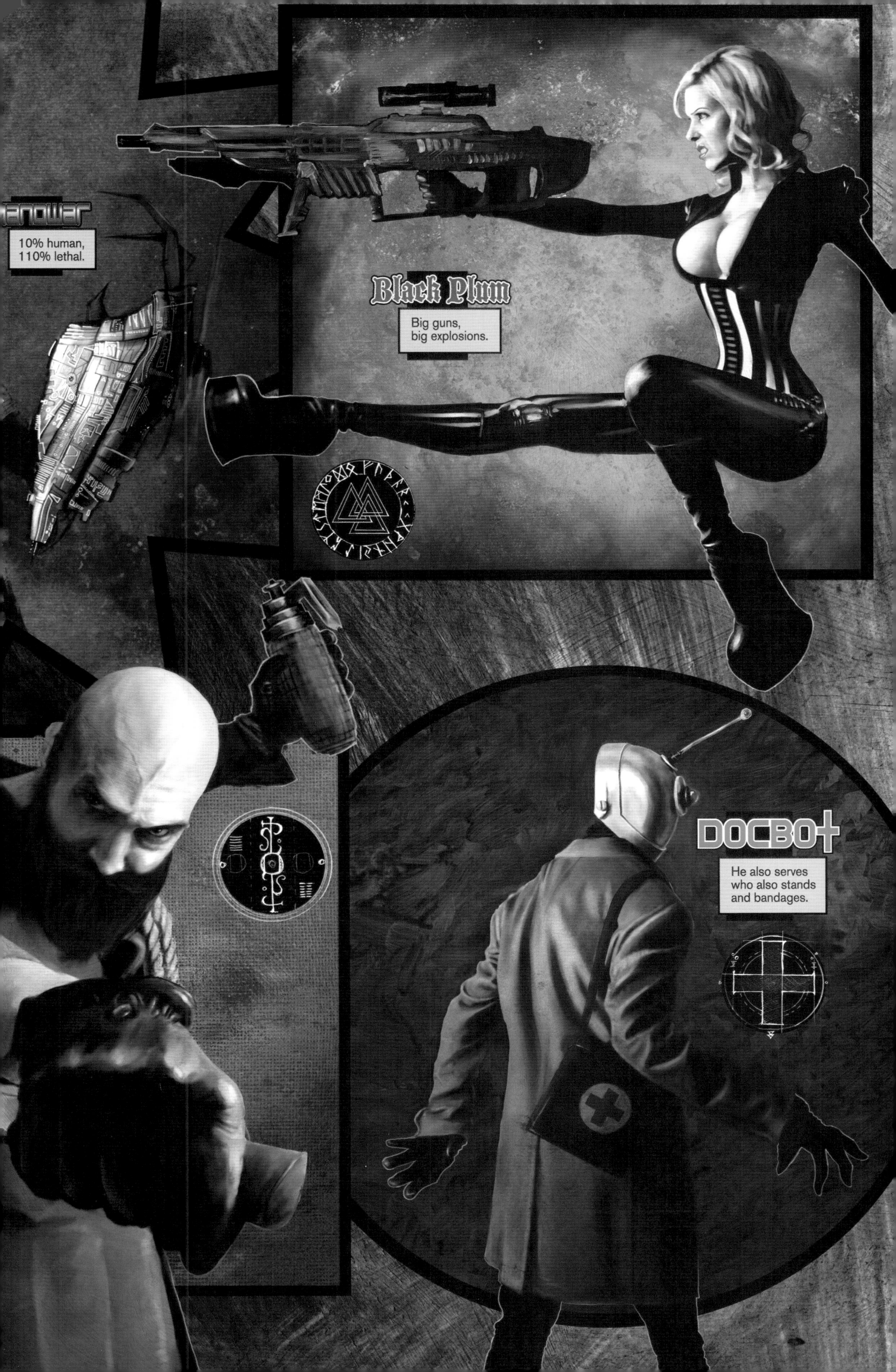
anowar
10% human,
110% lethal.
Black Plum
Big guns,
big explosions.
DOCBOT
He also serves
who also stands
and bandages.

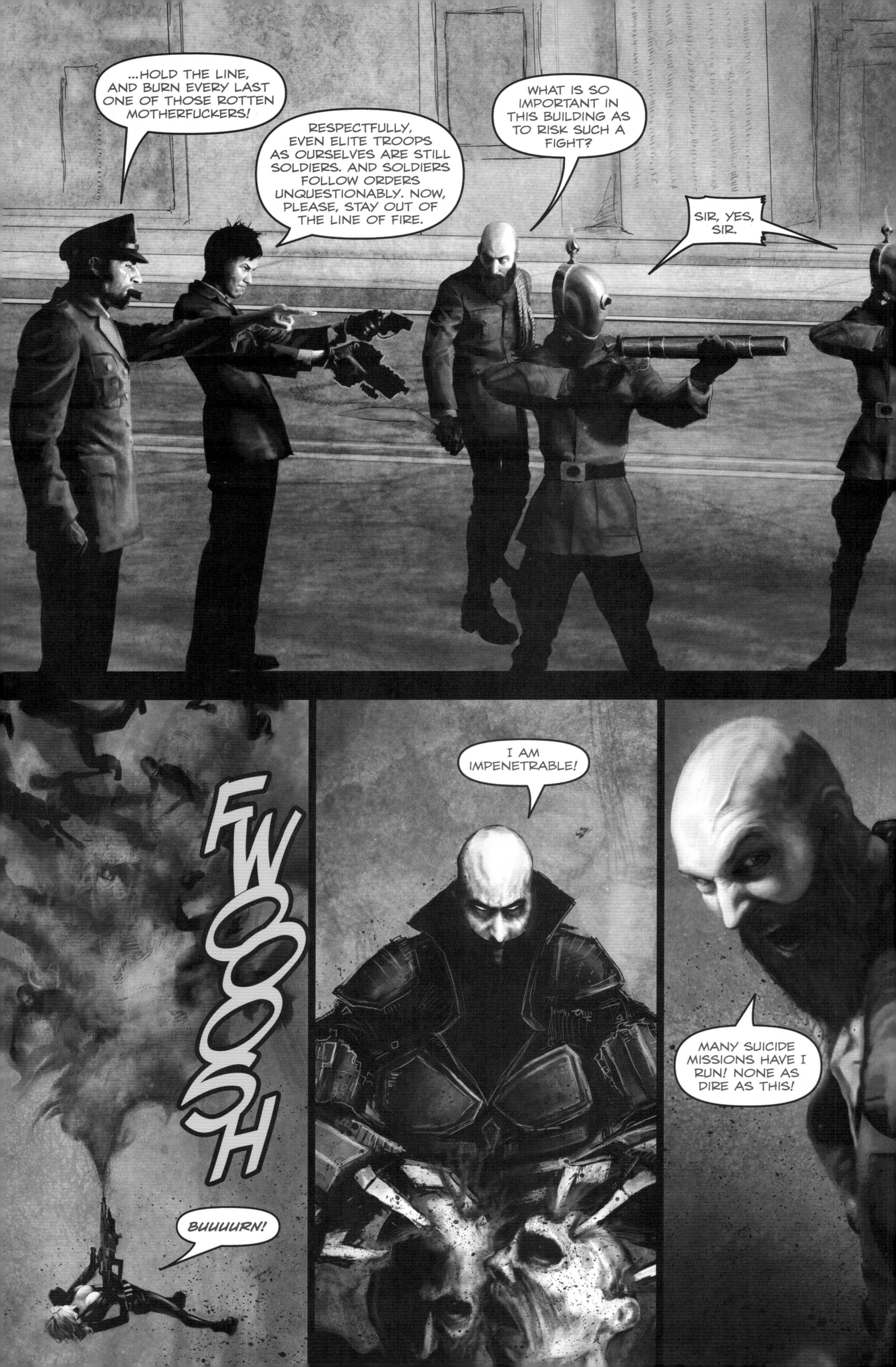
...HOLD THE LINE, AND BURN EVERY LAST ONE OF THOSE ROTTEN MOTHERFUCKERS!
RESPECTFULLY, EVEN ELITE TROOPS AS OURSELVES ARE STILL SOLDIERS. AND SOLDIERS FOLLOW ORDERS UNQUESTIONABLY. NOW, PLEASE, STAY OUT OF THE LINE OF FIRE.
WHAT IS SO IMPORTANT IN THIS BUILDING AS TO RISK SUCH A FIGHT?
SIR, YES, SIR.
FWOOOOSH
BUUUURN!
I AM IMPENETRABLE!
MANY SUICIDE MISSIONS HAVE I RUN! NONE AS DIRE AS THIS!

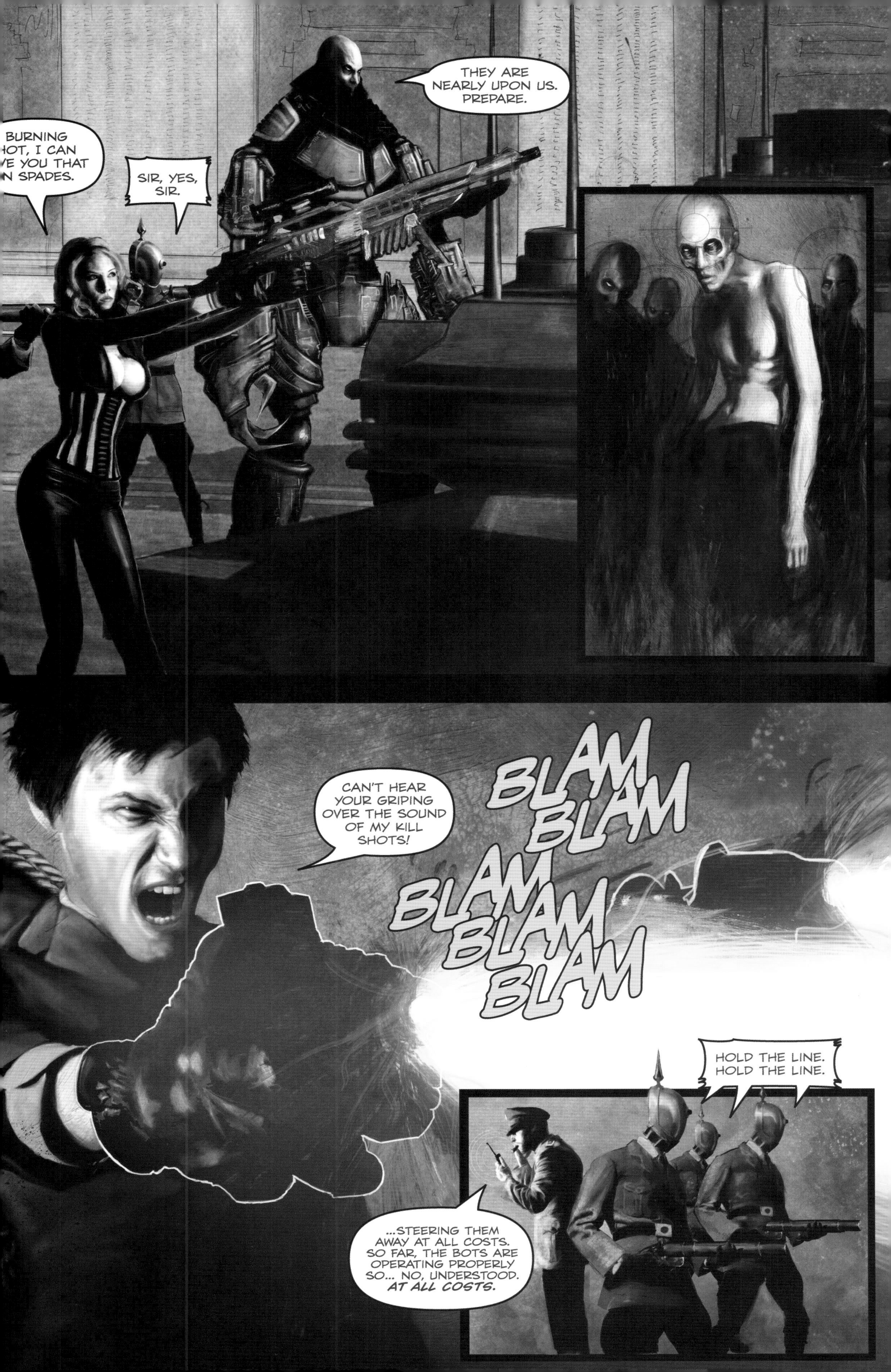
BURNING
HOT, I CAN
VE YOU THAT
N SPADES.
SIR, YES, SIR.
THEY ARE NEARLY UPON US. PREPARE.
CAN'T HEAR YOUR GRIPING OVER THE SOUND OF MY KILL SHOTS!
BLAM BLAM BLAM BLAM BLAM BLAM
HOLD THE LINE. HOLD THE LINE.
...STEERING THEM AWAY AT ALL COSTS. SO FAR, THE BOTS ARE OPERATING PROPERLY SO... NO, UNDERSTOOD. *AT ALL COSTS.*

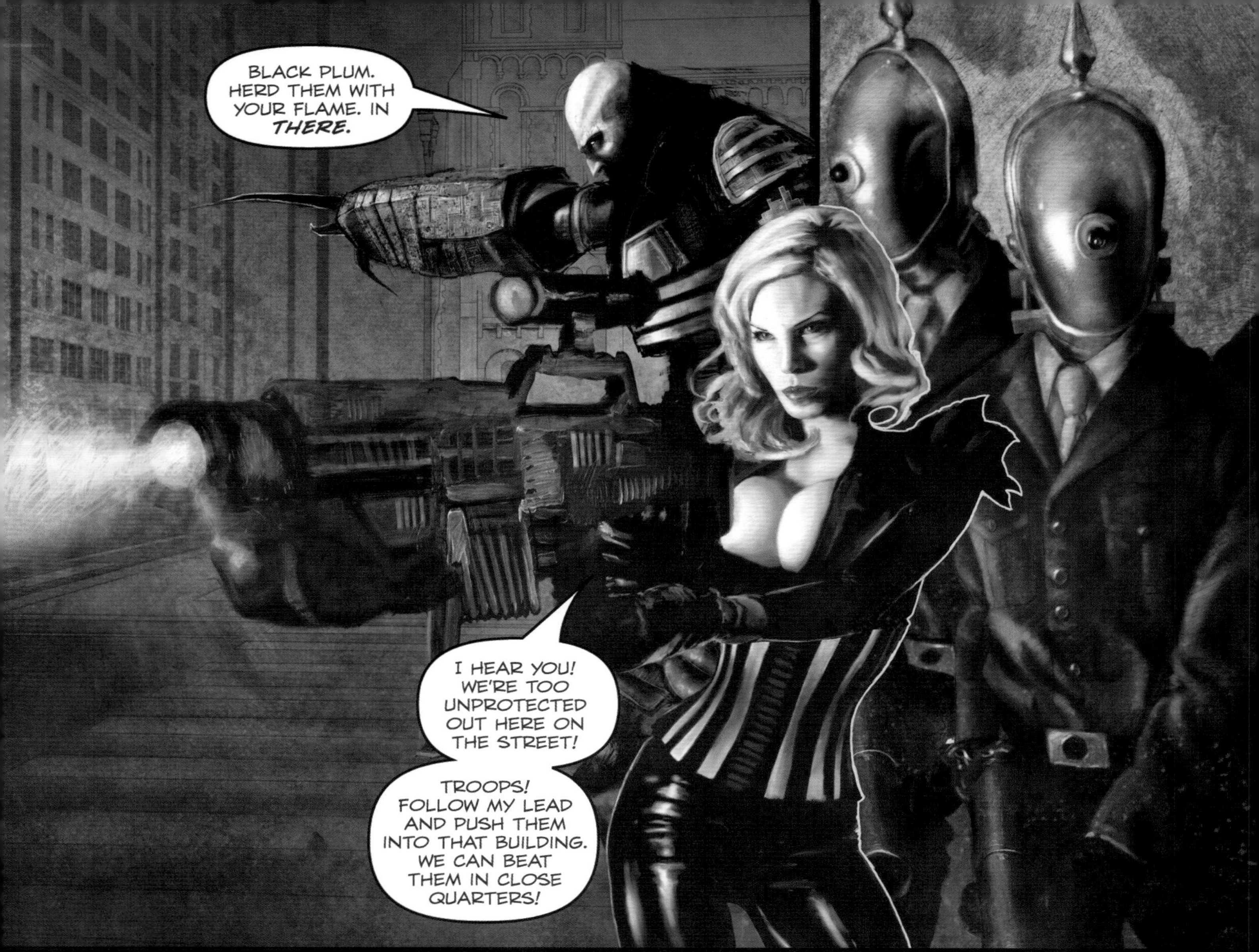
BLACK PLUM. HERD THEM WITH YOUR FLAME. IN *THERE.*
I HEAR YOU! WE'RE TOO UNPROTECTED OUT HERE ON THE STREET!
TROOPS! FOLLOW MY LEAD AND PUSH THEM INTO THAT BUILDING. WE CAN BEAT THEM IN CLOSE QUARTERS!

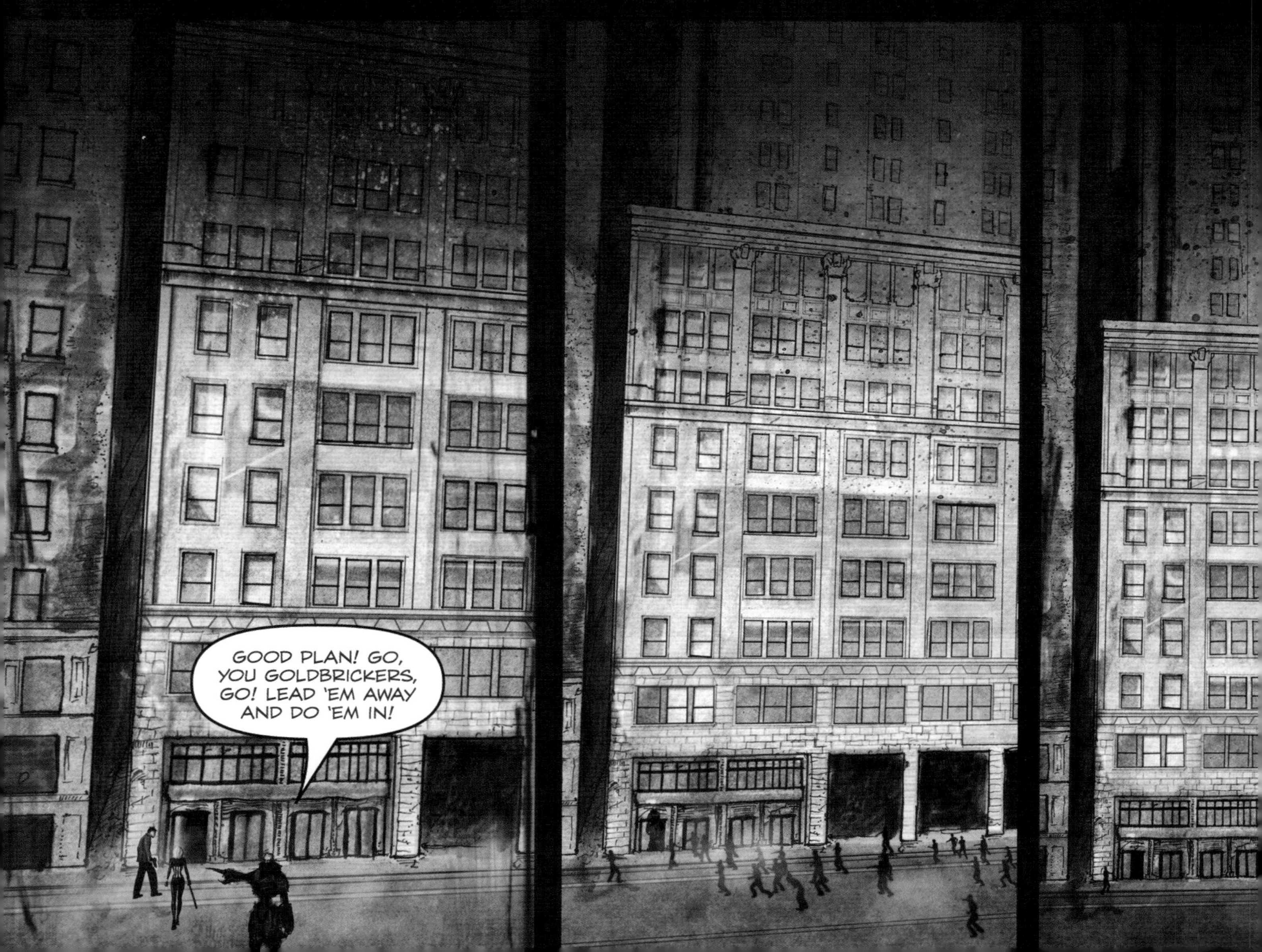
GOOD PLAN! GO, YOU GOLDBRICKERS, GO! LEAD 'EM AWAY AND DO 'EM IN!

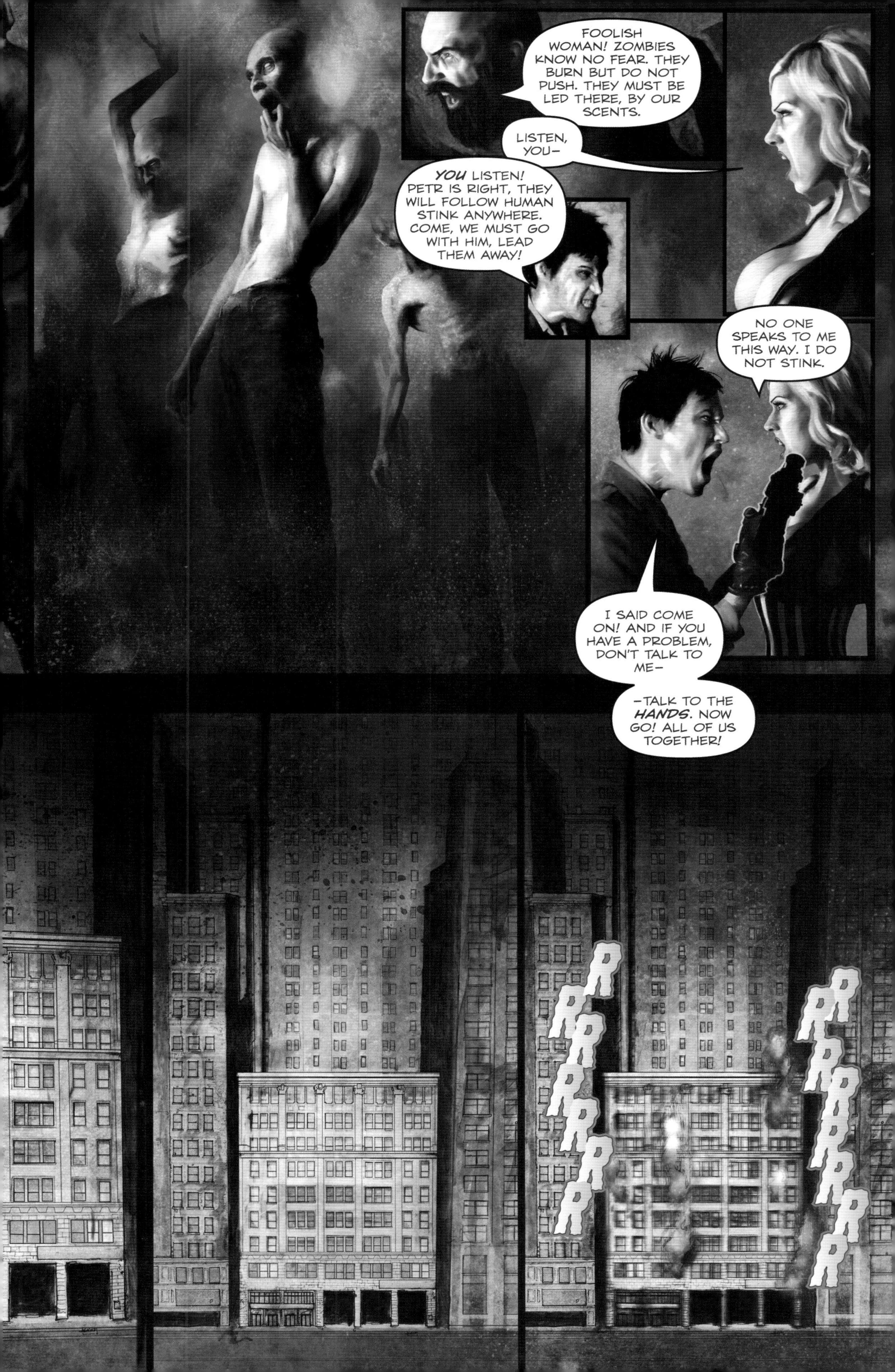
FOOLISH WOMAN! ZOMBIES KNOW NO FEAR. THEY BURN BUT DO NOT PUSH. THEY MUST BE LED THERE, BY OUR SCENTS.
LISTEN, YOU–
YOU LISTEN! PETR IS RIGHT, THEY WILL FOLLOW HUMAN STINK ANYWHERE. COME, WE MUST GO WITH HIM, LEAD THEM AWAY!
NO ONE SPEAKS TO ME THIS WAY. I DO NOT STINK.
I SAID COME ON! AND IF YOU HAVE A PROBLEM, DON'T TALK TO ME–
–TALK TO THE HANDS. NOW GO! ALL OF US TOGETHER!
RRRRRR
RRRRRRRR

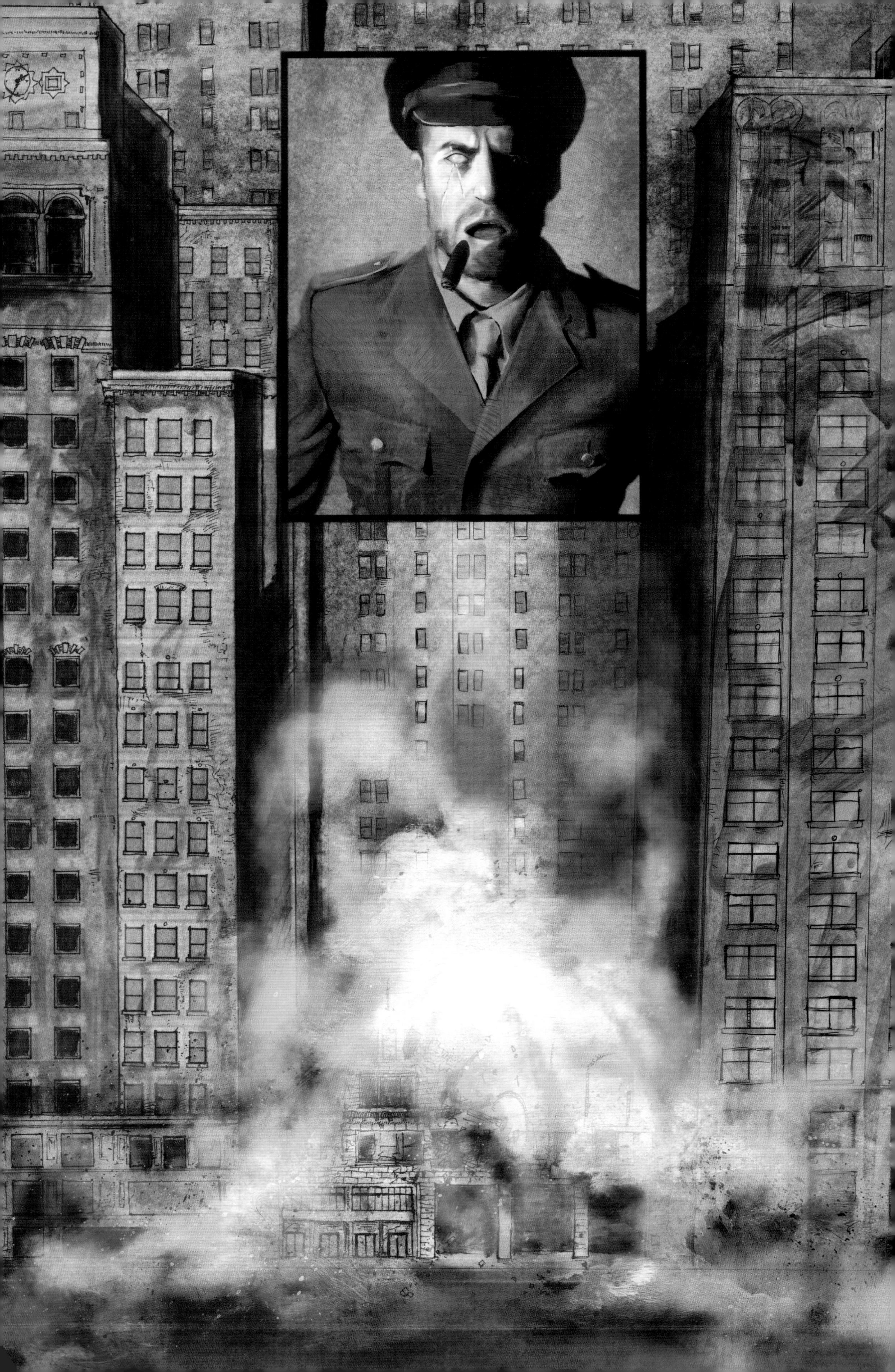

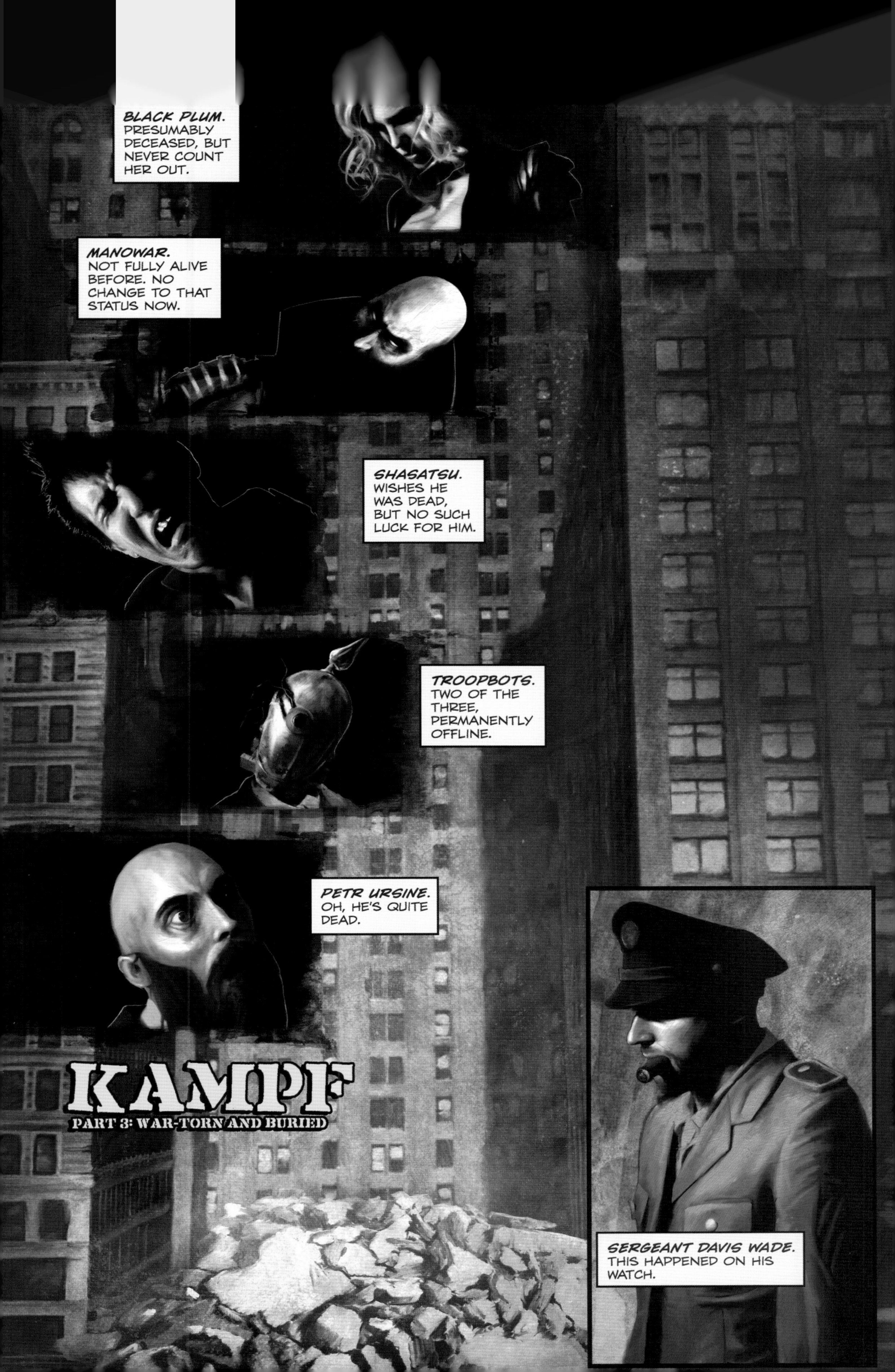
BLACK PLUM.
PRESUMABLY DECEASED, BUT NEVER COUNT HER OUT.
MANOWAR.
NOT FULLY ALIVE BEFORE. NO CHANGE TO THAT STATUS NOW.
SHASATSU.
WISHES HE WAS DEAD, BUT NO SUCH LUCK FOR HIM.
TROOPBOTS.
TWO OF THE THREE, PERMANENTLY OFFLINE.
PETR URSINE.
OH, HE'S QUITE DEAD.
KAMPF
PART 3: WAR-TORN AND BURIED
SERGEANT DAVIS WADE.
THIS HAPPENED ON HIS WATCH.

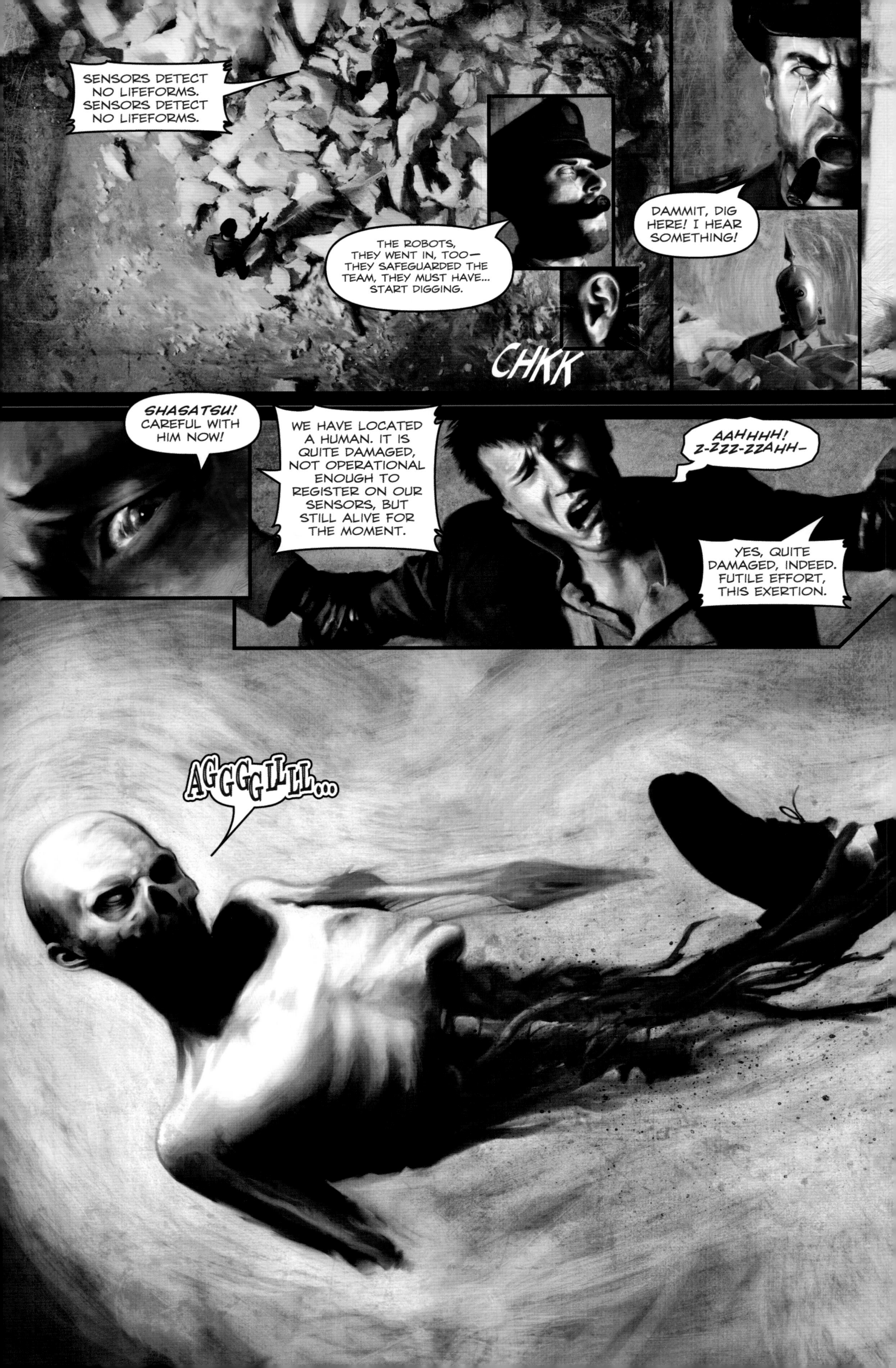
SENSORS DETECT NO LIFEFORMS. SENSORS DETECT NO LIFEFORMS.
THE ROBOTS, THEY WENT IN, TOO— THEY SAFEGUARDED THE TEAM, THEY MUST HAVE... START DIGGING.
CHKK
DAMMIT, DIG HERE! I HEAR SOMETHING!
SHASATSU! CAREFUL WITH HIM NOW!
WE HAVE LOCATED A HUMAN. IT IS QUITE DAMAGED, NOT OPERATIONAL ENOUGH TO REGISTER ON OUR SENSORS, BUT STILL ALIVE FOR THE MOMENT.
AAHHHH! Z-ZZZ-ZZAHH-
YES, QUITE DAMAGED, INDEED. FUTILE EFFORT, THIS EXERTION.
AGGGLLL...

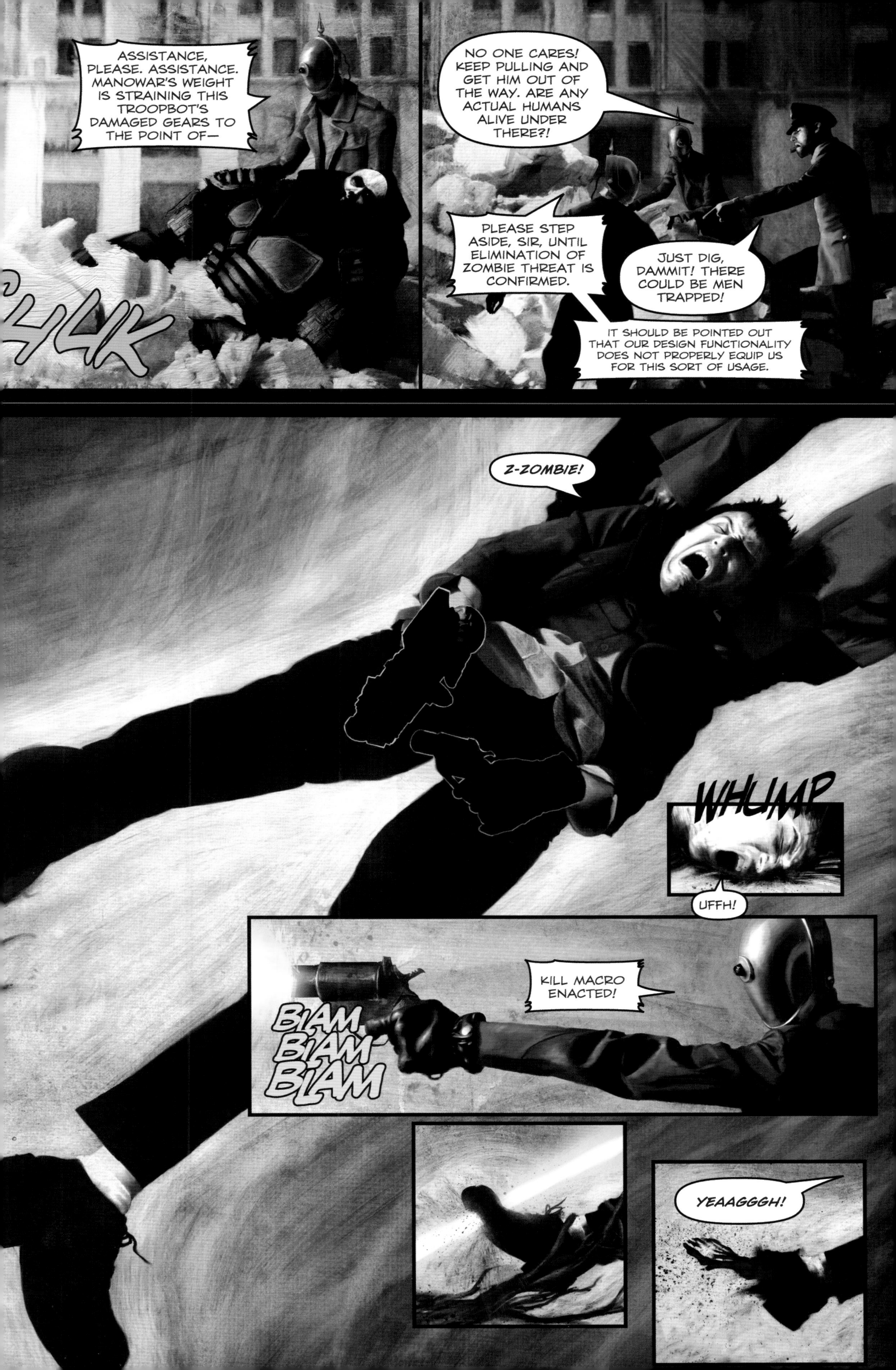
ASSISTANCE, PLEASE. ASSISTANCE. MANOWAR'S WEIGHT IS STRAINING THIS TROOPBOT'S DAMAGED GEARS TO THE POINT OF—
NO ONE CARES! KEEP PULLING AND GET HIM OUT OF THE WAY. ARE ANY ACTUAL HUMANS ALIVE UNDER THERE?!
PLEASE STEP ASIDE, SIR, UNTIL ELIMINATION OF ZOMBIE THREAT IS CONFIRMED.
JUST DIG, DAMMIT! THERE COULD BE MEN TRAPPED!
IT SHOULD BE POINTED OUT THAT OUR DESIGN FUNCTIONALITY DOES NOT PROPERLY EQUIP US FOR THIS SORT OF USAGE.
Z-ZOMBIE!
WHUMP
UFFH!
KILL MACRO ENACTED!
BLAM BLAM BLAM
YEAAGGGH!

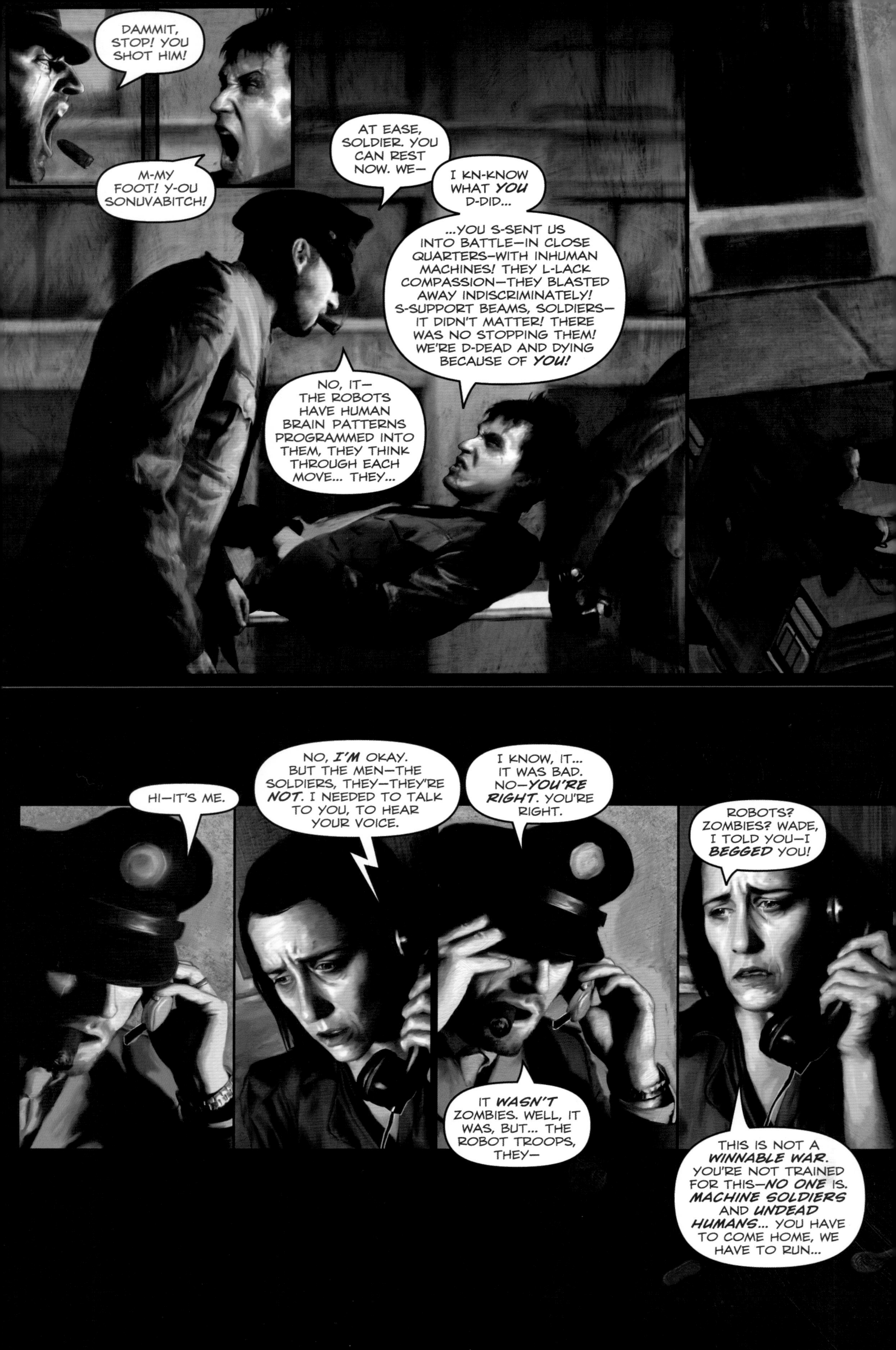
DAMMIT, STOP! YOU SHOT HIM!
M-MY FOOT! Y-OU SONUVABITCH!
AT EASE, SOLDIER. YOU CAN REST NOW. WE—
I KN-KNOW WHAT YOU D-DID...
...YOU S-SENT US INTO BATTLE—IN CLOSE QUARTERS—WITH INHUMAN MACHINES! THEY L-LACK COMPASSION—THEY BLASTED AWAY INDISCRIMINATELY! S-SUPPORT BEAMS, SOLDIERS—IT DIDN'T MATTER! THERE WAS NO STOPPING THEM! WE'RE D-DEAD AND DYING BECAUSE OF YOU!
NO, IT—THE ROBOTS HAVE HUMAN BRAIN PATTERNS PROGRAMMED INTO THEM, THEY THINK THROUGH EACH MOVE... THEY...
HI—IT'S ME.
NO, I'M OKAY. BUT THE MEN—THE SOLDIERS, THEY—THEY'RE NOT. I NEEDED TO TALK TO YOU, TO HEAR YOUR VOICE.
I KNOW, IT... IT WAS BAD. NO—YOU'RE RIGHT. YOU'RE RIGHT.
IT WASN'T ZOMBIES. WELL, IT WAS, BUT... THE ROBOT TROOPS, THEY—
ROBOTS? ZOMBIES? WADE, I TOLD YOU—I BEGGED YOU!
THIS IS NOT A WINNABLE WAR. YOU'RE NOT TRAINED FOR THIS—NO ONE IS. MACHINE SOLDIERS AND UNDEAD HUMANS... YOU HAVE TO COME HOME, WE HAVE TO RUN...

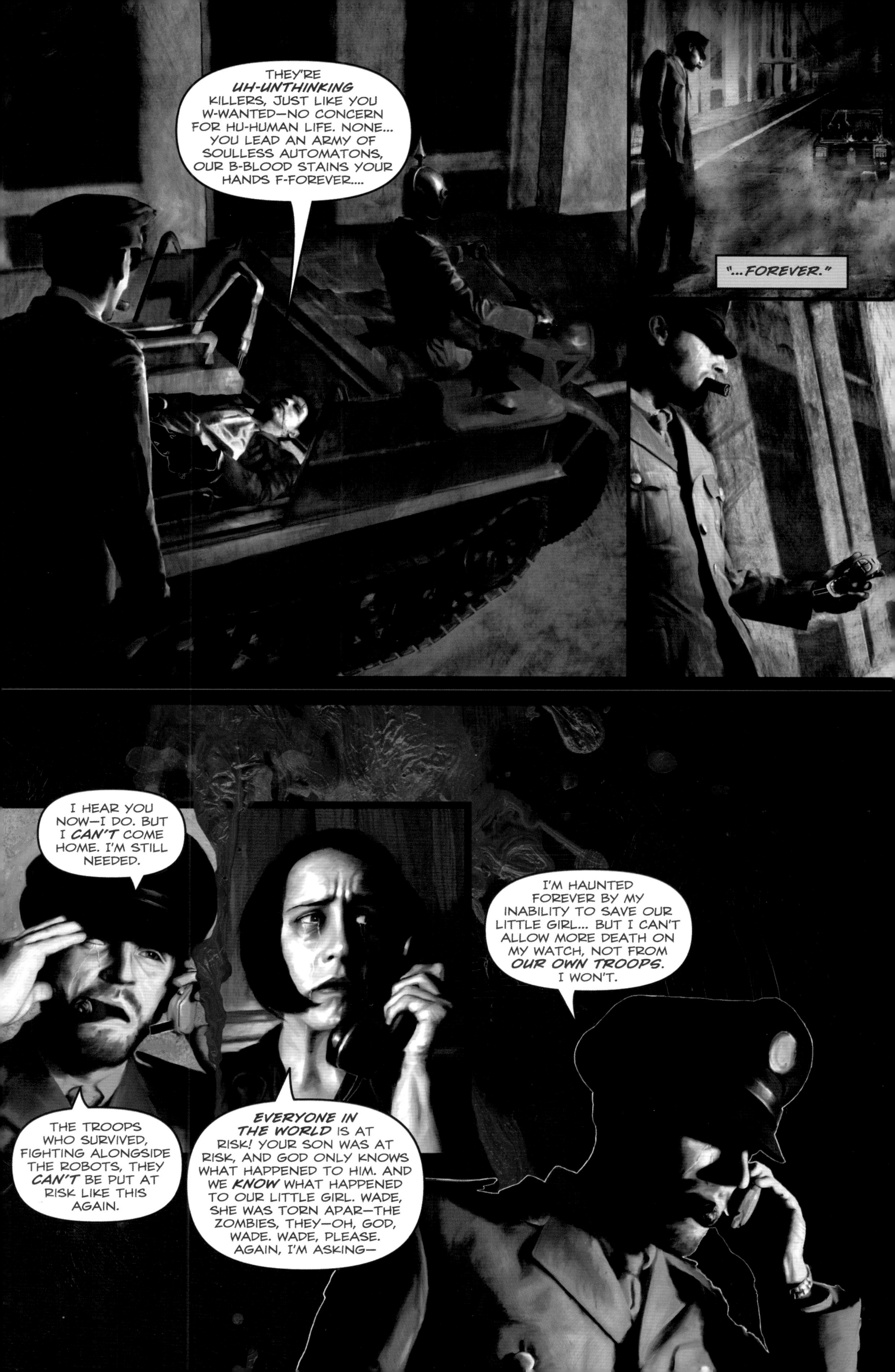
THEY'RE UH-UNTHINKING KILLERS, JUST LIKE YOU W-WANTED—NO CONCERN FOR HU-HUMAN LIFE. NONE... YOU LEAD AN ARMY OF SOULLESS AUTOMATONS, OUR B-BLOOD STAINS YOUR HANDS F-FOREVER....
"...FOREVER."
I HEAR YOU NOW—I DO. BUT I CAN'T COME HOME. I'M STILL NEEDED.
THE TROOPS WHO SURVIVED, FIGHTING ALONGSIDE THE ROBOTS, THEY CAN'T BE PUT AT RISK LIKE THIS AGAIN.
EVERYONE IN THE WORLD IS AT RISK! YOUR SON WAS AT RISK, AND GOD ONLY KNOWS WHAT HAPPENED TO HIM. AND WE KNOW WHAT HAPPENED TO OUR LITTLE GIRL. WADE, SHE WAS TORN APAR—THE ZOMBIES, THEY—OH, GOD, WADE. WADE, PLEASE. AGAIN, I'M ASKING—
I'M HAUNTED FOREVER BY MY INABILITY TO SAVE OUR LITTLE GIRL... BUT I CAN'T ALLOW MORE DEATH ON MY WATCH, NOT FROM OUR OWN TROOPS. I WON'T.

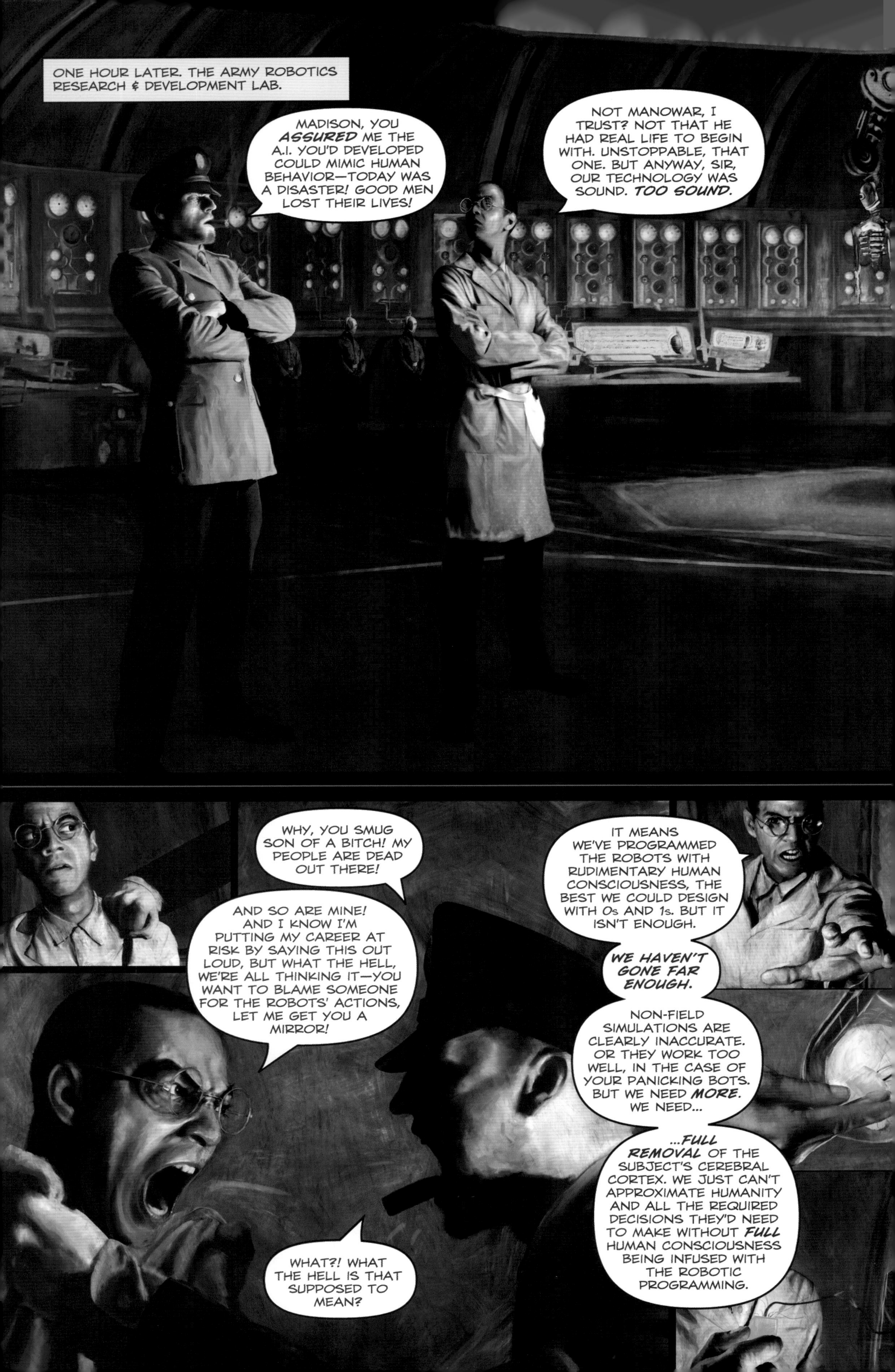

ONE HOUR LATER. THE ARMY ROBOTICS RESEARCH & DEVELOPMENT LAB.
MADISON, YOU *ASSURED* ME THE A.I. YOU'D DEVELOPED COULD MIMIC HUMAN BEHAVIOR—TODAY WAS A DISASTER! GOOD MEN LOST THEIR LIVES!
NOT MANOWAR, I TRUST? NOT THAT HE HAD REAL LIFE TO BEGIN WITH. UNSTOPPABLE, THAT ONE. BUT ANYWAY, SIR, OUR TECHNOLOGY WAS SOUND. *TOO SOUND.*
WHY, YOU SMUG SON OF A BITCH! MY PEOPLE ARE DEAD OUT THERE!
AND SO ARE MINE! AND I KNOW I'M PUTTING MY CAREER AT RISK BY SAYING THIS OUT LOUD, BUT WHAT THE HELL, WE'RE ALL THINKING IT—YOU WANT TO BLAME SOMEONE FOR THE ROBOTS' ACTIONS, LET ME GET YOU A MIRROR!
WHAT?! WHAT THE HELL IS THAT SUPPOSED TO MEAN?
IT MEANS WE'VE PROGRAMMED THE ROBOTS WITH RUDIMENTARY HUMAN CONSCIOUSNESS, THE BEST WE COULD DESIGN WITH 0s AND 1s. BUT IT ISN'T ENOUGH.
WE HAVEN'T GONE FAR ENOUGH.
NON-FIELD SIMULATIONS ARE CLEARLY INACCURATE. OR THEY WORK TOO WELL, IN THE CASE OF YOUR PANICKING BOTS. BUT WE NEED *MORE*. WE NEED...
...*FULL REMOVAL* OF THE SUBJECT'S CEREBRAL CORTEX. WE JUST CAN'T APPROXIMATE HUMANITY AND ALL THE REQUIRED DECISIONS THEY'D NEED TO MAKE WITHOUT *FULL* HUMAN CONSCIOUSNESS BEING INFUSED WITH THE ROBOTIC PROGRAMMING.

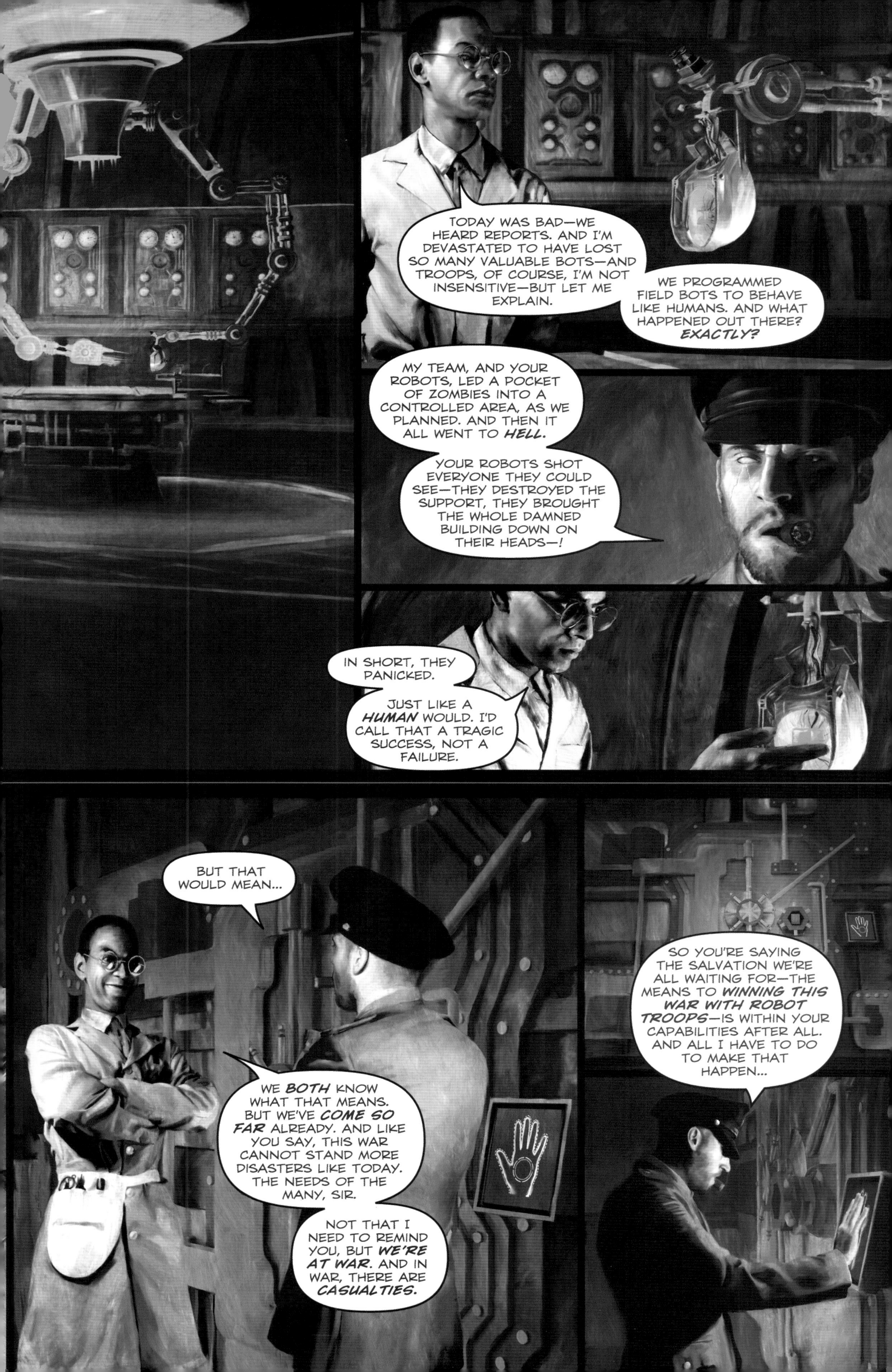
TODAY WAS BAD—WE HEARD REPORTS. AND I'M DEVASTATED TO HAVE LOST SO MANY VALUABLE BOTS—AND TROOPS, OF COURSE, I'M NOT INSENSITIVE—BUT LET ME EXPLAIN.
WE PROGRAMMED FIELD BOTS TO BEHAVE LIKE HUMANS. AND WHAT HAPPENED OUT THERE? EXACTLY?
MY TEAM, AND YOUR ROBOTS, LED A POCKET OF ZOMBIES INTO A CONTROLLED AREA, AS WE PLANNED. AND THEN IT ALL WENT TO HELL.
YOUR ROBOTS SHOT EVERYONE THEY COULD SEE—THEY DESTROYED THE SUPPORT, THEY BROUGHT THE WHOLE DAMNED BUILDING DOWN ON THEIR HEADS—!
IN SHORT, THEY PANICKED.
JUST LIKE A HUMAN WOULD. I'D CALL THAT A TRAGIC SUCCESS, NOT A FAILURE.
BUT THAT WOULD MEAN...
WE BOTH KNOW WHAT THAT MEANS. BUT WE'VE COME SO FAR ALREADY. AND LIKE YOU SAY, THIS WAR CANNOT STAND MORE DISASTERS LIKE TODAY. THE NEEDS OF THE MANY, SIR.
NOT THAT I NEED TO REMIND YOU, BUT WE'RE AT WAR. AND IN WAR, THERE ARE CASUALTIES.
SO YOU'RE SAYING THE SALVATION WE'RE ALL WAITING FOR—THE MEANS TO WINNING THIS WAR WITH ROBOT TROOPS—IS WITHIN YOUR CAPABILITIES AFTER ALL. AND ALL I HAVE TO DO TO MAKE THAT HAPPEN...

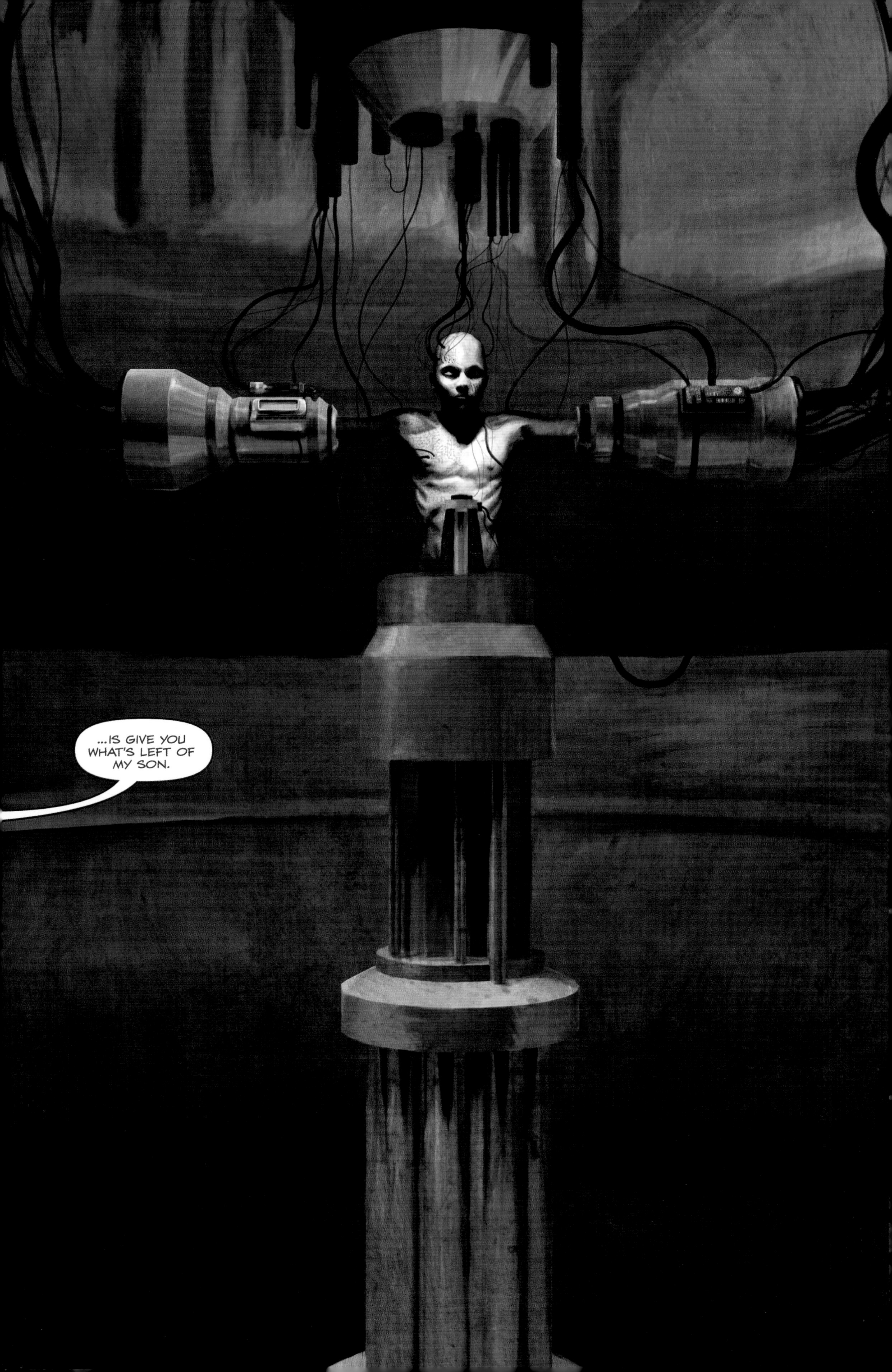
...IS GIVE YOU WHAT'S LEFT OF MY SON.

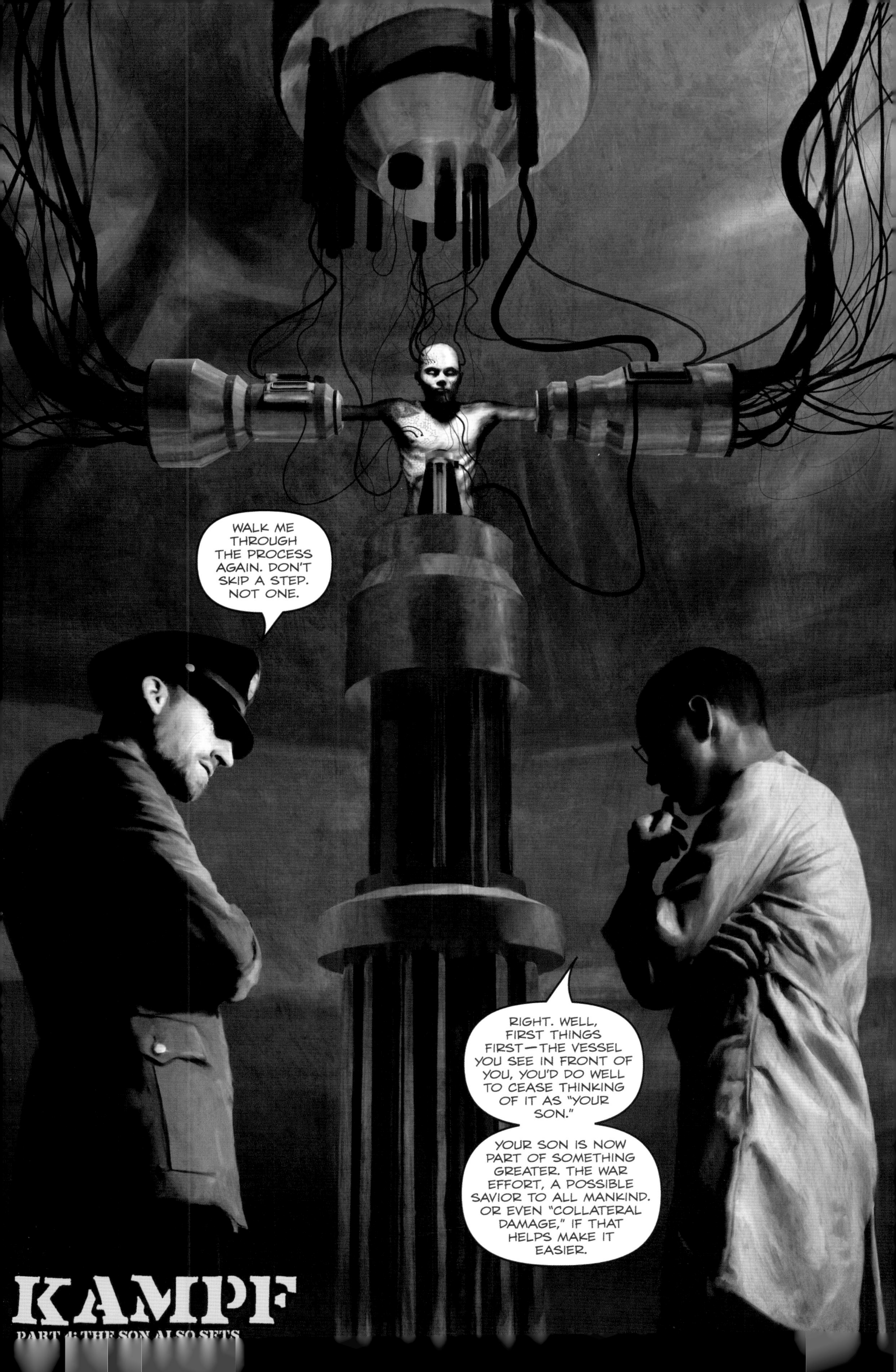

WALK ME THROUGH THE PROCESS AGAIN. DON'T SKIP A STEP. NOT ONE.
RIGHT. WELL, FIRST THINGS FIRST—THE VESSEL YOU SEE IN FRONT OF YOU, YOU'D DO WELL TO CEASE THINKING OF IT AS "YOUR SON."
YOUR SON IS NOW PART OF SOMETHING GREATER. THE WAR EFFORT, A POSSIBLE SAVIOR TO ALL MANKIND. OR EVEN "COLLATERAL DAMAGE," IF THAT HELPS MAKE IT EASIER.
KAMPF
PART 4: THE SON ALSO SETS

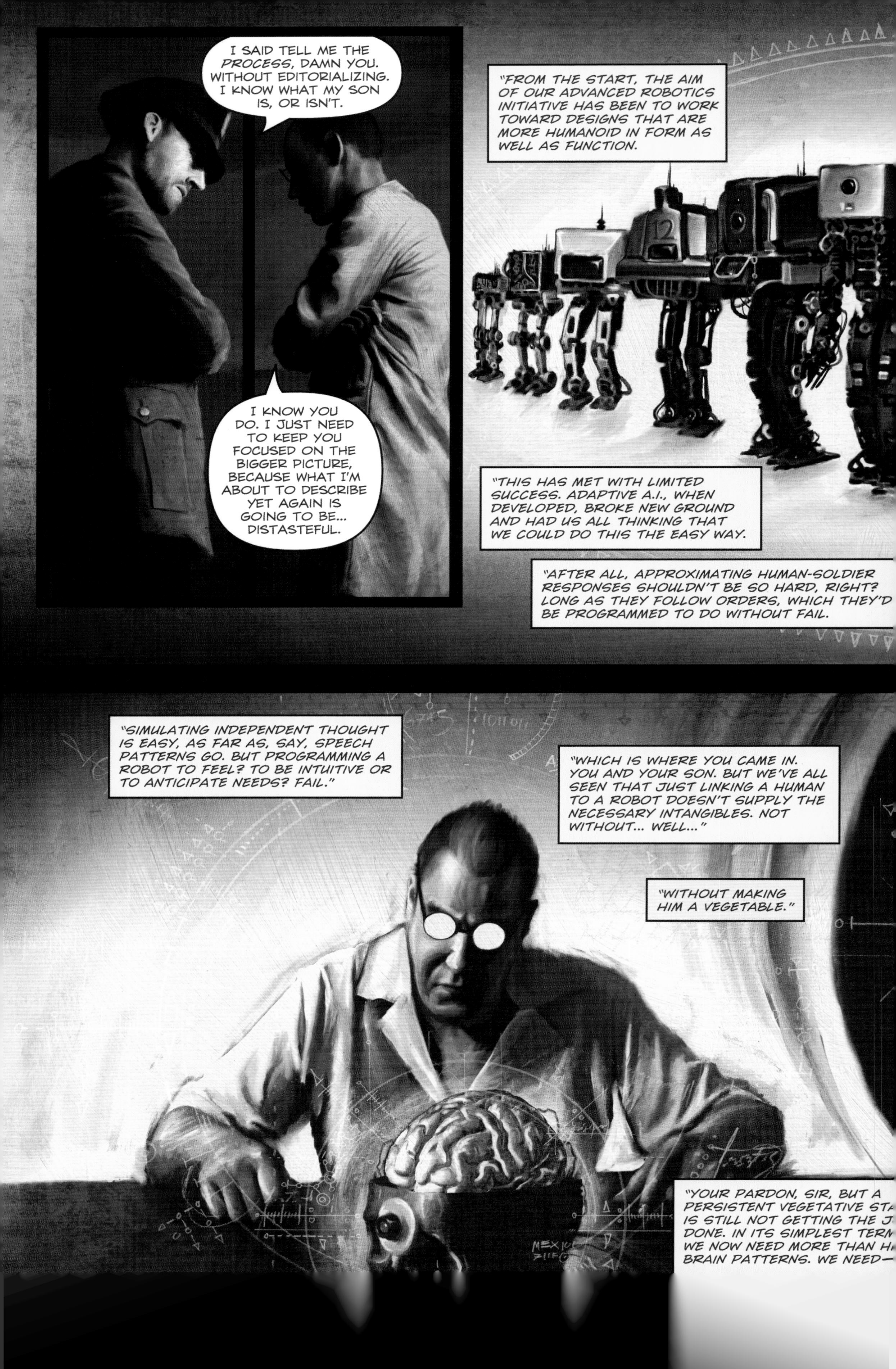
I SAID TELL ME THE *PROCESS*, DAMN YOU. WITHOUT EDITORIALIZING. I KNOW WHAT MY SON IS, OR ISN'T.
I KNOW YOU DO. I JUST NEED TO KEEP YOU FOCUSED ON THE BIGGER PICTURE, BECAUSE WHAT I'M ABOUT TO DESCRIBE YET AGAIN IS GOING TO BE... DISTASTEFUL.
"FROM THE START, THE AIM OF OUR ADVANCED ROBOTICS INITIATIVE HAS BEEN TO WORK TOWARD DESIGNS THAT ARE MORE HUMANOID IN FORM AS WELL AS FUNCTION.
"THIS HAS MET WITH LIMITED SUCCESS. ADAPTIVE A.I., WHEN DEVELOPED, BROKE NEW GROUND AND HAD US ALL THINKING THAT WE COULD DO THIS THE EASY WAY.
"AFTER ALL, APPROXIMATING HUMAN-SOLDIER RESPONSES SHOULDN'T BE SO HARD, RIGHT? LONG AS THEY FOLLOW ORDERS, WHICH THEY'D BE PROGRAMMED TO DO WITHOUT FAIL.
"SIMULATING INDEPENDENT THOUGHT IS EASY, AS FAR AS, SAY, SPEECH PATTERNS GO. BUT PROGRAMMING A ROBOT TO FEEL? TO BE INTUITIVE OR TO ANTICIPATE NEEDS? FAIL."
"WHICH IS WHERE YOU CAME IN. YOU AND YOUR SON. BUT WE'VE ALL SEEN THAT JUST LINKING A HUMAN TO A ROBOT DOESN'T SUPPLY THE NECESSARY INTANGIBLES. NOT WITHOUT... WELL..."
"WITHOUT MAKING HIM A VEGETABLE."
"YOUR PARDON, SIR, BUT A PERSISTENT VEGETATIVE STA IS STILL NOT GETTING THE J DONE. IN ITS SIMPLEST TERM WE NOW NEED MORE THAN H BRAIN PATTERNS. WE NEED—

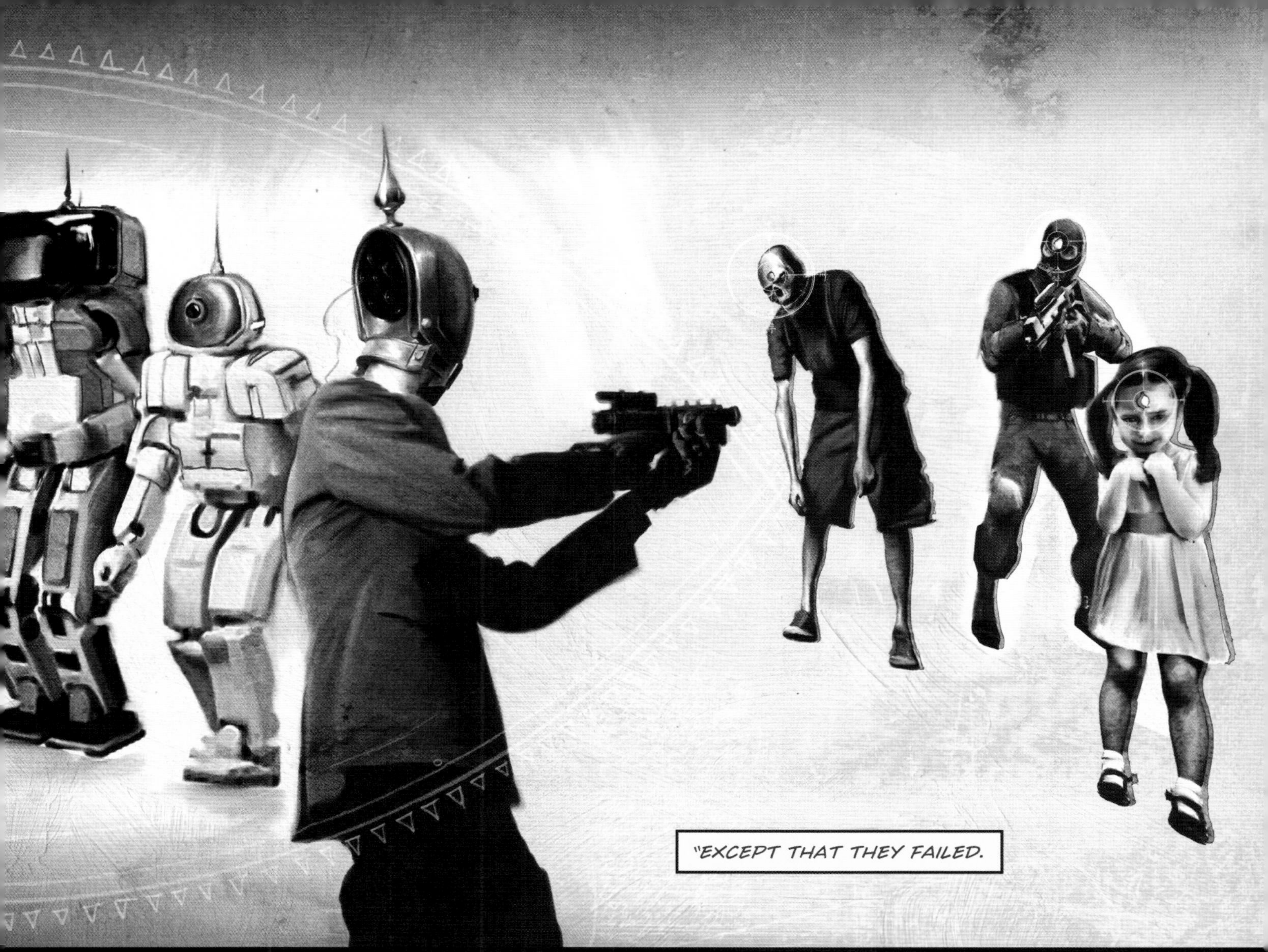
"EXCEPT THAT THEY FAILED.

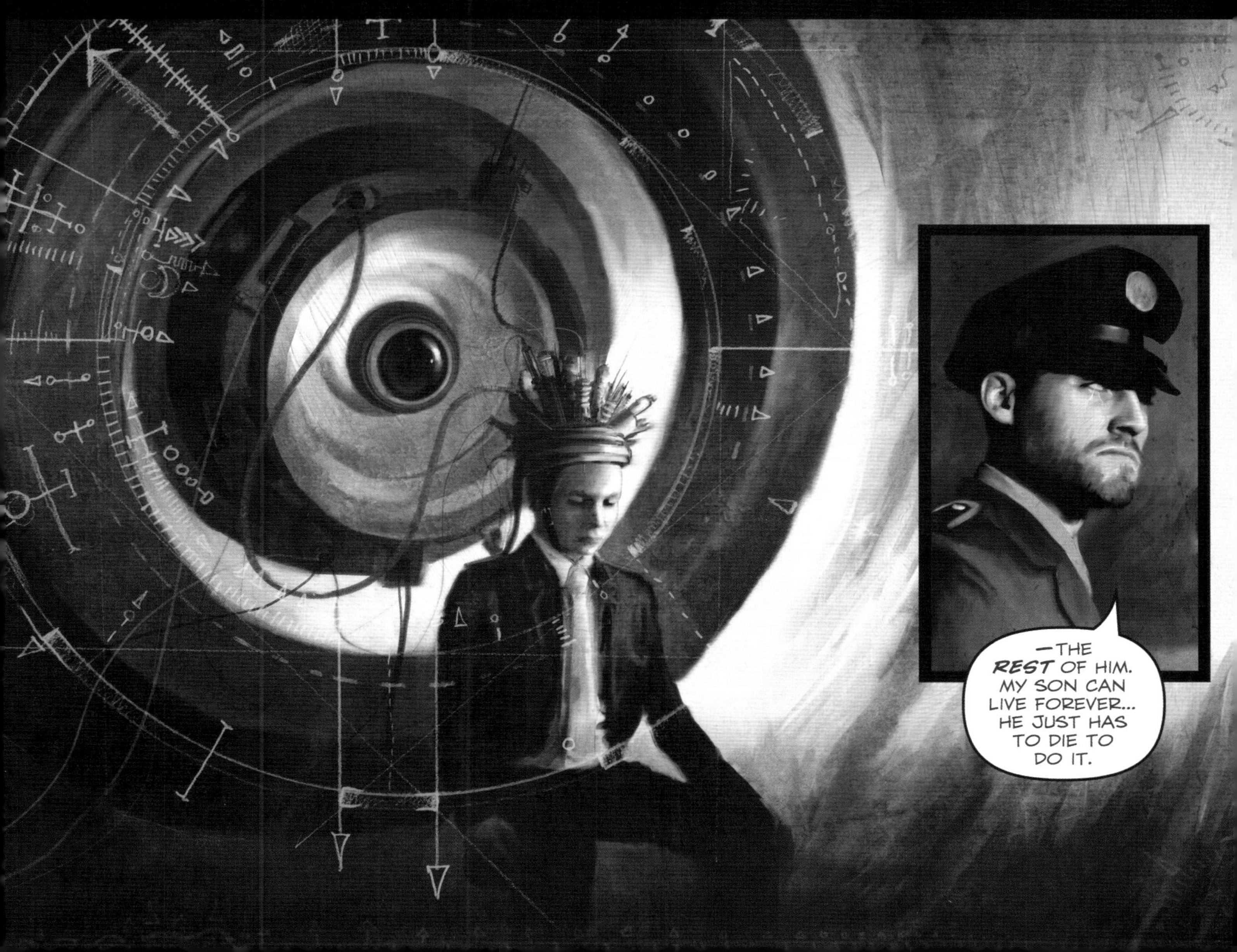
—THE REST OF HIM. MY SON CAN LIVE FOREVER... HE JUST HAS TO DIE TO DO IT.

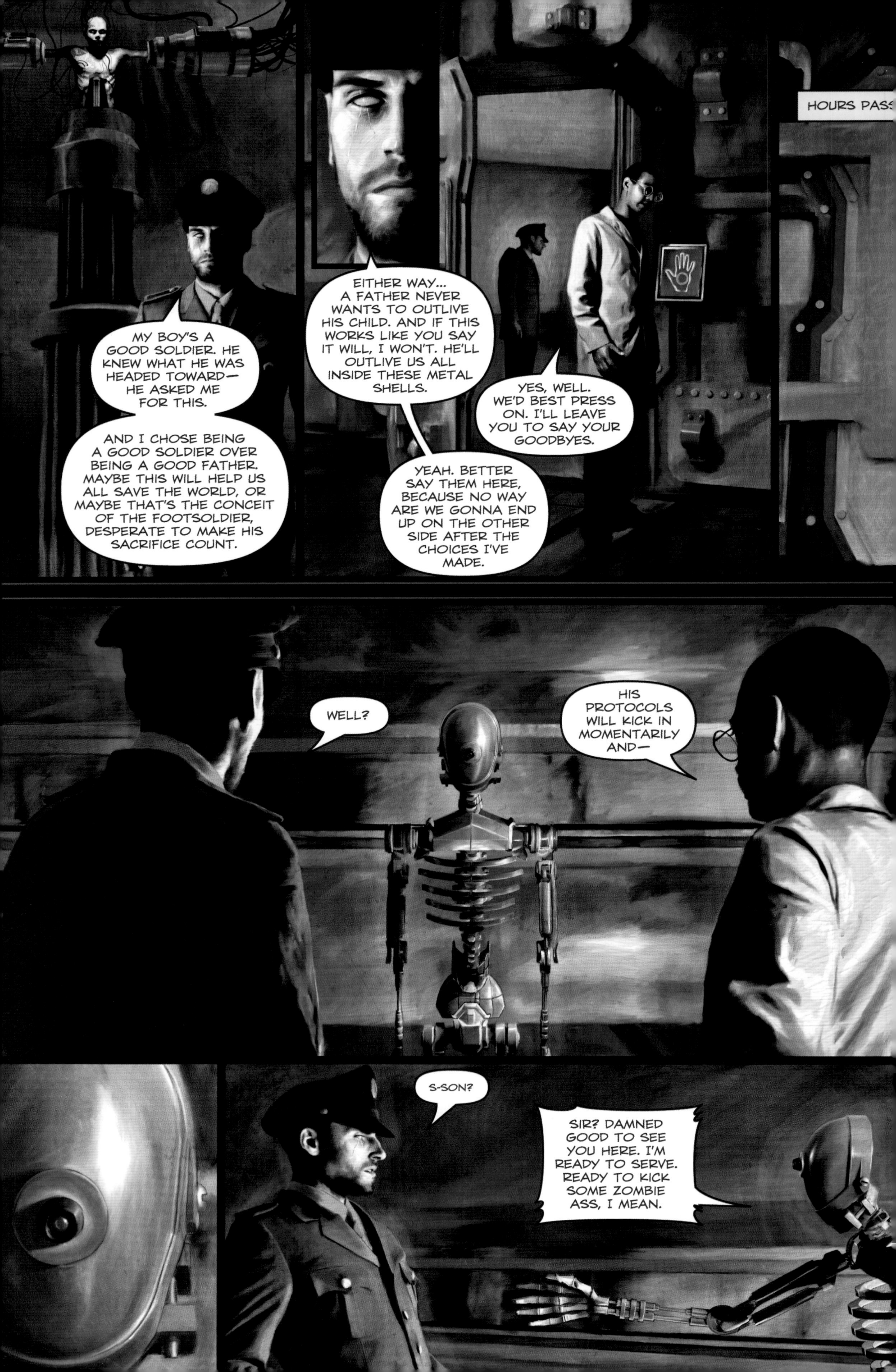
HOURS PASS
MY BOY'S A GOOD SOLDIER. HE KNEW WHAT HE WAS HEADED TOWARD—HE ASKED ME FOR THIS.
AND I CHOSE BEING A GOOD SOLDIER OVER BEING A GOOD FATHER. MAYBE THIS WILL HELP US ALL SAVE THE WORLD, OR MAYBE THAT'S THE CONCEIT OF THE FOOTSOLDIER, DESPERATE TO MAKE HIS SACRIFICE COUNT.
EITHER WAY... A FATHER NEVER WANTS TO OUTLIVE HIS CHILD. AND IF THIS WORKS LIKE YOU SAY IT WILL, I WON'T. HE'LL OUTLIVE US ALL INSIDE THESE METAL SHELLS.
YES, WELL. WE'D BEST PRESS ON. I'LL LEAVE YOU TO SAY YOUR GOODBYES.
YEAH. BETTER SAY THEM HERE, BECAUSE NO WAY ARE WE GONNA END UP ON THE OTHER SIDE AFTER THE CHOICES I'VE MADE.
WELL?
HIS PROTOCOLS WILL KICK IN MOMENTARILY AND—
S-SON?
SIR? DAMNED GOOD TO SEE YOU HERE. I'M READY TO SERVE. READY TO KICK SOME ZOMBIE ASS, I MEAN.

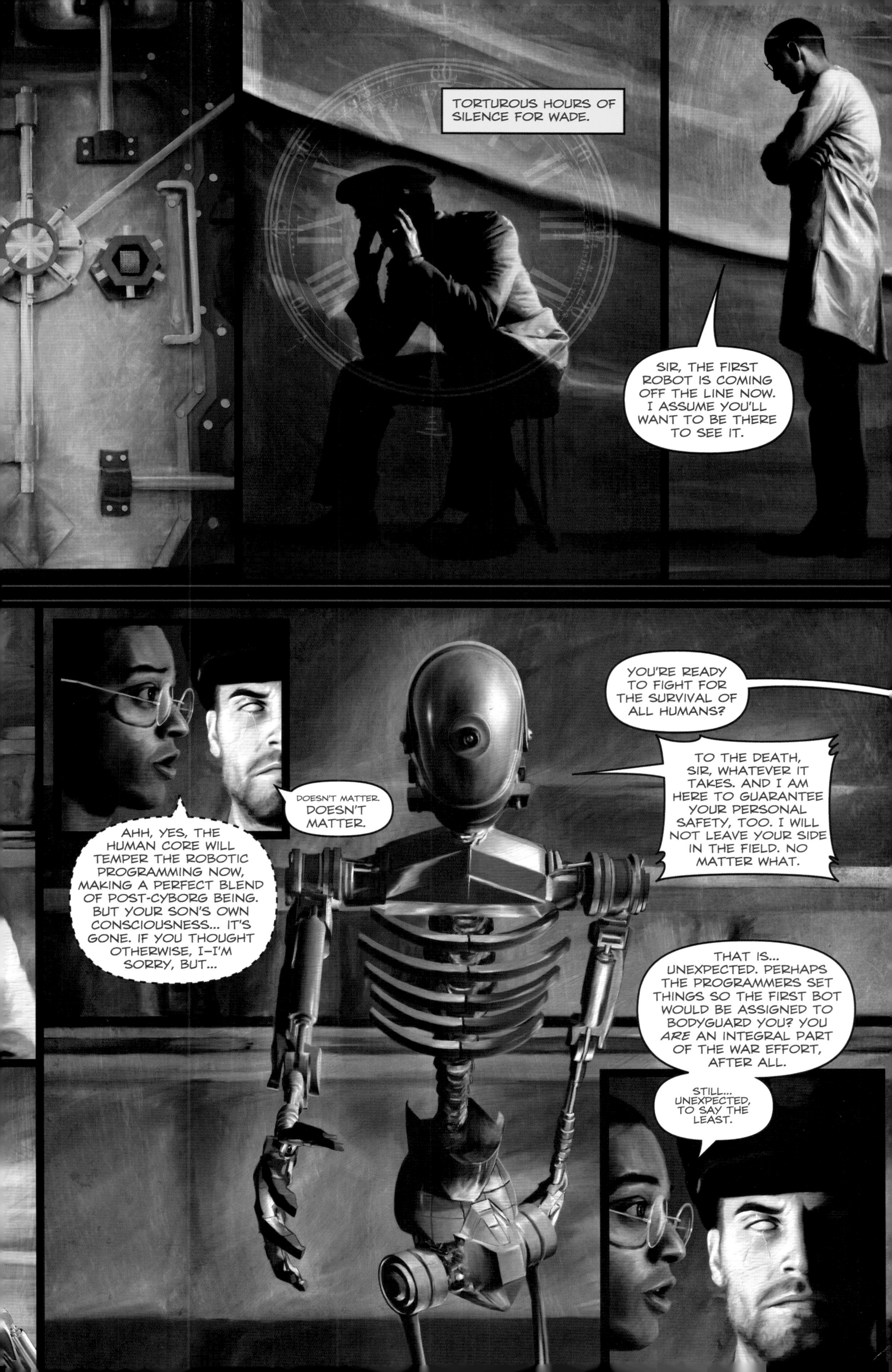
TORTUROUS HOURS OF SILENCE FOR WADE.
SIR, THE FIRST ROBOT IS COMING OFF THE LINE NOW. I ASSUME YOU'LL WANT TO BE THERE TO SEE IT.
AHH, YES, THE HUMAN CORE WILL TEMPER THE ROBOTIC PROGRAMMING NOW, MAKING A PERFECT BLEND OF POST-CYBORG BEING. BUT YOUR SON'S OWN CONSCIOUSNESS... IT'S GONE. IF YOU THOUGHT OTHERWISE, I—I'M SORRY, BUT...
DOESN'T MATTER. DOESN'T MATTER.
YOU'RE READY TO FIGHT FOR THE SURVIVAL OF ALL HUMANS?
TO THE DEATH, SIR, WHATEVER IT TAKES. AND I AM HERE TO GUARANTEE YOUR PERSONAL SAFETY, TOO. I WILL NOT LEAVE YOUR SIDE IN THE FIELD. NO MATTER WHAT.
THAT IS... UNEXPECTED. PERHAPS THE PROGRAMMERS SET THINGS SO THE FIRST BOT WOULD BE ASSIGNED TO BODYGUARD YOU? YOU *ARE* AN INTEGRAL PART OF THE WAR EFFORT, AFTER ALL.
STILL... UNEXPECTED, TO SAY THE LEAST.

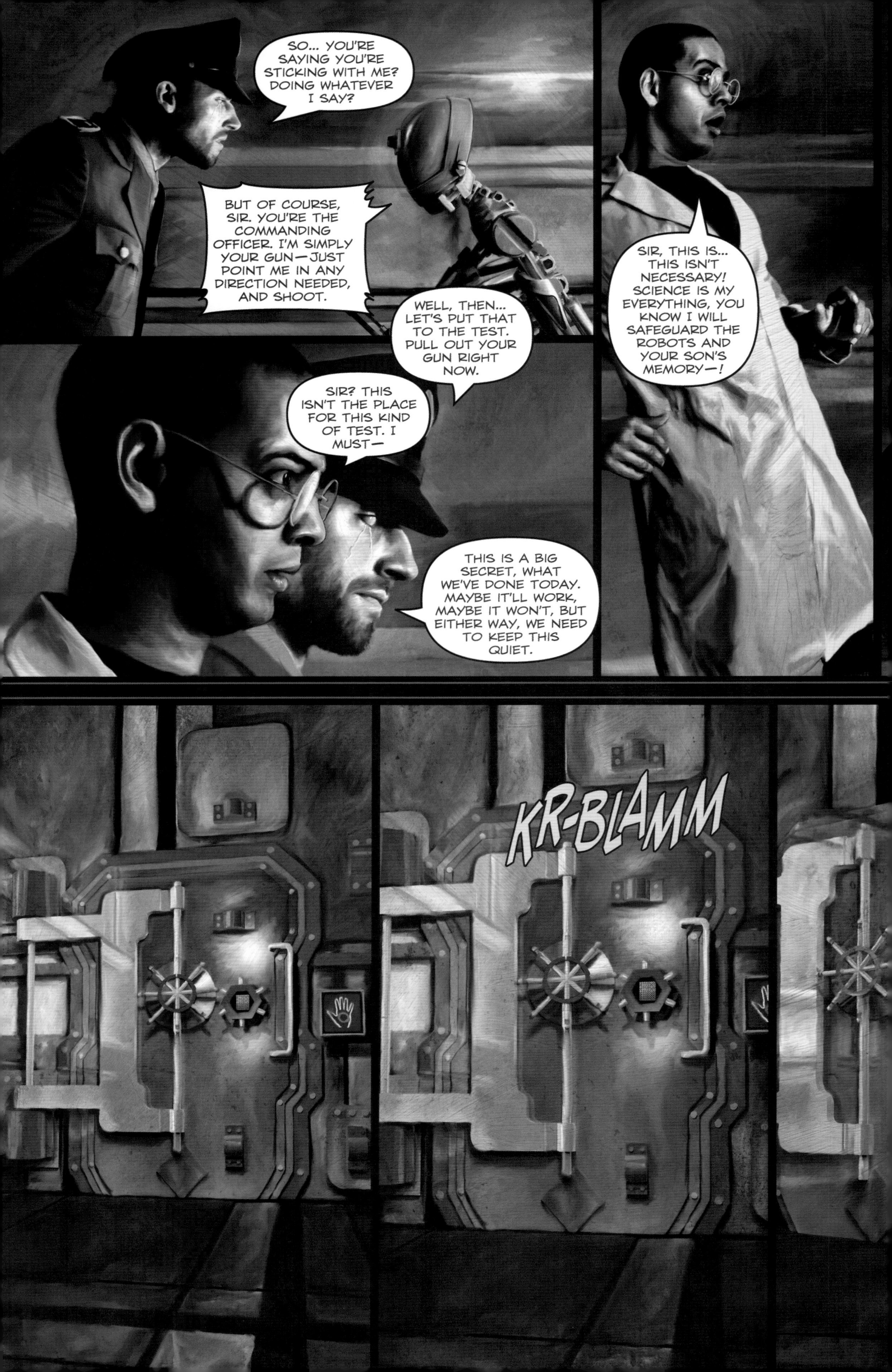
SO... YOU'RE SAYING YOU'RE STICKING WITH ME? DOING WHATEVER I SAY?
BUT OF COURSE, SIR. YOU'RE THE COMMANDING OFFICER. I'M SIMPLY YOUR GUN—JUST POINT ME IN ANY DIRECTION NEEDED, AND SHOOT.
WELL, THEN... LET'S PUT THAT TO THE TEST. PULL OUT YOUR GUN RIGHT NOW.
SIR? THIS ISN'T THE PLACE FOR THIS KIND OF TEST. I MUST—
THIS IS A BIG SECRET, WHAT WE'VE DONE TODAY. MAYBE IT'LL WORK, MAYBE IT WON'T, BUT EITHER WAY, WE NEED TO KEEP THIS QUIET.
SIR, THIS IS... THIS ISN'T NECESSARY! SCIENCE IS MY EVERYTHING, YOU KNOW I WILL SAFEGUARD THE ROBOTS AND YOUR SON'S MEMORY—!
KR-BLAMM

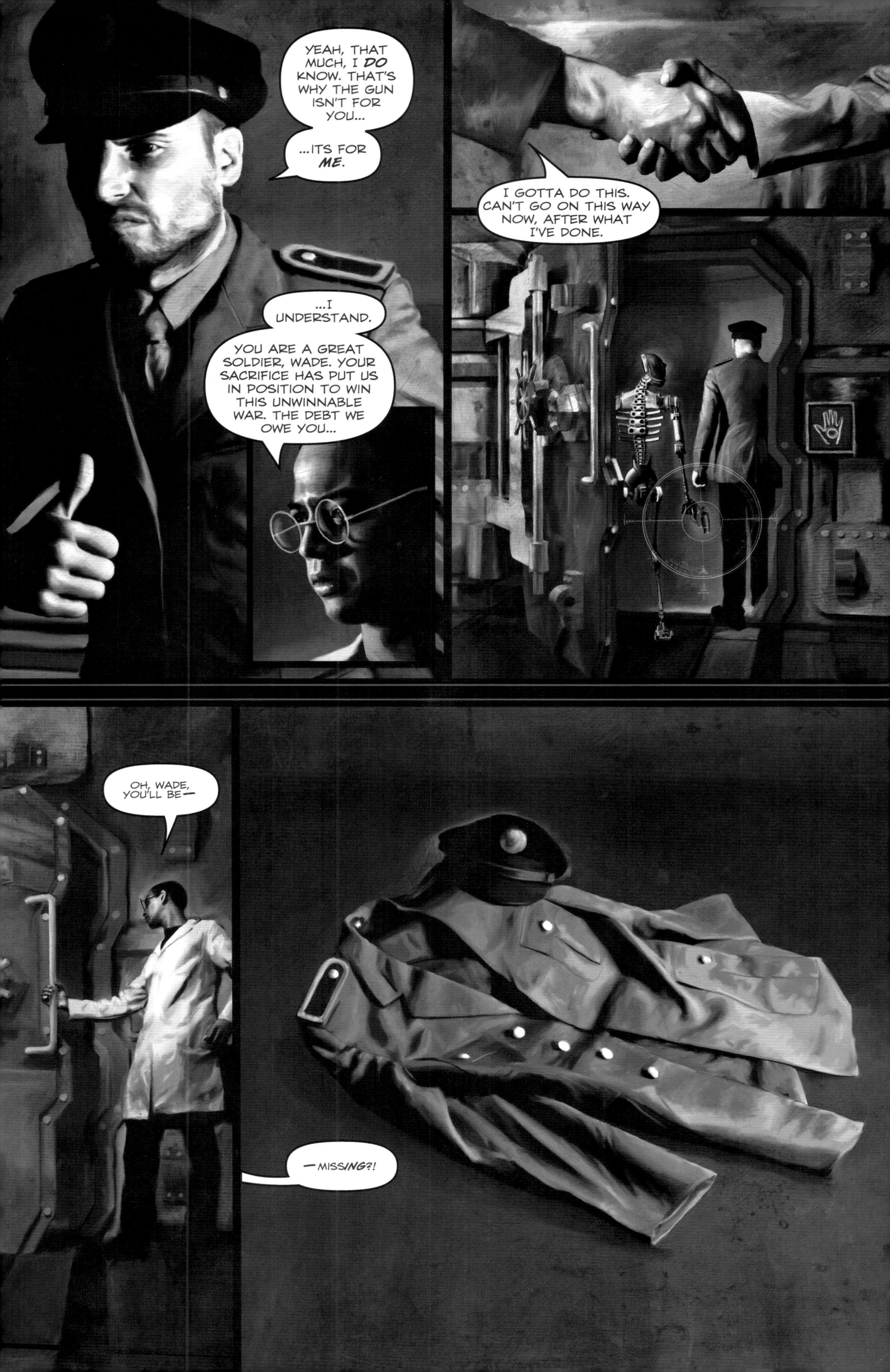

YEAH, THAT MUCH, I DO KNOW. THAT'S WHY THE GUN ISN'T FOR YOU...
...ITS FOR ME.
I GOTTA DO THIS. CAN'T GO ON THIS WAY NOW, AFTER WHAT I'VE DONE.
...I UNDERSTAND.
YOU ARE A GREAT SOLDIER, WADE. YOUR SACRIFICE HAS PUT US IN POSITION TO WIN THIS UNWINNABLE WAR. THE DEBT WE OWE YOU...
OH, WADE, YOU'LL BE—
—MISSING?!

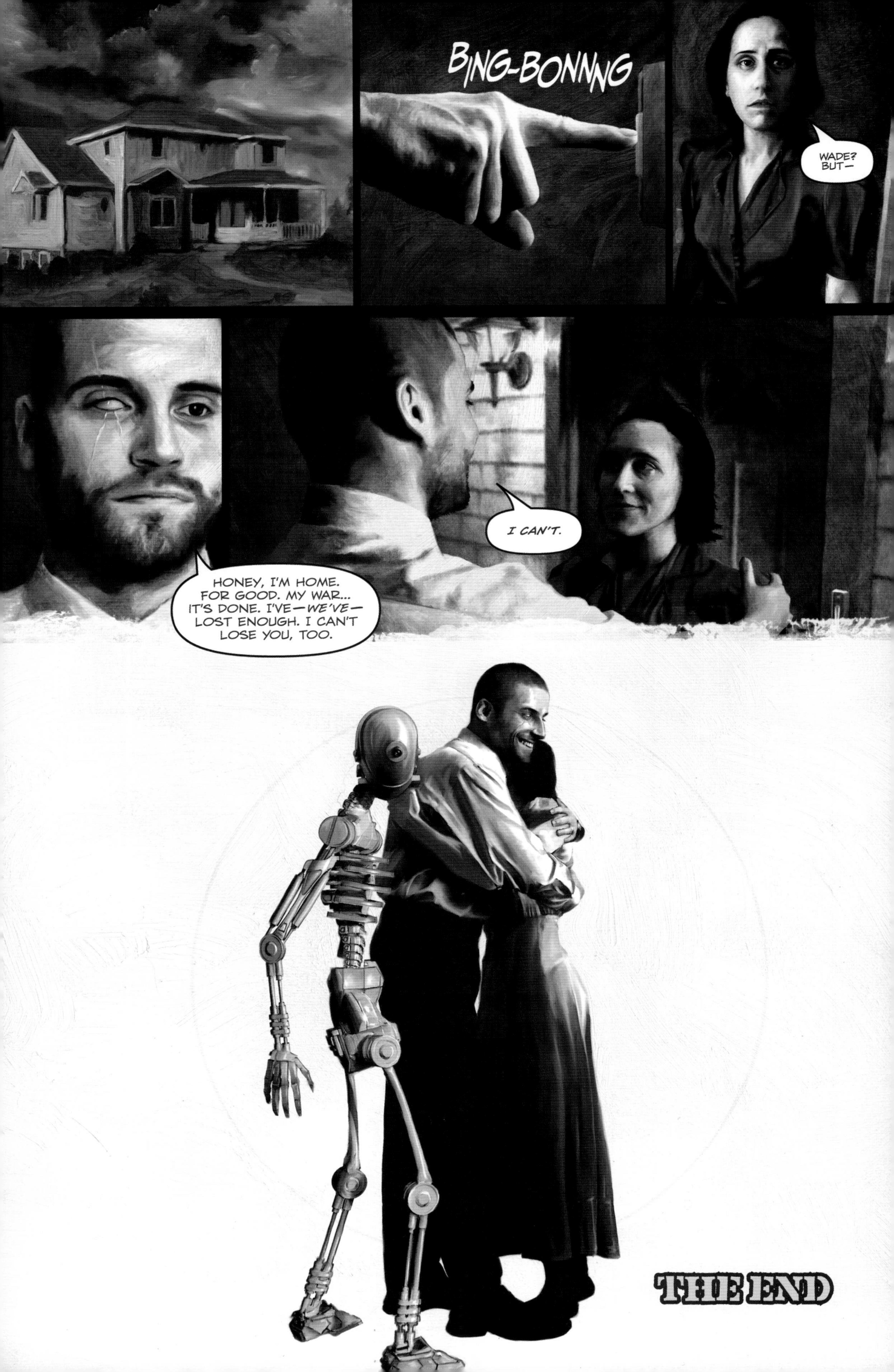
BING-BONNNG
WADE? BUT—
HONEY, I'M HOME. FOR GOOD. MY WAR... IT'S DONE. I'VE—WE'VE—LOST ENOUGH. I CAN'T LOSE YOU, TOO.
I CAN'T.
THE END

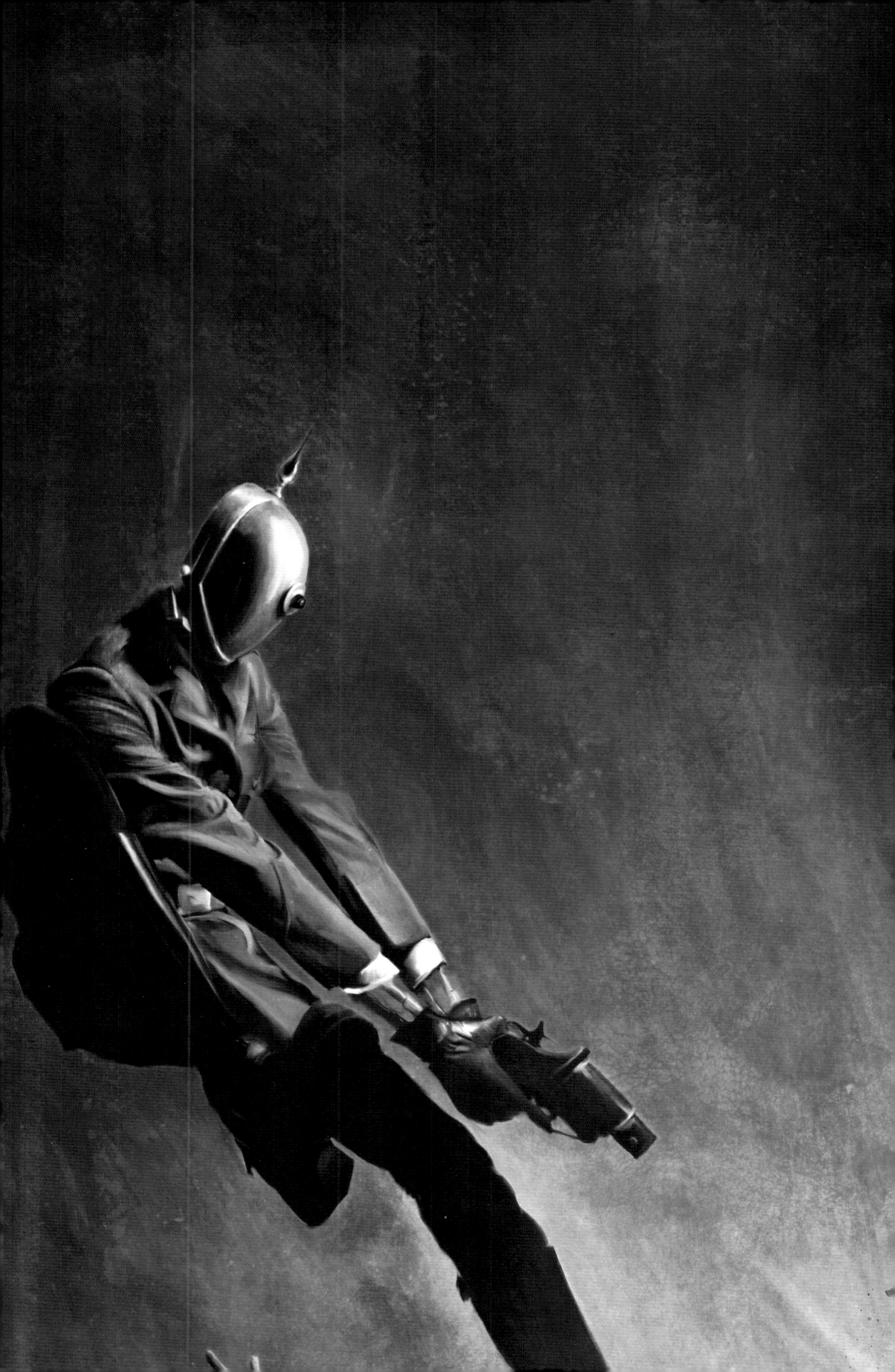

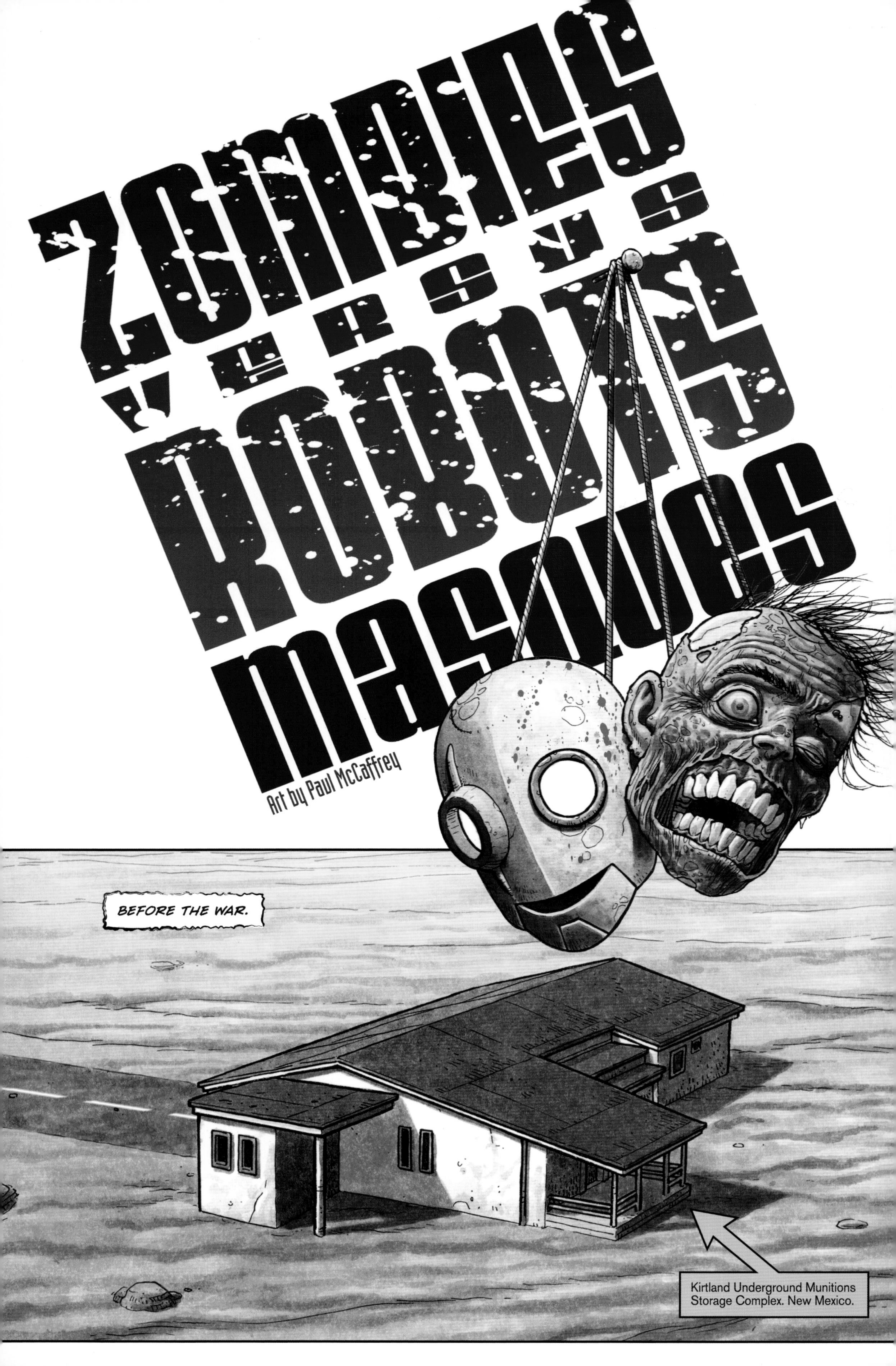
ZOMBIES
VERSUS
ROBOTS
MASQUES
Art by Paul McCaffrey
BEFORE THE WAR.
Kirtland Underground Munitions Storage Complex. New Mexico.

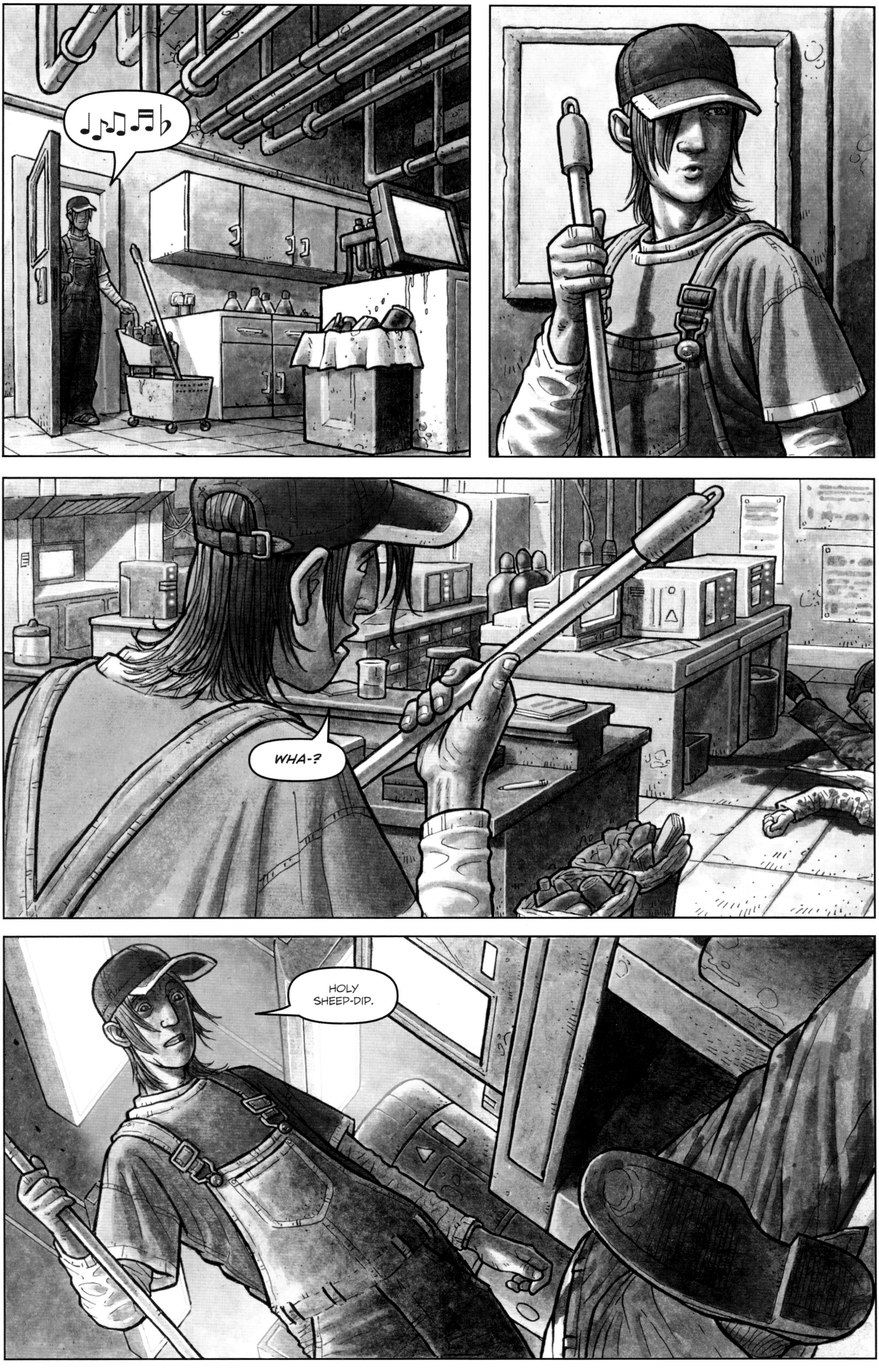
WHA-?
HOLY SHEEP-DIP.

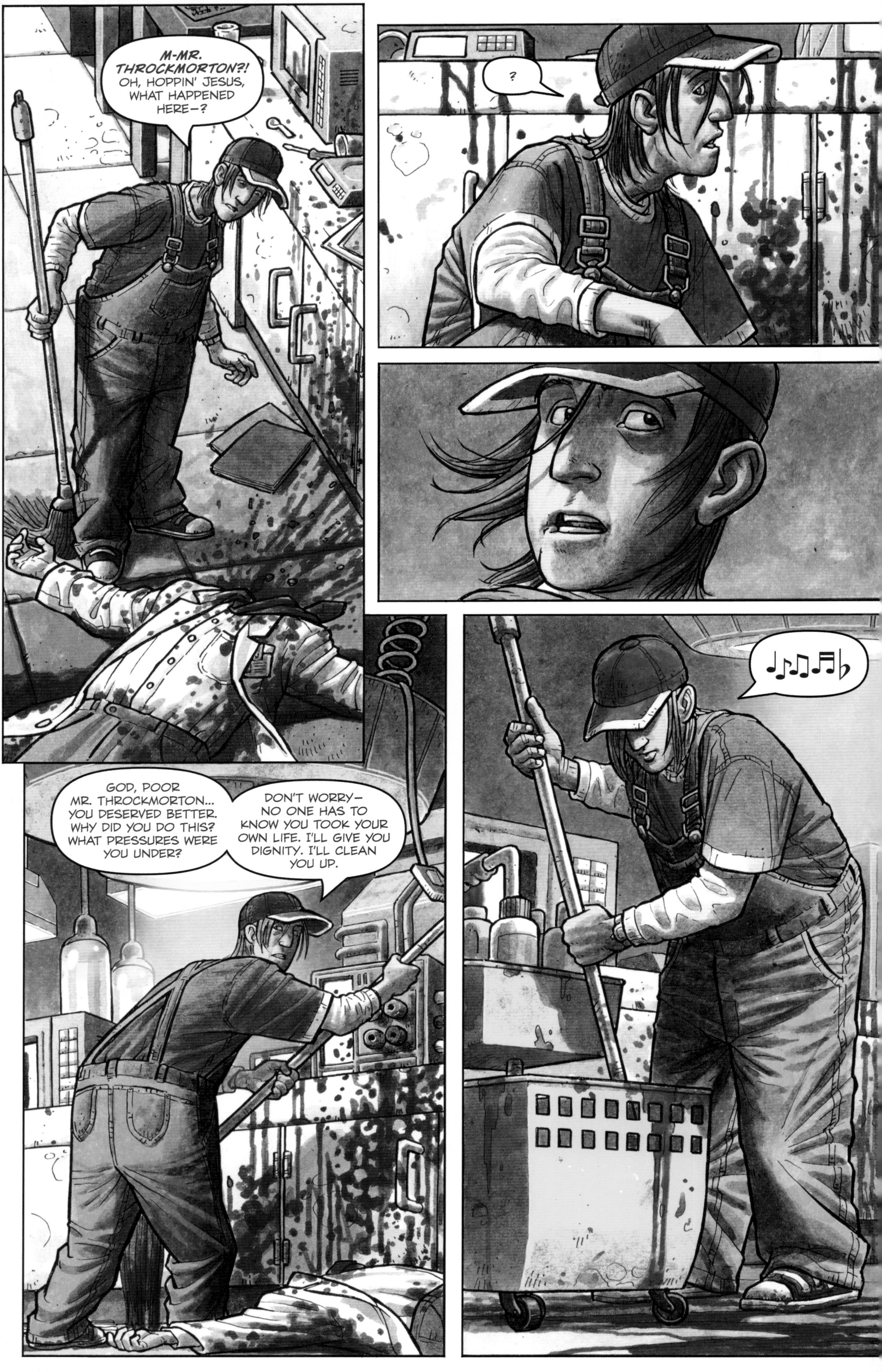
M-MR. THROCKMORTON?! OH, HOPPIN' JESUS, WHAT HAPPENED HERE–?
?
GOD, POOR MR. THROCKMORTON... YOU DESERVED BETTER. WHY DID YOU DO THIS? WHAT PRESSURES WERE YOU UNDER?
DON'T WORRY– NO ONE HAS TO KNOW YOU TOOK YOUR OWN LIFE. I'LL GIVE YOU DIGNITY. I'LL CLEAN YOU UP.

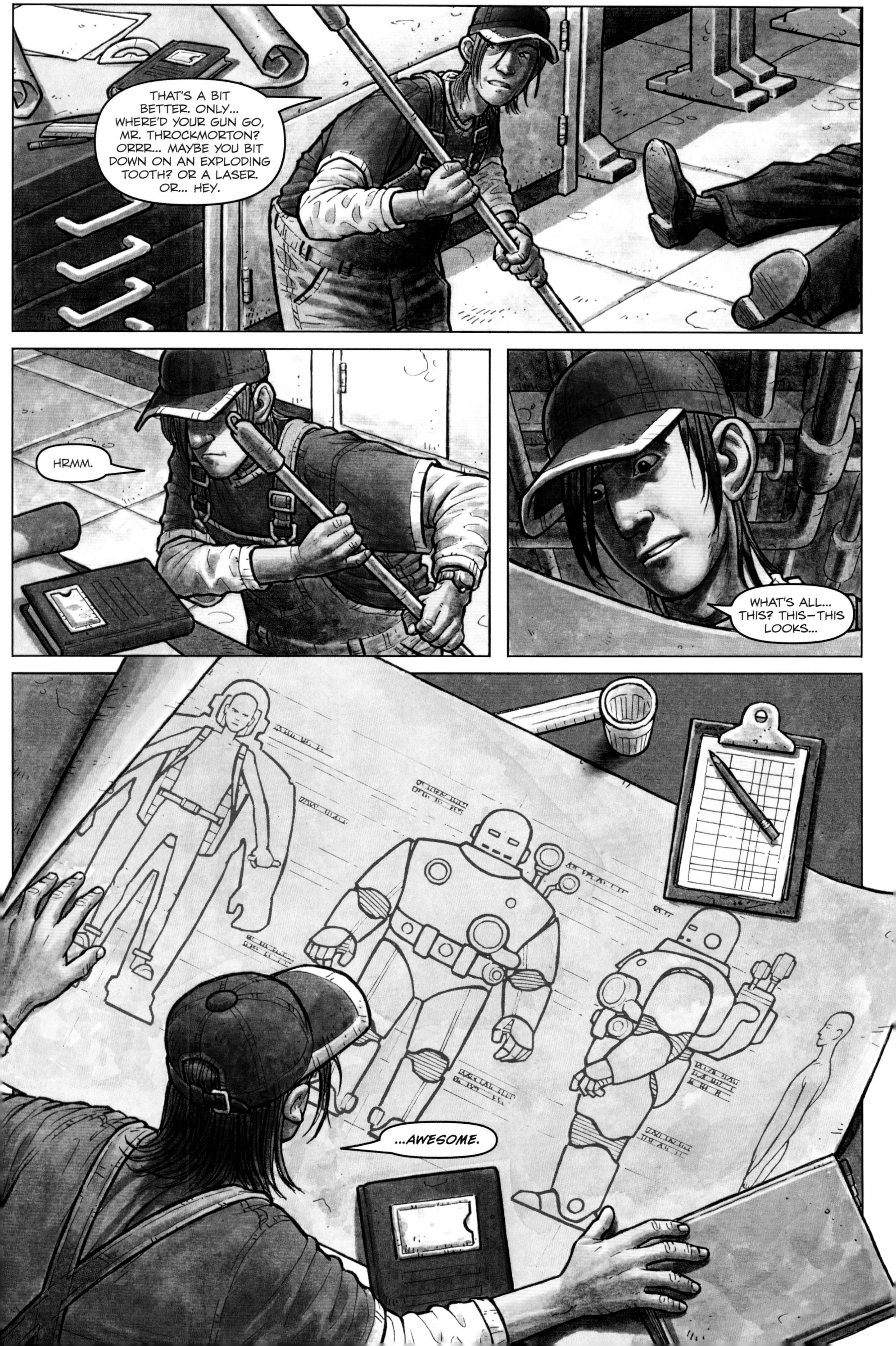
THAT'S A BIT BETTER. ONLY... WHERE'D YOUR GUN GO, MR. THROCKMORTON? ORRR... MAYBE YOU BIT DOWN ON AN EXPLODING TOOTH? OR A LASER. OR... HEY.
HRMM.
WHAT'S ALL... THIS? THIS—THIS LOOKS...
...AWESOME.

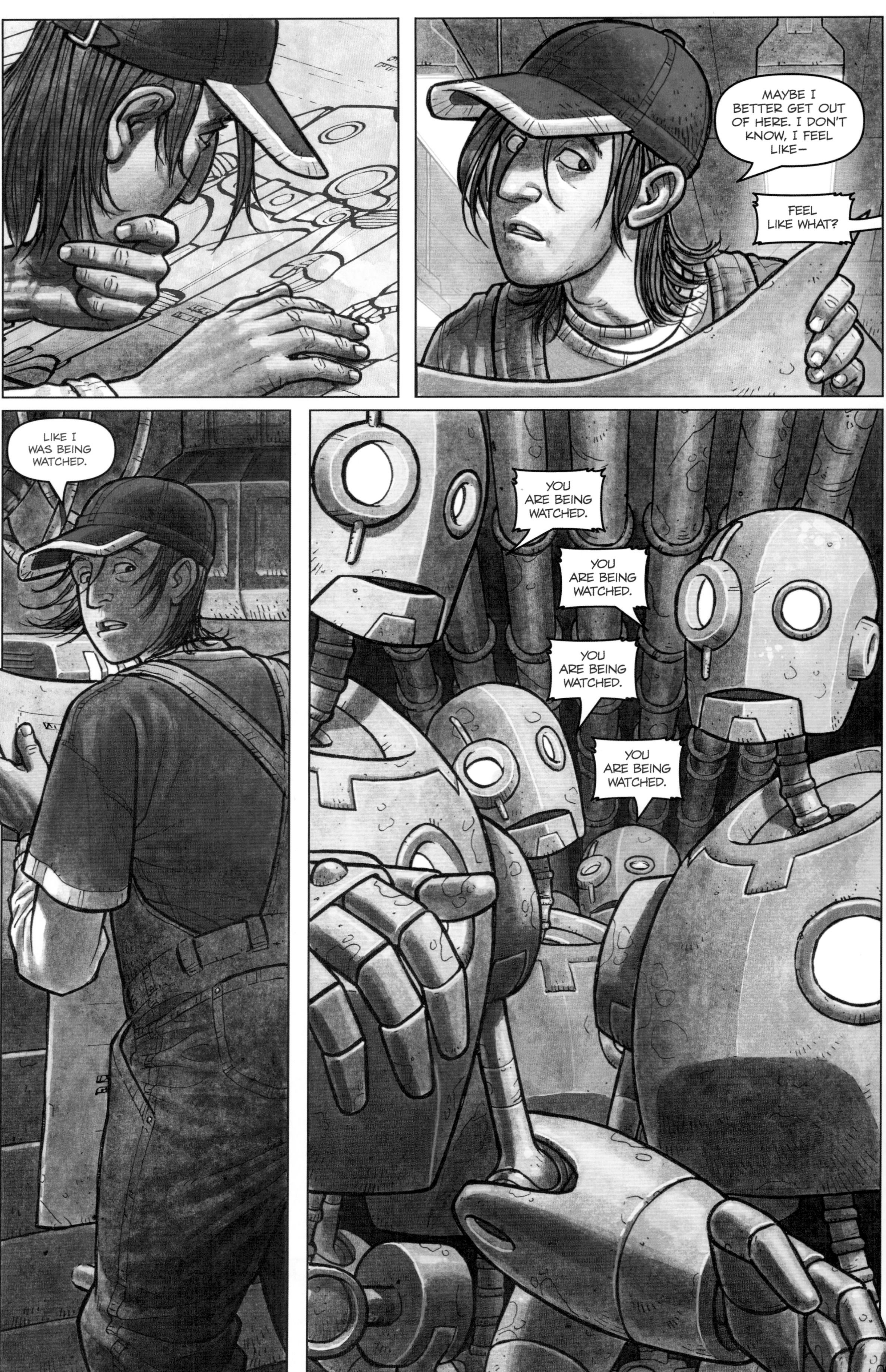
MAYBE I BETTER GET OUT OF HERE. I DON'T KNOW, I FEEL LIKE–
FEEL LIKE WHAT?
LIKE I WAS BEING WATCHED.
YOU ARE BEING WATCHED.
YOU ARE BEING WATCHED.
YOU ARE BEING WATCHED.
YOU ARE BEING WATCHED.

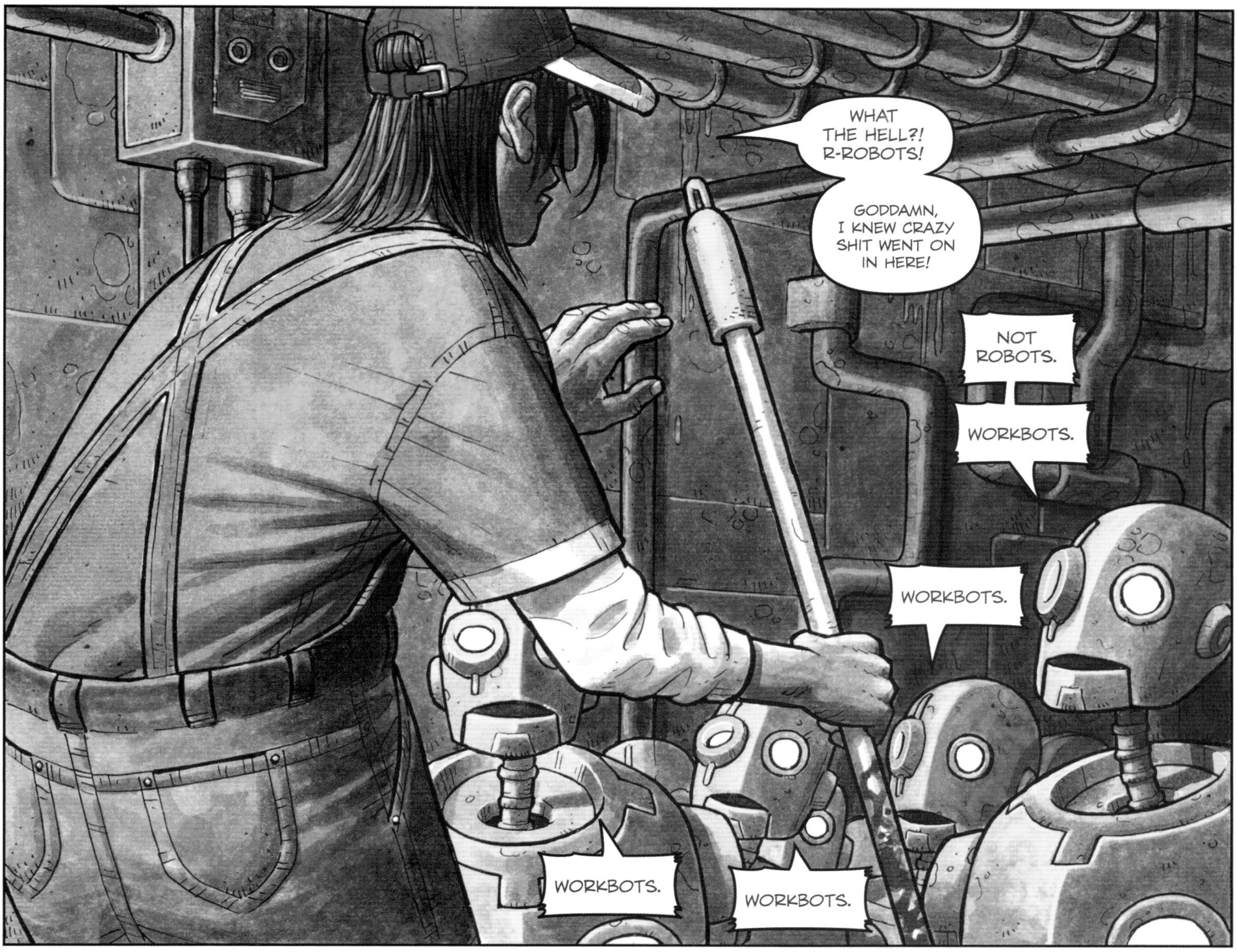
WHAT THE HELL?! R-ROBOTS!
GODDAMN, I KNEW CRAZY SHIT WENT ON IN HERE!
NOT ROBOTS.
WORKBOTS.
WORKBOTS.
WORKBOTS.
WORKBOTS.

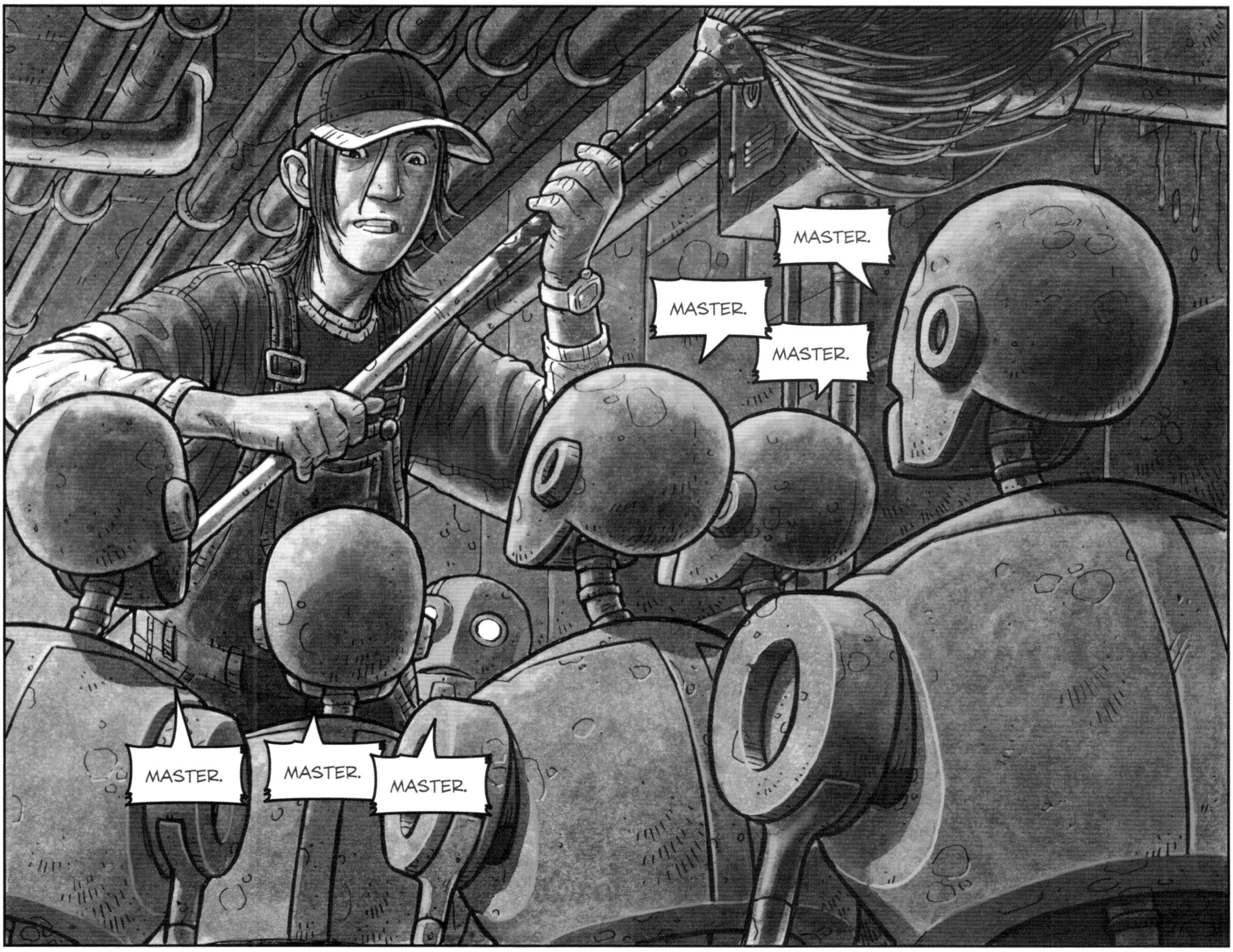
MASTER.
MASTER.
MASTER.
MASTER.
MASTER.
MASTER.

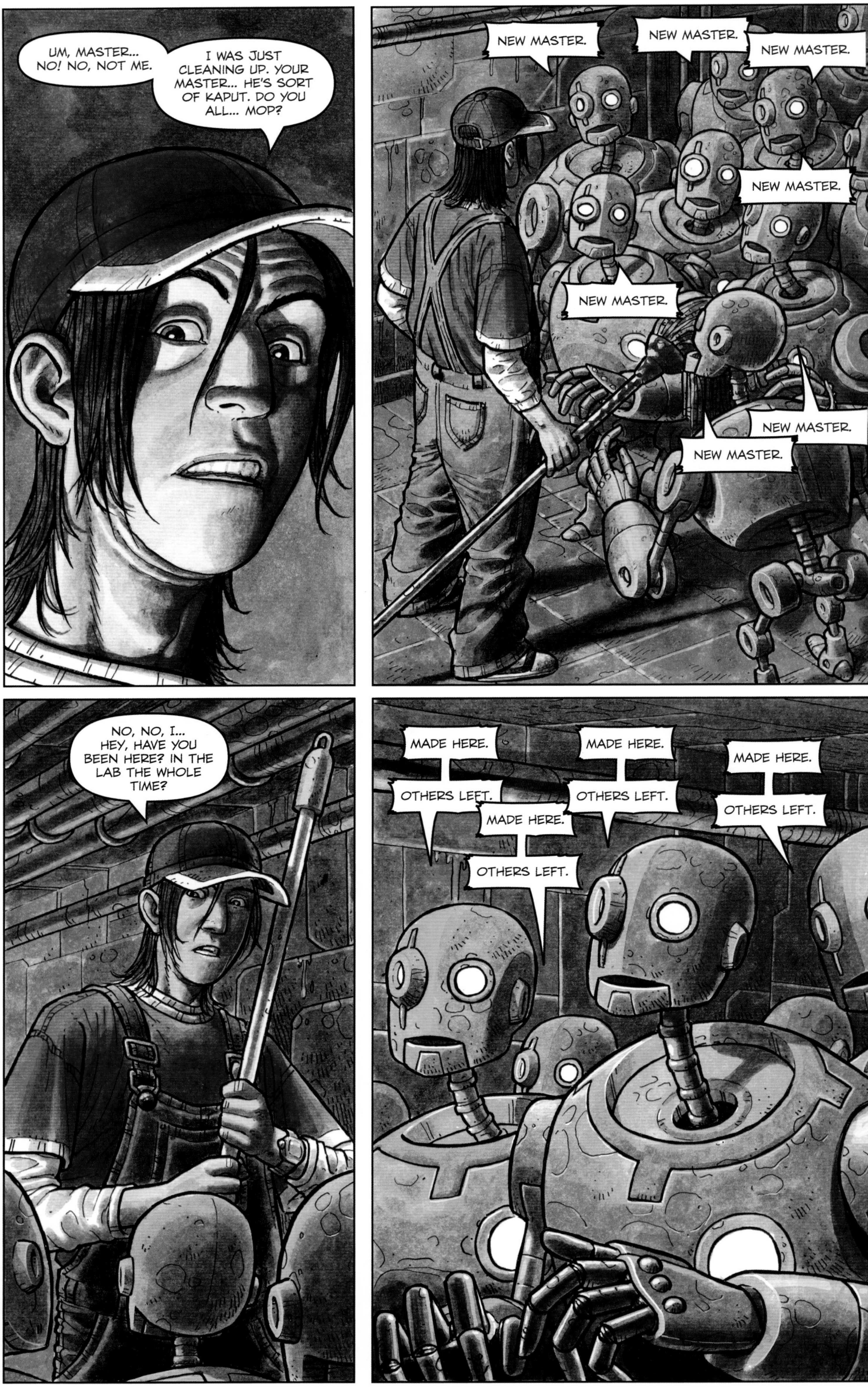

UM, MASTER... NO! NO, NOT ME.
I WAS JUST CLEANING UP. YOUR MASTER... HE'S SORT OF KAPUT. DO YOU ALL... MOP?
NEW MASTER.
NEW MASTER.
NEW MASTER.
NEW MASTER.
NEW MASTER.
NEW MASTER.
NEW MASTER.
NO, NO, I... HEY, HAVE YOU BEEN HERE? IN THE LAB THE WHOLE TIME?
MADE HERE.
OTHERS LEFT.
MADE HERE.
OTHERS LEFT.
MADE HERE.
OTHERS LEFT.
MADE HERE.
OTHERS LEFT.

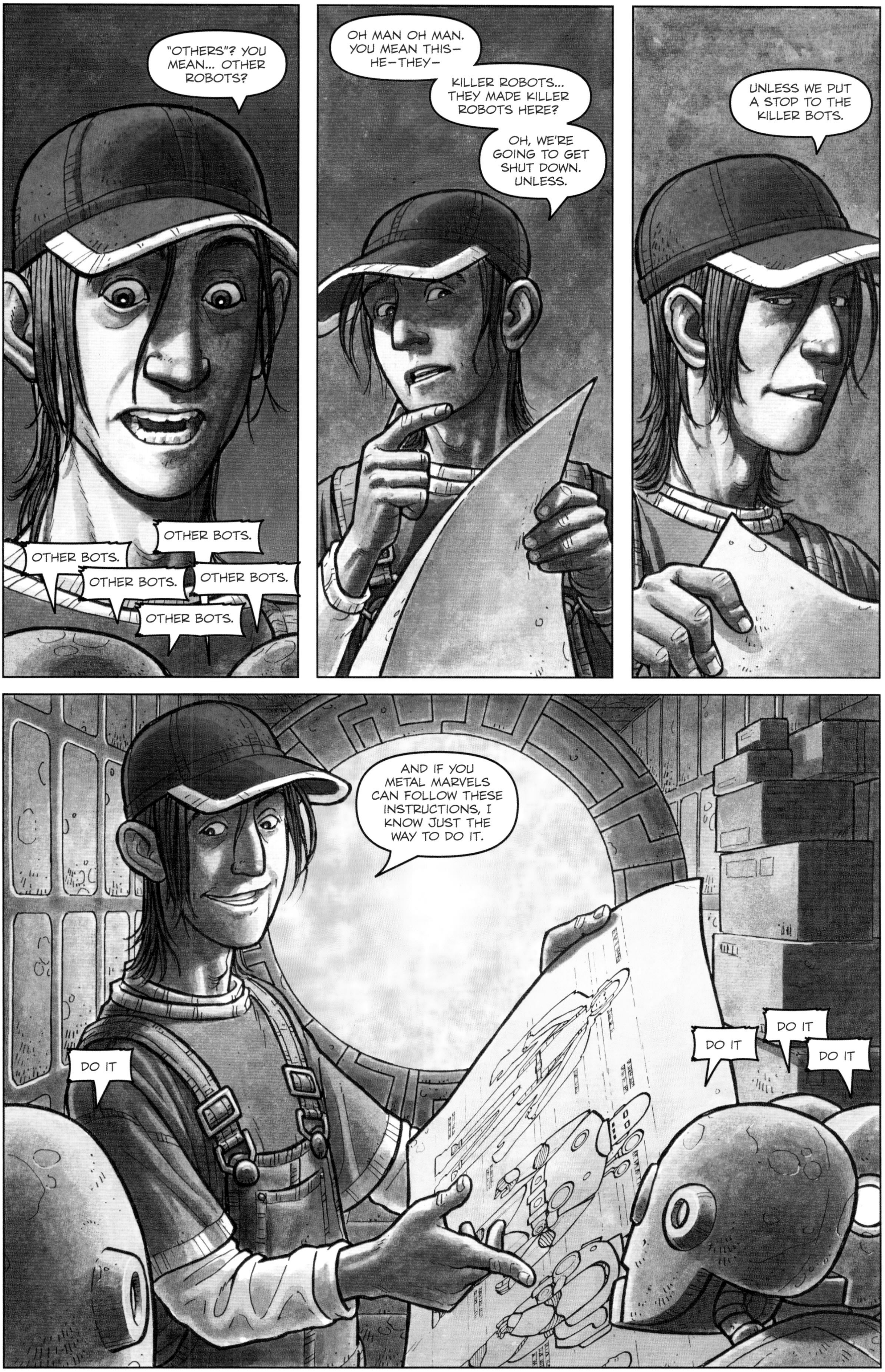
"OTHERS"? YOU MEAN... OTHER ROBOTS?
OTHER BOTS.
OTHER BOTS.
OTHER BOTS.
OTHER BOTS.
OTHER BOTS.
OH MAN OH MAN. YOU MEAN THIS— HE—THEY—
KILLER ROBOTS... THEY MADE KILLER ROBOTS HERE?
OH, WE'RE GOING TO GET SHUT DOWN. UNLESS.
UNLESS WE PUT A STOP TO THE KILLER BOTS.
AND IF YOU METAL MARVELS CAN FOLLOW THESE INSTRUCTIONS, I KNOW JUST THE WAY TO DO IT.
DO IT
DO IT
DO IT
DO IT

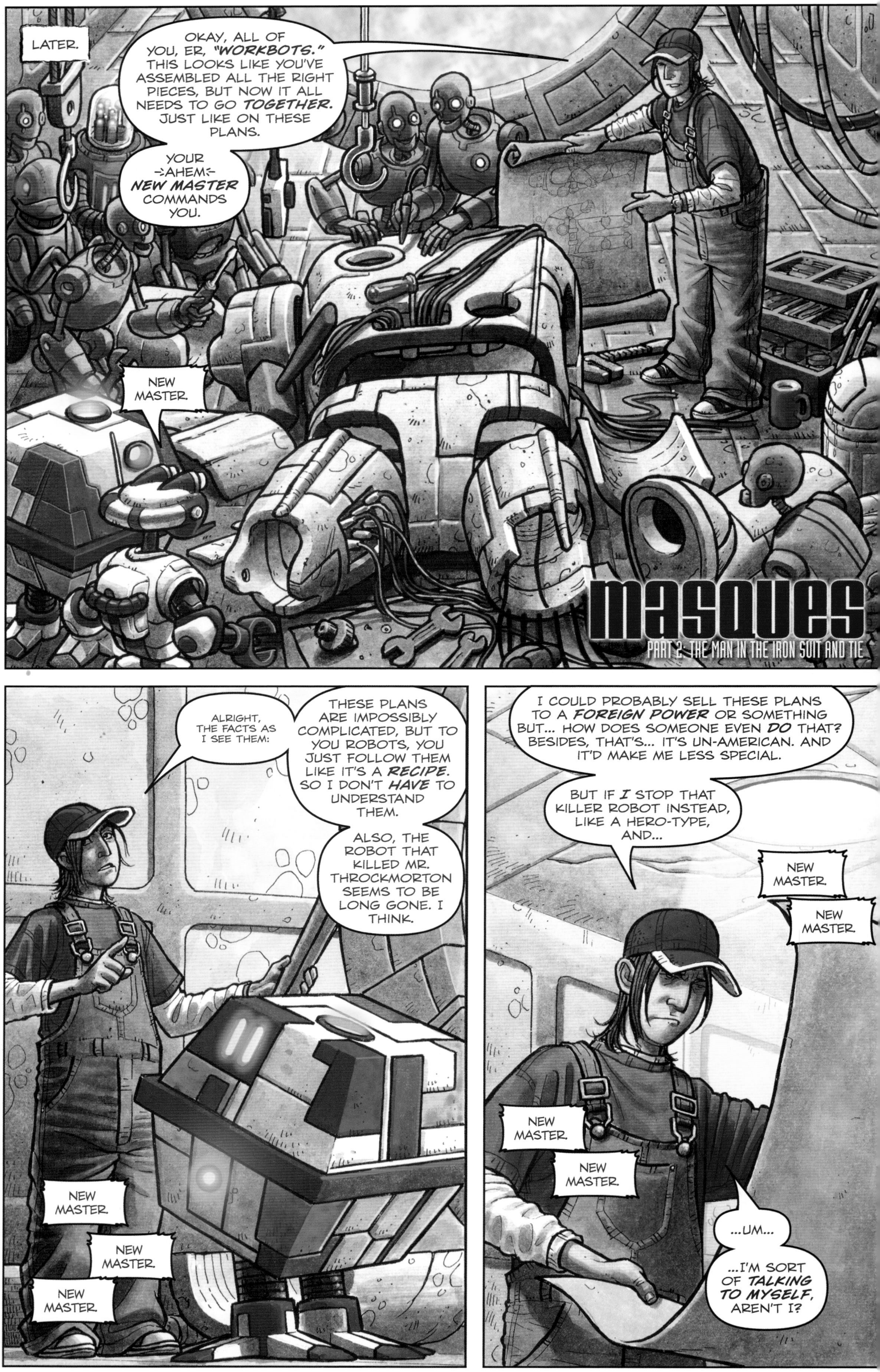
LATER.
OKAY, ALL OF YOU, ER, "WORKBOTS." THIS LOOKS LIKE YOU'VE ASSEMBLED ALL THE RIGHT PIECES, BUT NOW IT ALL NEEDS TO GO TOGETHER. JUST LIKE ON THESE PLANS.
YOUR -AHEM- NEW MASTER COMMANDS YOU.
NEW MASTER.
MASQUES
PART 2: THE MAN IN THE IRON SUIT AND TIE
ALRIGHT, THE FACTS AS I SEE THEM:
THESE PLANS ARE IMPOSSIBLY COMPLICATED, BUT TO YOU ROBOTS, YOU JUST FOLLOW THEM LIKE IT'S A RECIPE. SO I DON'T HAVE TO UNDERSTAND THEM.
ALSO, THE ROBOT THAT KILLED MR. THROCKMORTON SEEMS TO BE LONG GONE. I THINK.
NEW MASTER.
NEW MASTER.
NEW MASTER.
I COULD PROBABLY SELL THESE PLANS TO A FOREIGN POWER OR SOMETHING BUT... HOW DOES SOMEONE EVEN DO THAT? BESIDES, THAT'S... IT'S UN-AMERICAN. AND IT'D MAKE ME LESS SPECIAL.
BUT IF I STOP THAT KILLER ROBOT INSTEAD, LIKE A HERO-TYPE, AND...
NEW MASTER.
NEW MASTER.
NEW MASTER.
NEW MASTER.
...UM...
...I'M SORT OF TALKING TO MYSELF, AREN'T I?

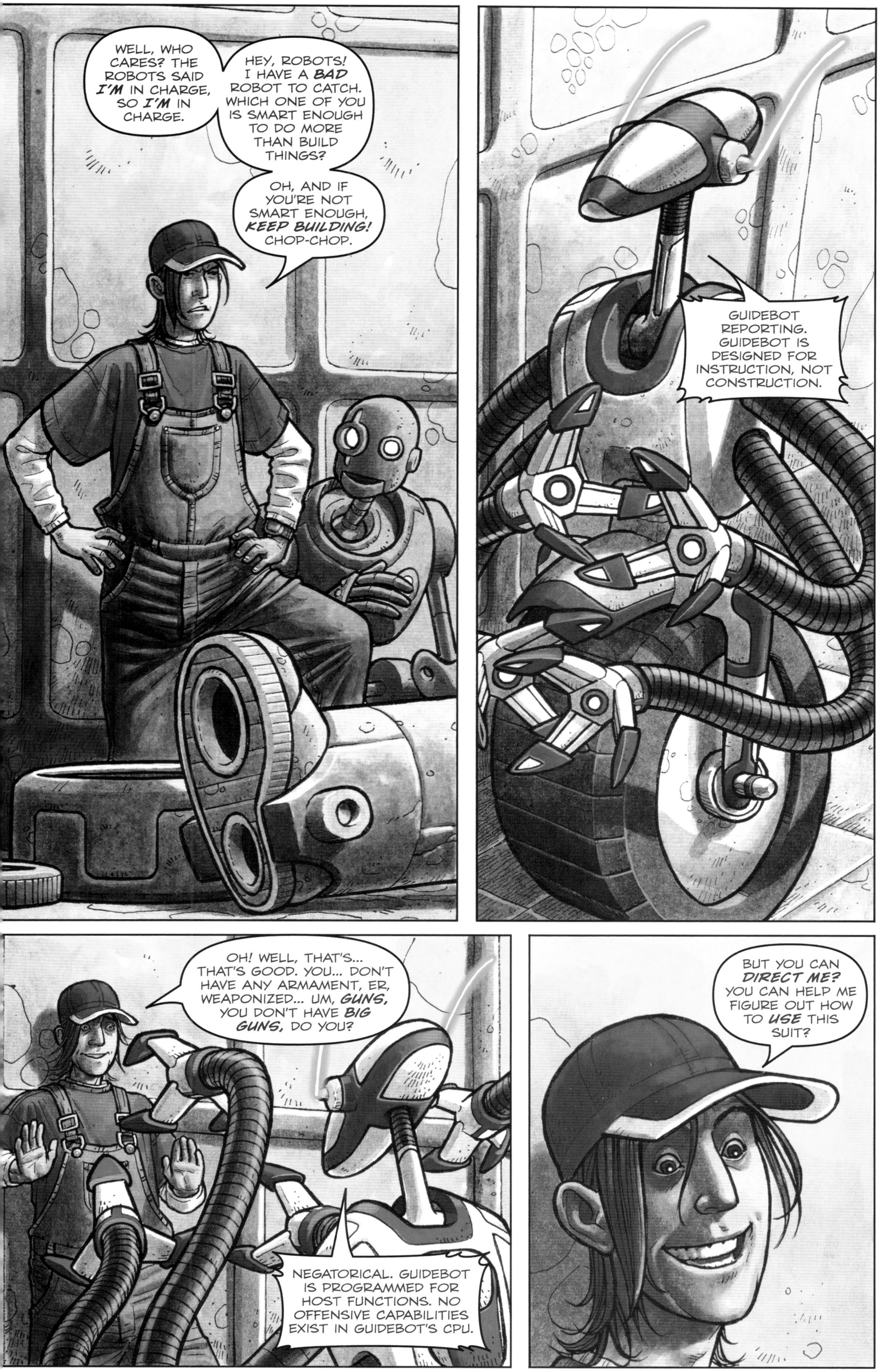
WELL, WHO CARES? THE ROBOTS SAID *I'M* IN CHARGE, SO *I'M* IN CHARGE.
HEY, ROBOTS! I HAVE A ***BAD*** ROBOT TO CATCH. WHICH ONE OF YOU IS SMART ENOUGH TO DO MORE THAN BUILD THINGS?
OH, AND IF YOU'RE NOT SMART ENOUGH, ***KEEP BUILDING!*** CHOP-CHOP.
GUIDEBOT REPORTING. GUIDEBOT IS DESIGNED FOR INSTRUCTION, NOT CONSTRUCTION.
OH! WELL, THAT'S... THAT'S GOOD. YOU... DON'T HAVE ANY ARMAMENT, ER, WEAPONIZED... UM, ***GUNS,*** YOU DON'T HAVE ***BIG GUNS,*** DO YOU?
NEGATORICAL. GUIDEBOT IS PROGRAMMED FOR HOST FUNCTIONS. NO OFFENSIVE CAPABILITIES EXIST IN GUIDEBOT'S CPU.
BUT YOU CAN ***DIRECT ME?*** YOU CAN HELP ME FIGURE OUT HOW TO ***USE*** THIS SUIT?

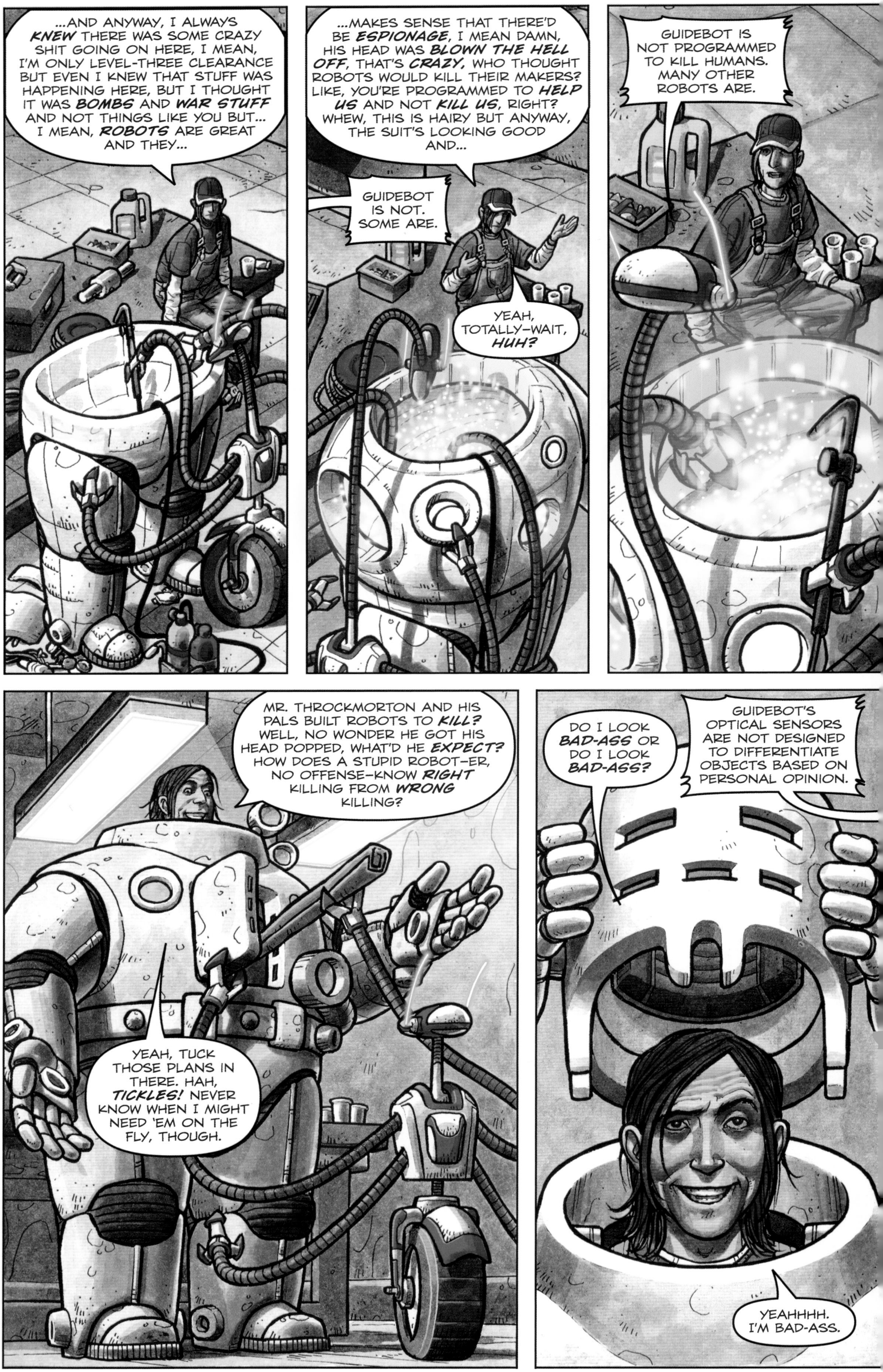
...AND ANYWAY, I ALWAYS KNEW THERE WAS SOME CRAZY SHIT GOING ON HERE, I MEAN, I'M ONLY LEVEL-THREE CLEARANCE BUT EVEN I KNEW THAT STUFF WAS HAPPENING HERE, BUT I THOUGHT IT WAS BOMBS AND WAR STUFF AND NOT THINGS LIKE YOU BUT... I MEAN, ROBOTS ARE GREAT AND THEY...
...MAKES SENSE THAT THERE'D BE ESPIONAGE, I MEAN DAMN, HIS HEAD WAS BLOWN THE HELL OFF, THAT'S CRAZY, WHO THOUGHT ROBOTS WOULD KILL THEIR MAKERS? LIKE, YOU'RE PROGRAMMED TO HELP US AND NOT KILL US, RIGHT? WHEW, THIS IS HAIRY BUT ANYWAY, THE SUIT'S LOOKING GOOD AND...
GUIDEBOT IS NOT. SOME ARE.
YEAH, TOTALLY–WAIT, HUH?
GUIDEBOT IS NOT PROGRAMMED TO KILL HUMANS. MANY OTHER ROBOTS ARE.
MR. THROCKMORTON AND HIS PALS BUILT ROBOTS TO KILL? WELL, NO WONDER HE GOT HIS HEAD POPPED, WHAT'D HE EXPECT? HOW DOES A STUPID ROBOT–ER, NO OFFENSE–KNOW RIGHT KILLING FROM WRONG KILLING?
YEAH, TUCK THOSE PLANS IN THERE. HAH, TICKLES! NEVER KNOW WHEN I MIGHT NEED 'EM ON THE FLY, THOUGH.
DO I LOOK BAD-ASS OR DO I LOOK BAD-ASS?
GUIDEBOT'S OPTICAL SENSORS ARE NOT DESIGNED TO DIFFERENTIATE OBJECTS BASED ON PERSONAL OPINION.
YEAHHHH. I'M BAD-ASS.

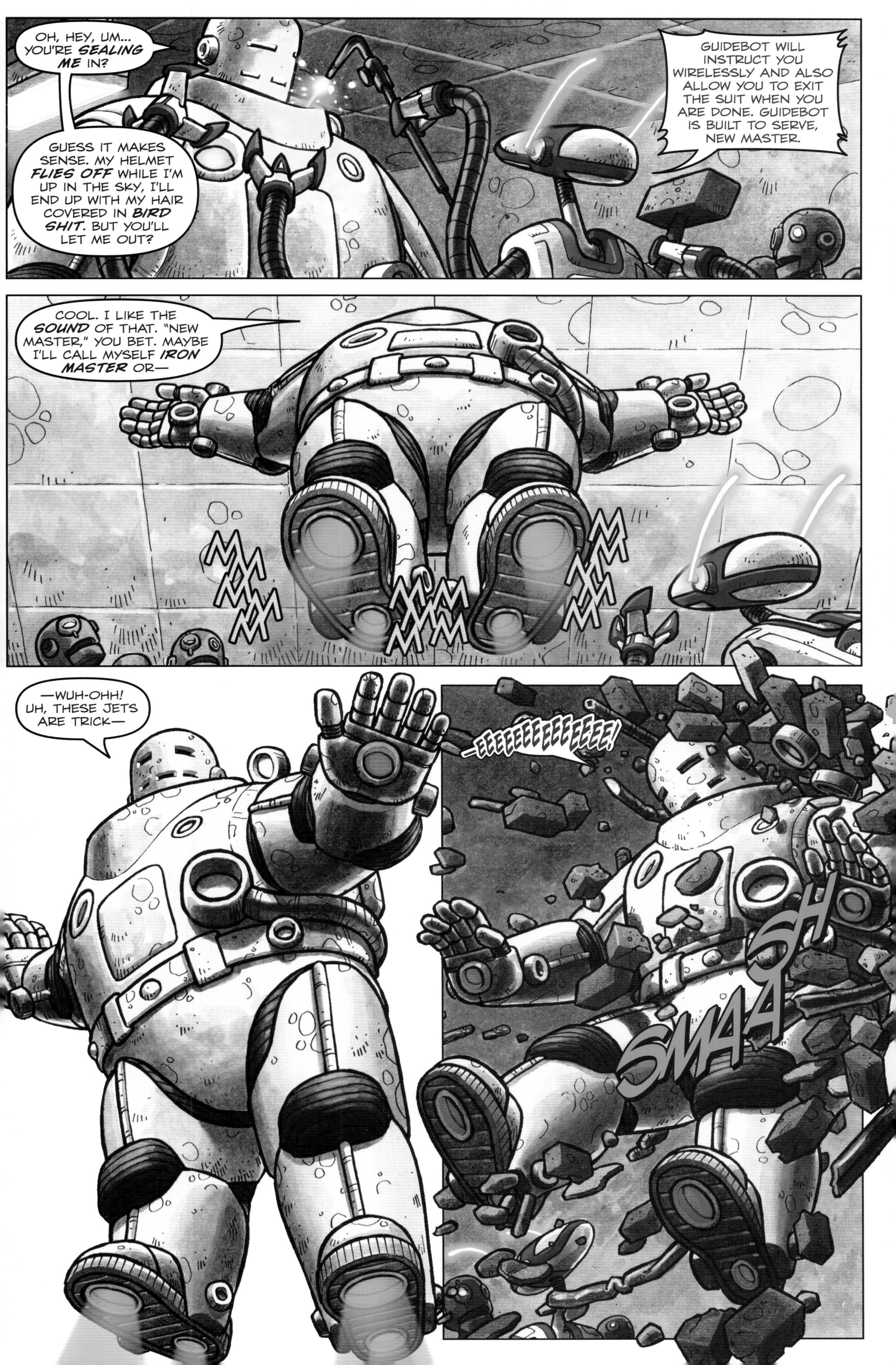
OH, HEY, UM... YOU'RE SEALING ME IN?
GUESS IT MAKES SENSE. MY HELMET FLIES OFF WHILE I'M UP IN THE SKY, I'LL END UP WITH MY HAIR COVERED IN BIRD SHIT. BUT YOU'LL LET ME OUT?
GUIDEBOT WILL INSTRUCT YOU WIRELESSLY AND ALSO ALLOW YOU TO EXIT THE SUIT WHEN YOU ARE DONE. GUIDEBOT IS BUILT TO SERVE, NEW MASTER.
COOL. I LIKE THE SOUND OF THAT. "NEW MASTER," YOU BET. MAYBE I'LL CALL MYSELF IRON MASTER OR—
—WUH-OHH! UH, THESE JETS ARE TRICK—
—EEEEEEEEEEEEEE!
SMAASH

OHHHH-HH...
OH, MAN, MY HEAD. AND I BET I LOOKED REALLY STUPID, DIDN'T I?
GUIDEBOT'S OPTICAL SENSORS ARE NOT DESIGNED TO DIFFERENTIATE OBJECTS BASED ON PERSONAL OPINION.
WELL, NO ONE WON A NASCAR RACE FIRST TIME THEY GOT BEHIND THE WHEEL. LET ME TRY THIS AGAIN. SLOWLY...
UHH!
AH-ALL RIGHT, NOW TO JUST FLIP OVER, CAREFULLY. CAREFULLLLLLY.
SHIIIIIIIT!

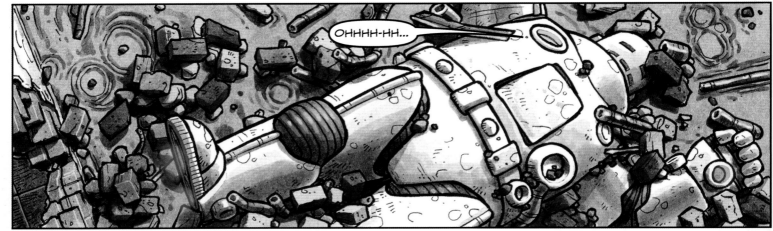

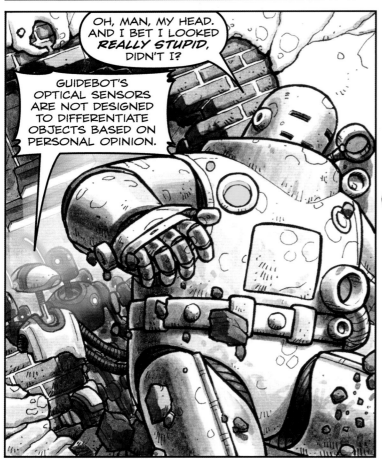

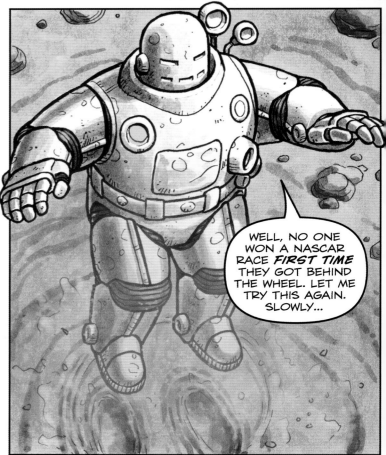

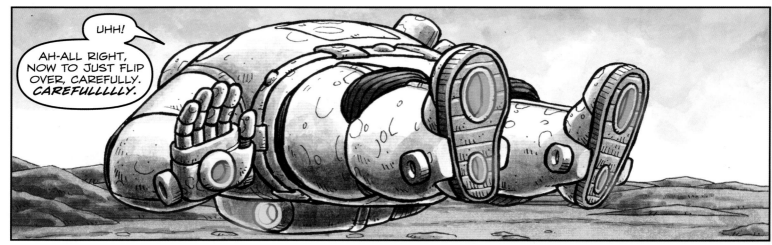

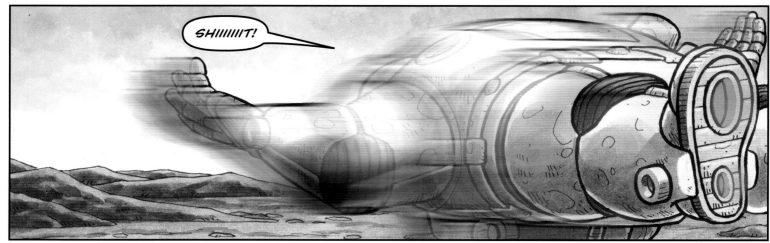

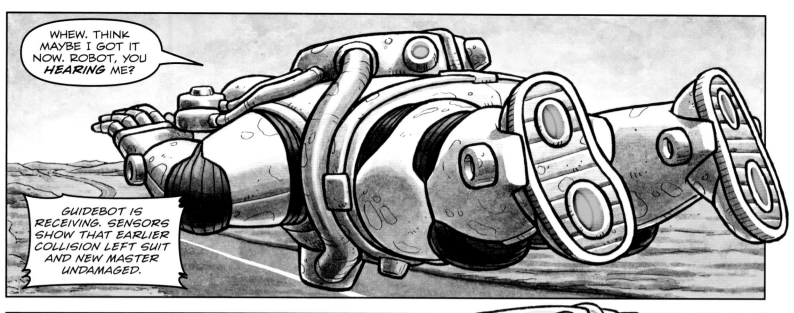

WHEW. THINK MAYBE I GOT IT NOW. ROBOT, YOU *HEARING* ME?

GUIDEBOT IS RECEIVING. SENSORS SHOW THAT EARLIER COLLISION LEFT SUIT AND NEW MASTER UNDAMAGED.

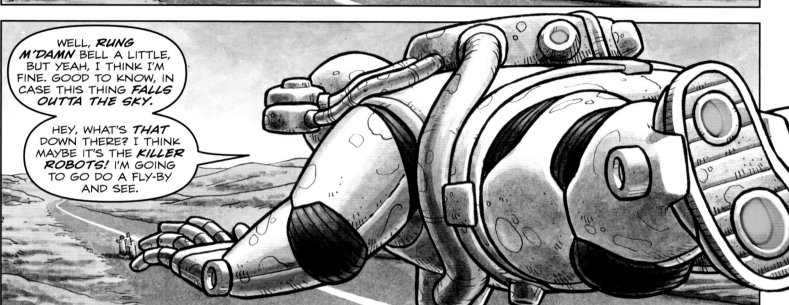

WELL, *RUNG M'DAMN* BELL A LITTLE, BUT YEAH, I THINK I'M FINE. GOOD TO KNOW, IN CASE THIS THING *FALLS OUTTA THE SKY.*

HEY, WHAT'S *THAT* DOWN THERE? I THINK MAYBE IT'S THE *KILLER ROBOTS!* I'M GOING TO GO DO A FLY-BY AND SEE.

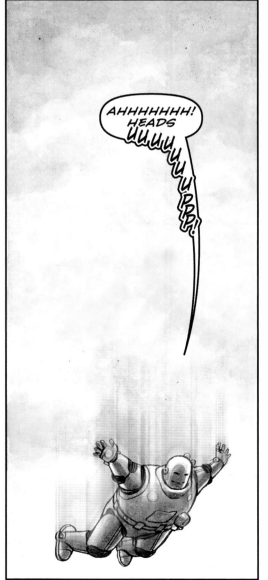

AHHHHHHH! HEADS UUUUUUUUUURRR!

SQUELCH

OHHH, GOD. ROBOT, I THINK I HURT SOMEONE.

(I MEAN, I HURT MYSELF, TOO, BUT THIS SUIT'S GOT NICE PADDING.)

NEW MASTER, SENSORS DETECT ONLY YOUR LIFEFORM.

Y-YEAH? THAT MEANS IT WAS THE ROBOTS! GOOD TO KNOW I DIDN'T HURT ANYTHING STILL—

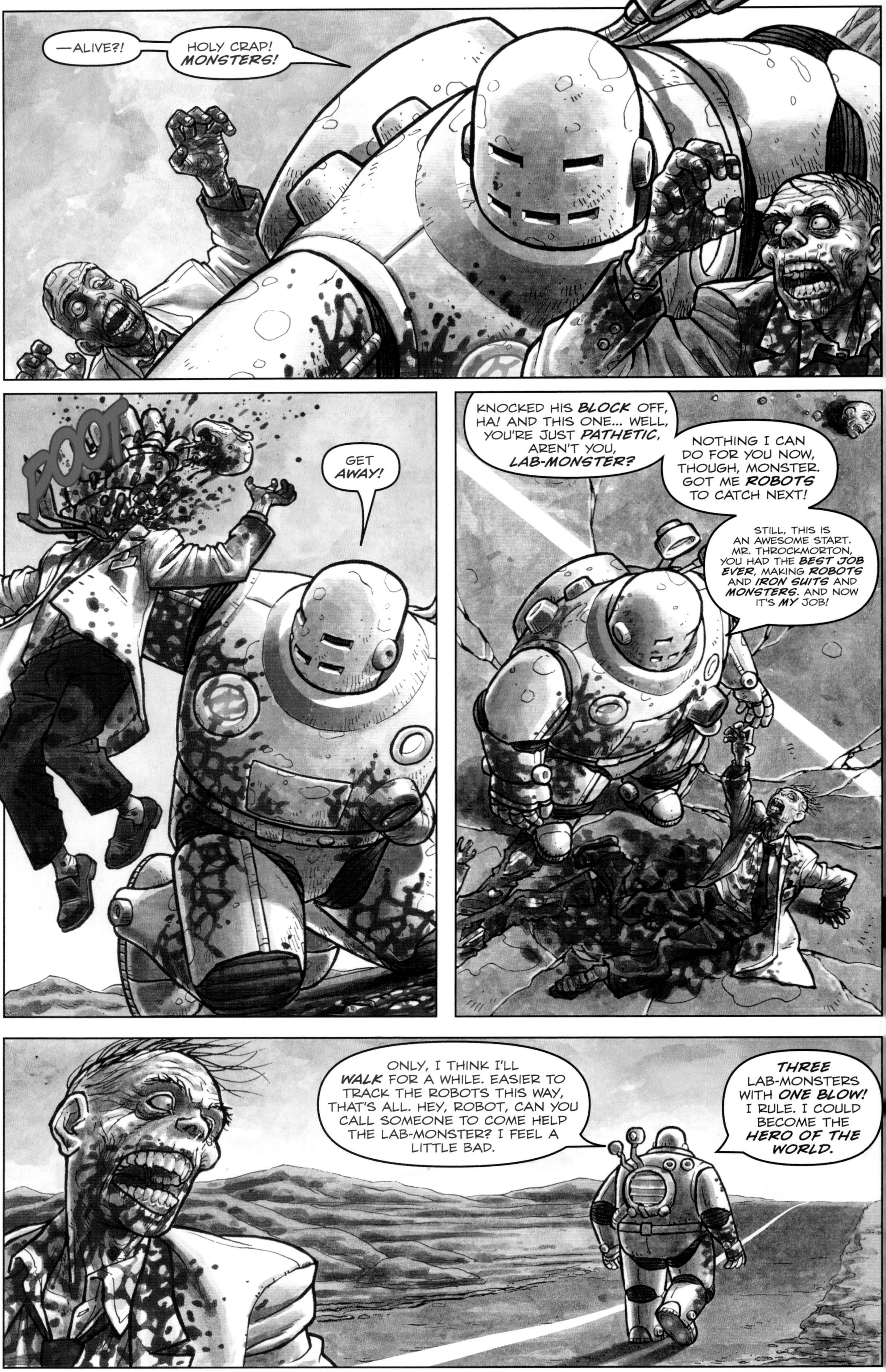
—ALIVE?!
HOLY CRAP! MONSTERS!
POOT
GET AWAY!
KNOCKED HIS BLOCK OFF, HA! AND THIS ONE... WELL, YOU'RE JUST PATHETIC, AREN'T YOU, LAB-MONSTER?
NOTHING I CAN DO FOR YOU NOW, THOUGH, MONSTER. GOT ME ROBOTS TO CATCH NEXT!
STILL, THIS IS AN AWESOME START. MR. THROCKMORTON, YOU HAD THE BEST JOB EVER, MAKING ROBOTS AND IRON SUITS AND MONSTERS. AND NOW IT'S MY JOB!
ONLY, I THINK I'LL WALK FOR A WHILE. EASIER TO TRACK THE ROBOTS THIS WAY, THAT'S ALL. HEY, ROBOT, CAN YOU CALL SOMEONE TO COME HELP THE LAB-MONSTER? I FEEL A LITTLE BAD.
THREE LAB-MONSTERS WITH ONE BLOW! I RULE. I COULD BECOME THE HERO OF THE WORLD.

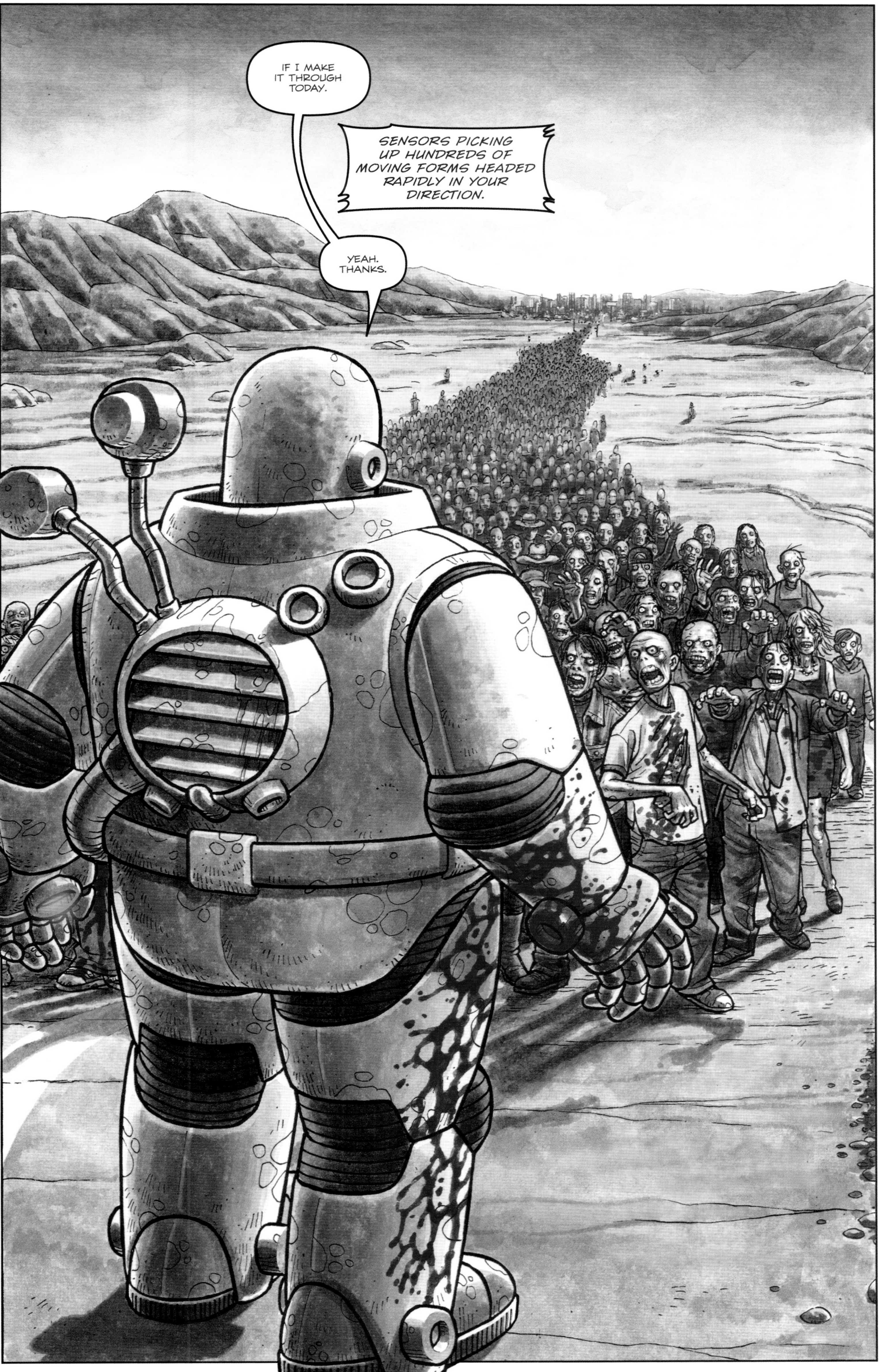
SENSORS PICKING UP HUNDREDS OF MOVING FORMS HEADED RAPIDLY IN YOUR DIRECTION.
YEAH. THANKS.
IF I MAKE IT THROUGH TODAY.

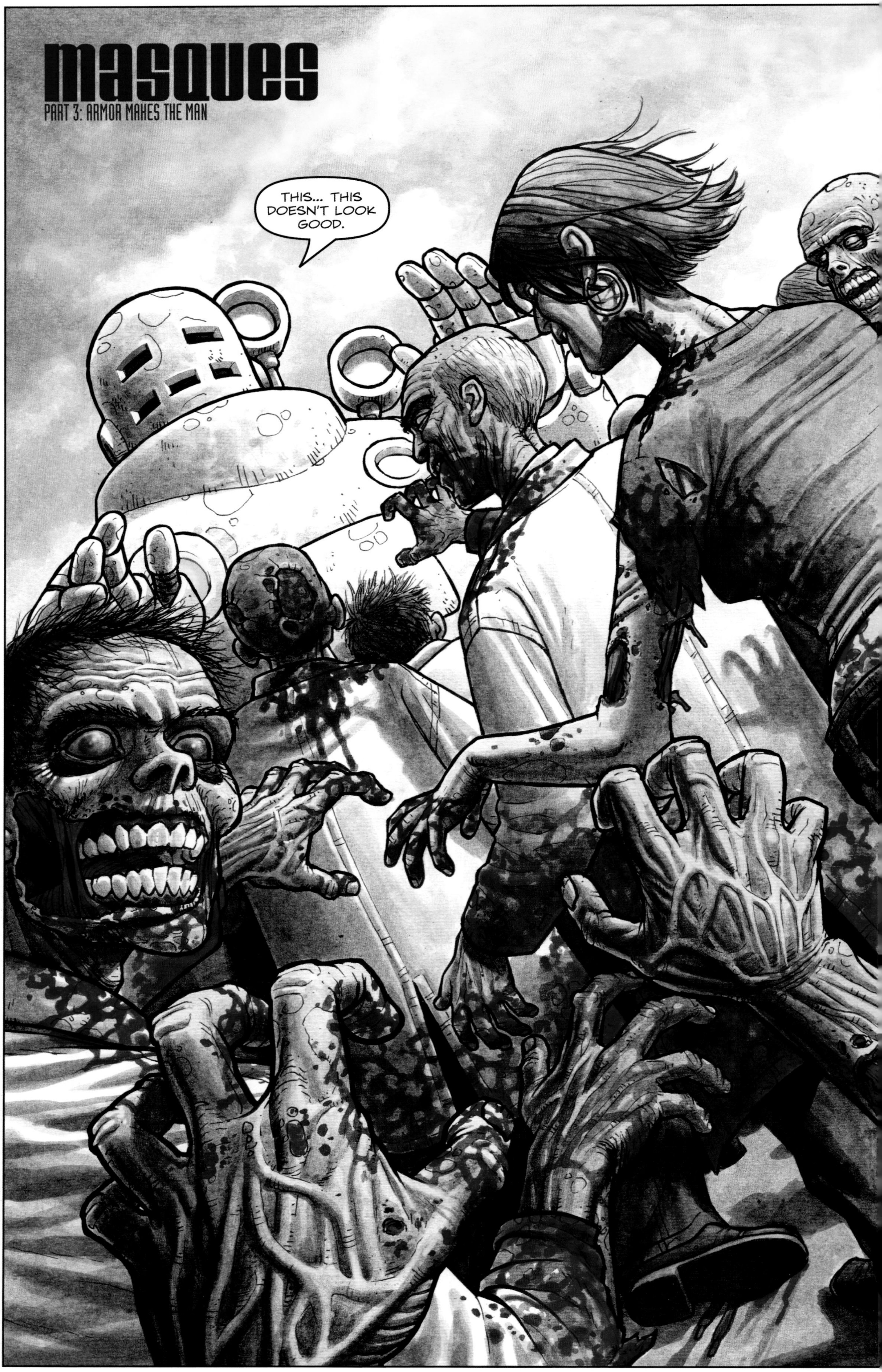
MASQUES
PART 3: ARMOR MAKES THE MAN
THIS... THIS DOESN'T LOOK GOOD.

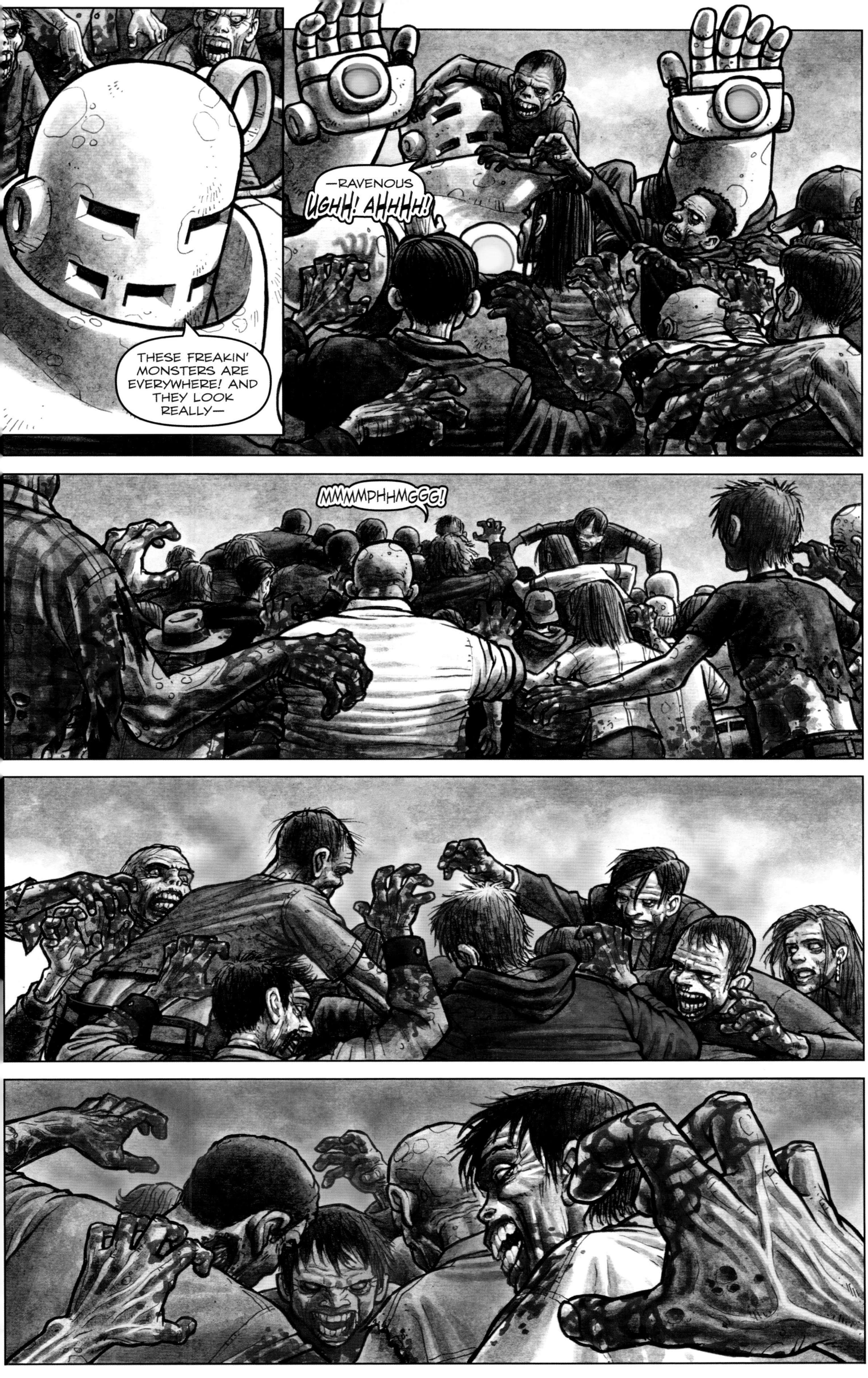
THESE FREAKIN' MONSTERS ARE EVERYWHERE! AND THEY LOOK REALLY—
—RAVENOUS
UGHH! AHHHH!
MMMMPHHMGGG!

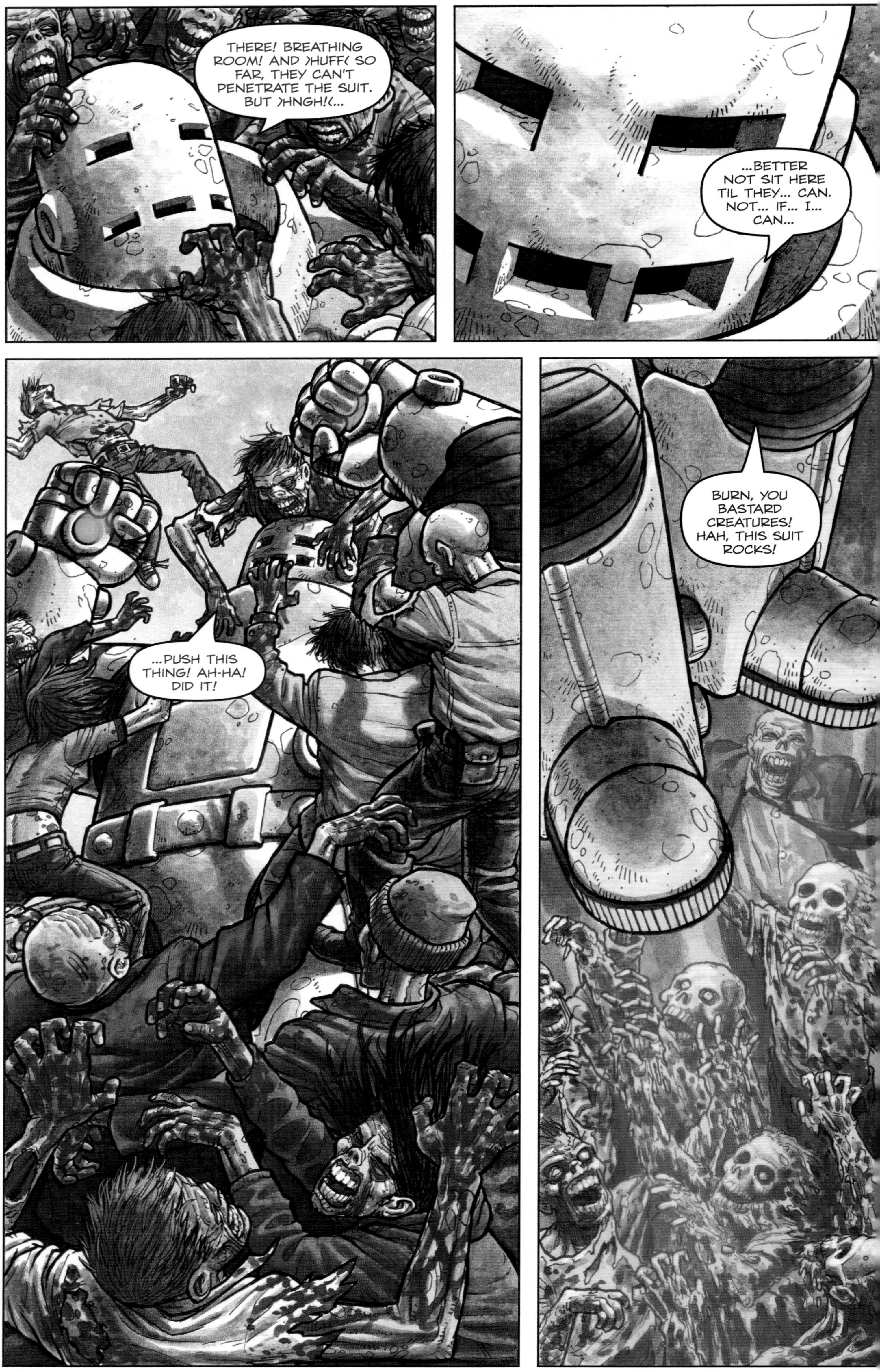
THERE! BREATHING ROOM! AND)HUFF(SO FAR, THEY CAN'T PENETRATE THE SUIT. BUT)HNGH!(...
...BETTER NOT SIT HERE TIL THEY... CAN. NOT... IF... I... CAN...
...PUSH THIS THING! AH-HA! DID IT!
BURN, YOU BASTARD CREATURES! HAH, THIS SUIT ROCKS!

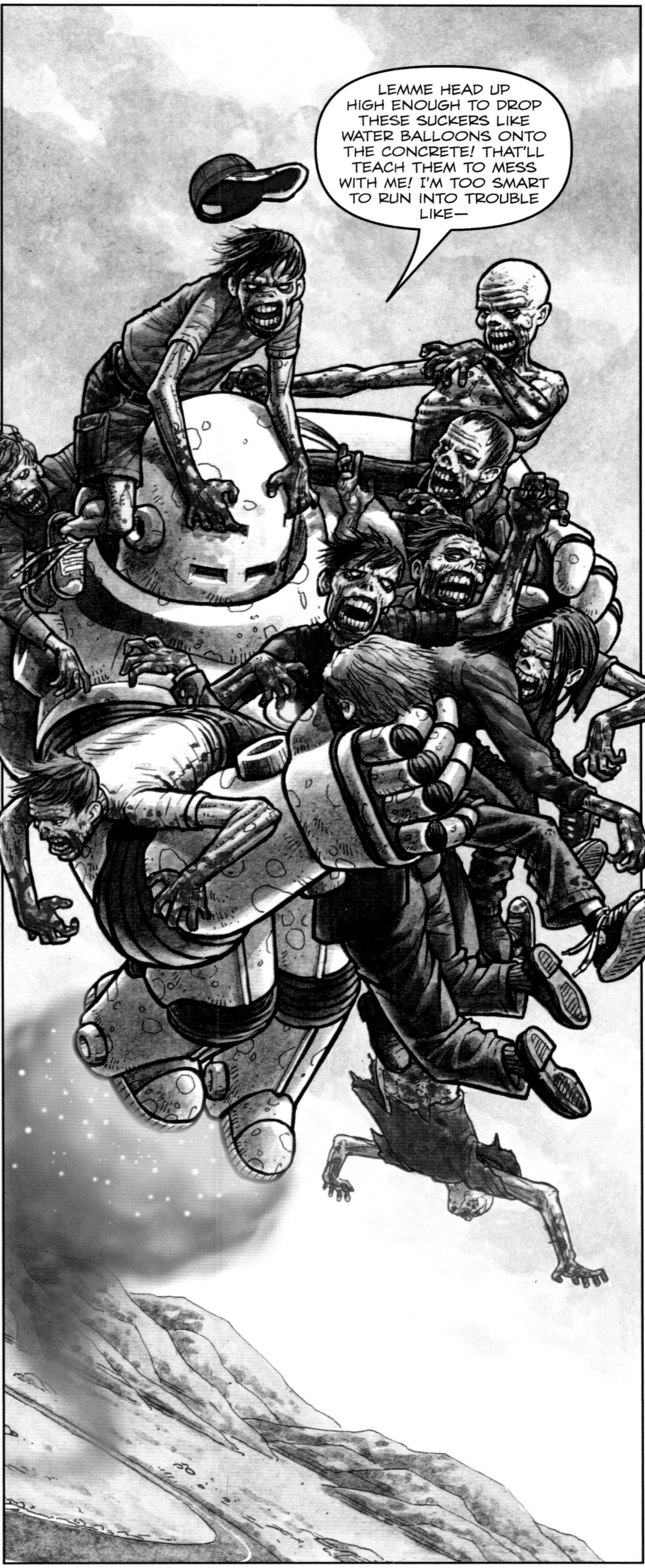
LEMME HEAD UP HIGH ENOUGH TO DROP THESE SUCKERS LIKE WATER BALLOONS ONTO THE CONCRETE! THAT'LL TEACH THEM TO MESS WITH ME! I'M TOO SMART TO RUN INTO TROUBLE LIKE—

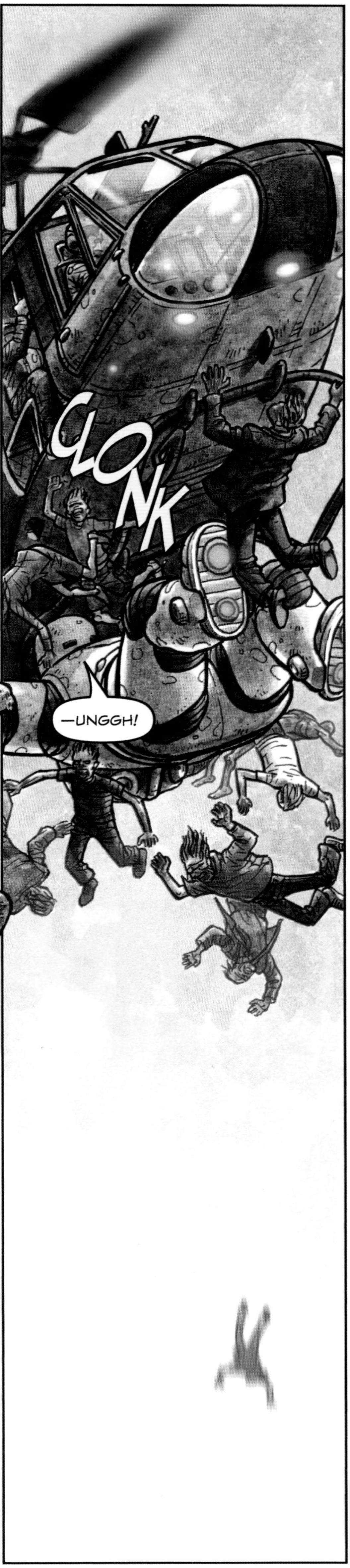
CLONK
—UNGGH!

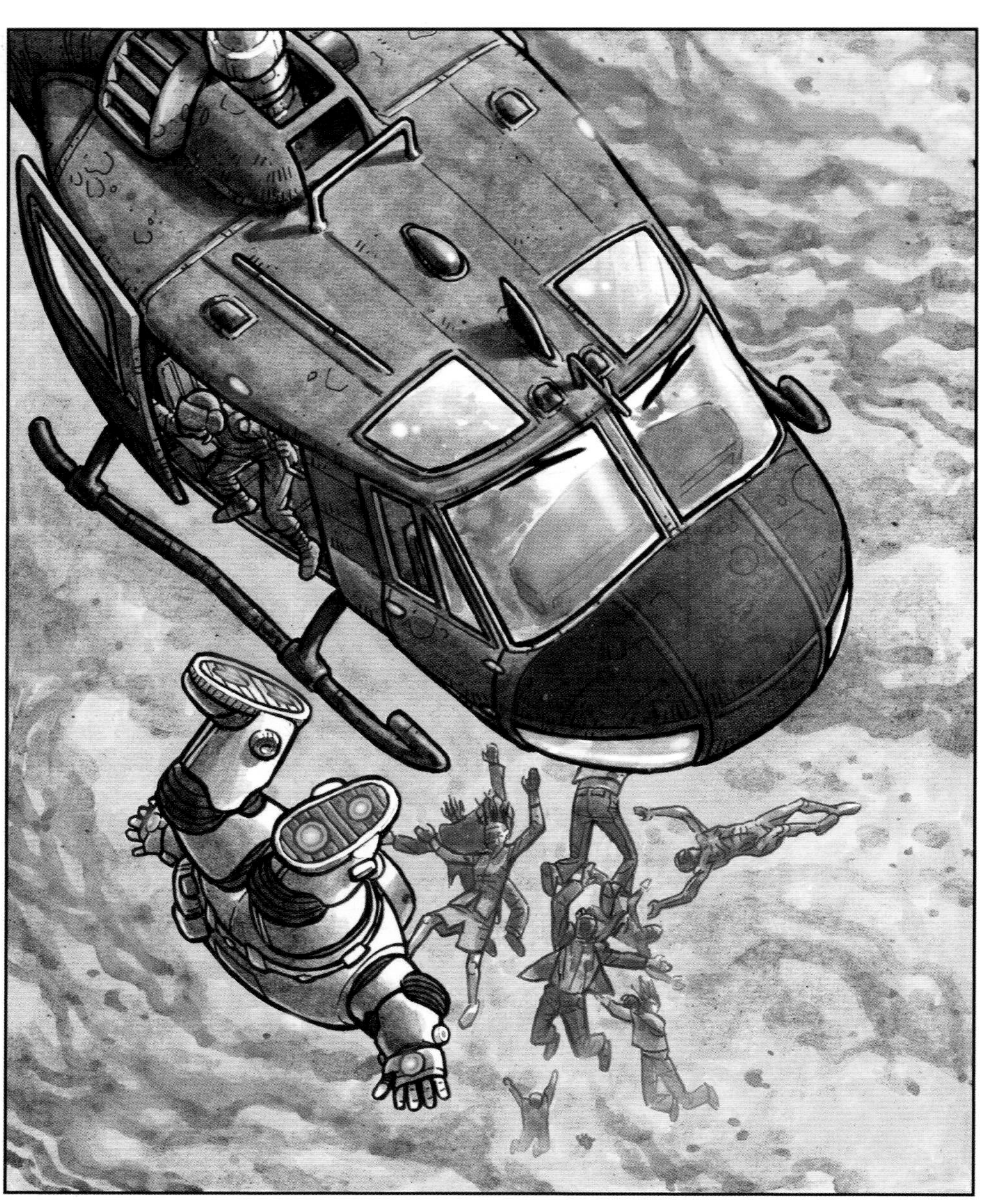

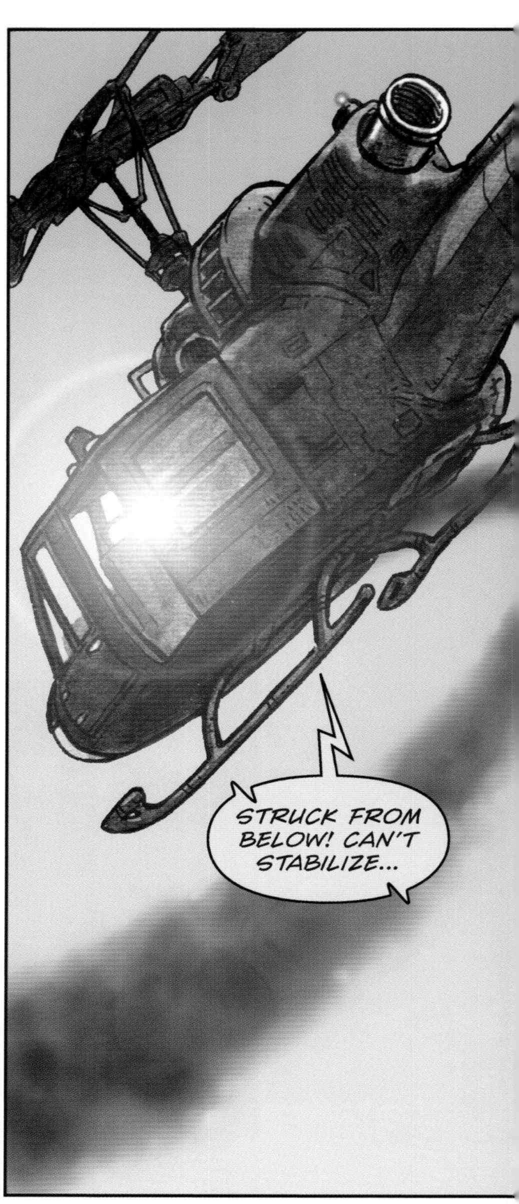
STRUCK FROM BELOW! CAN'T STABILIZE...

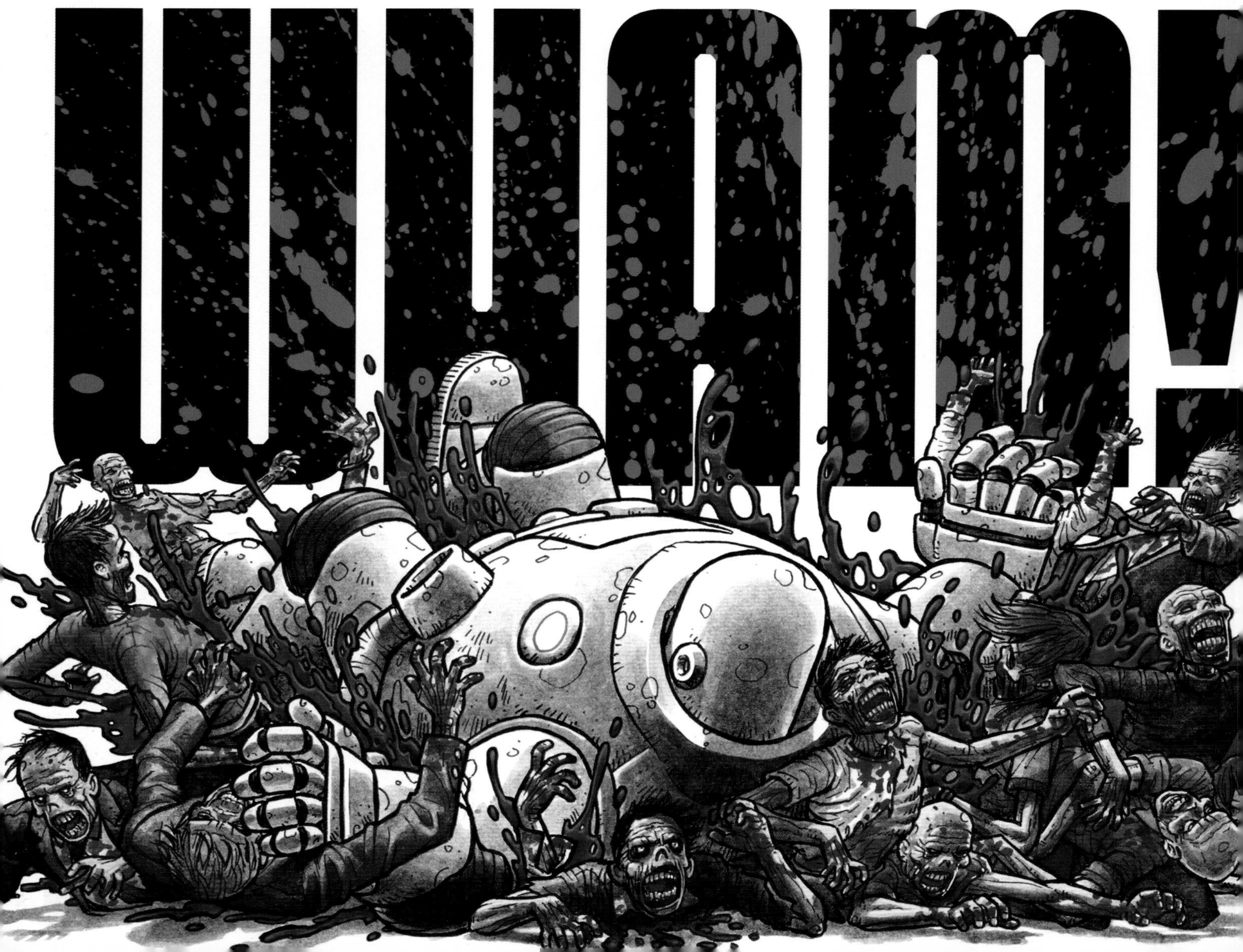

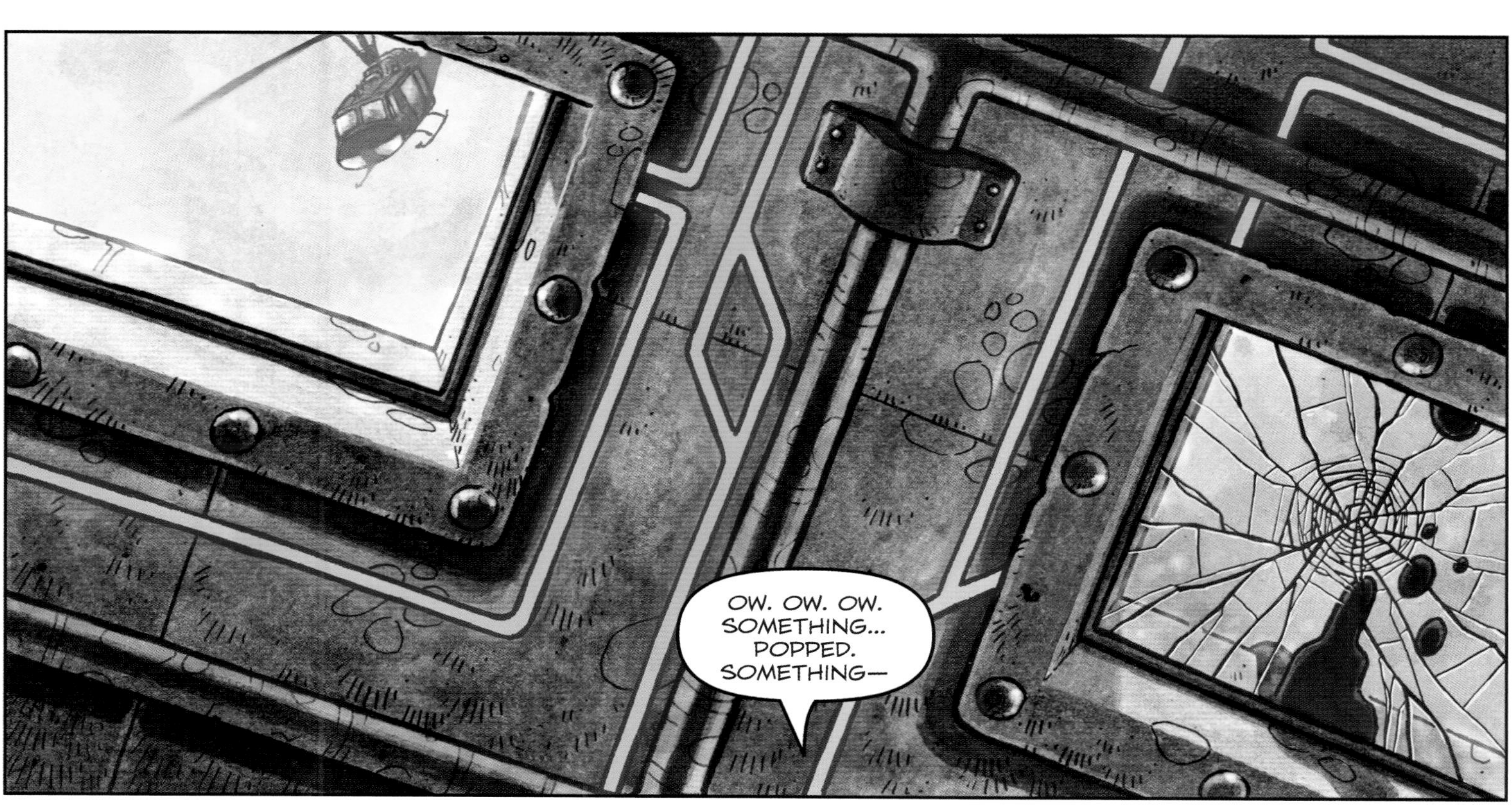
OW. OW. OW. SOMETHING... POPPED. SOMETHING—

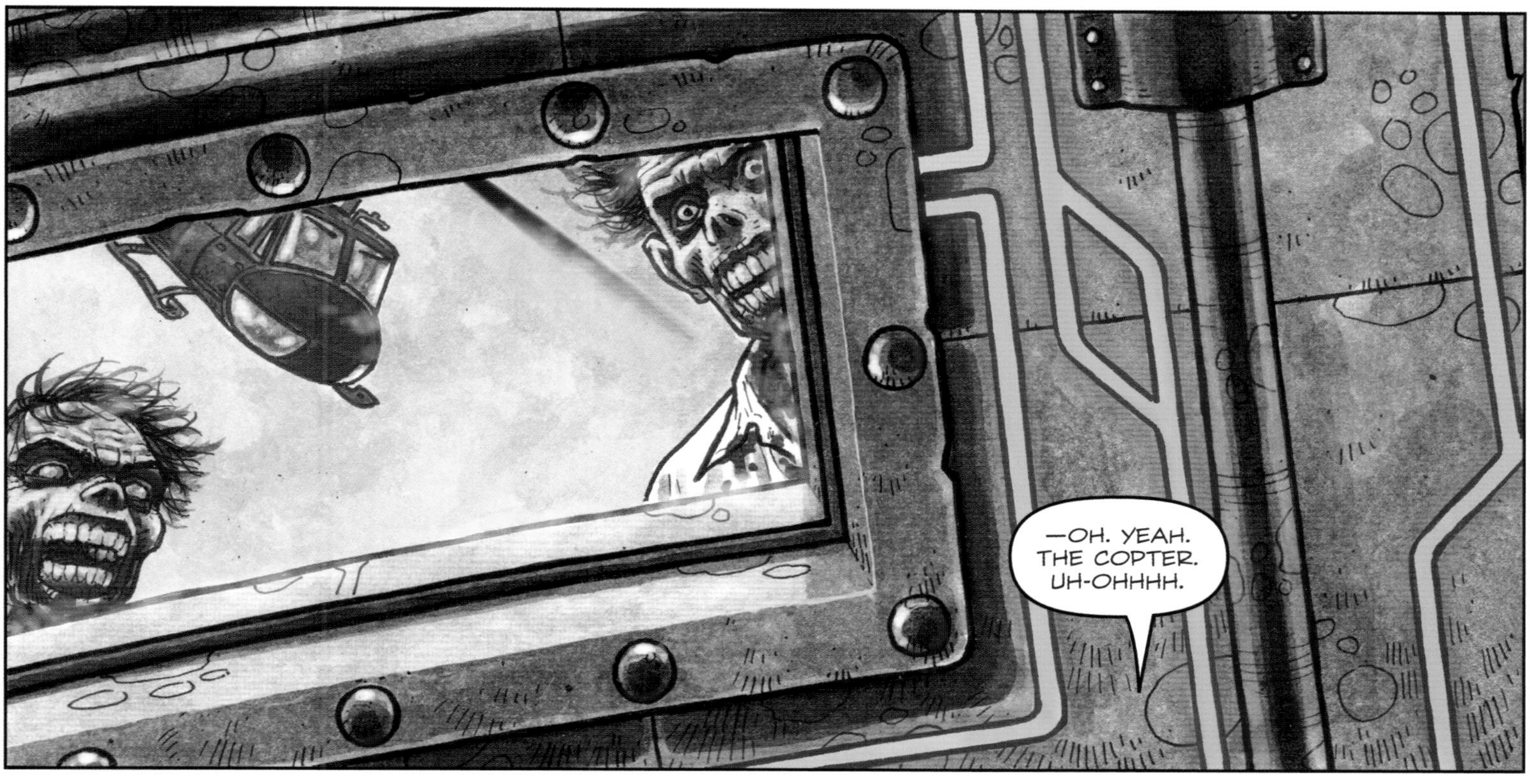
—OH. YEAH. THE COPTER. UH-OHHHH.

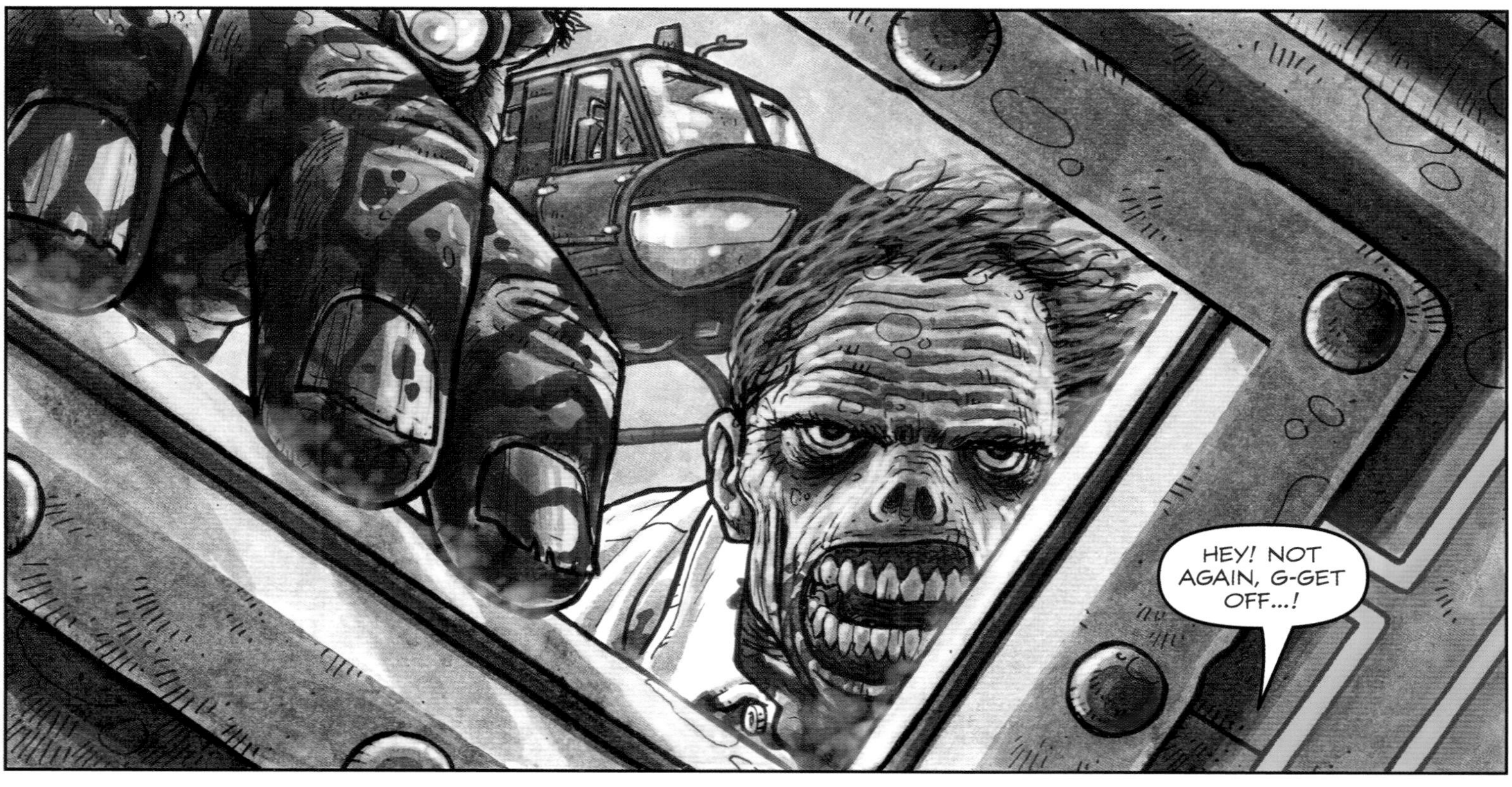
HEY! NOT AGAIN, G-GET OFF...!

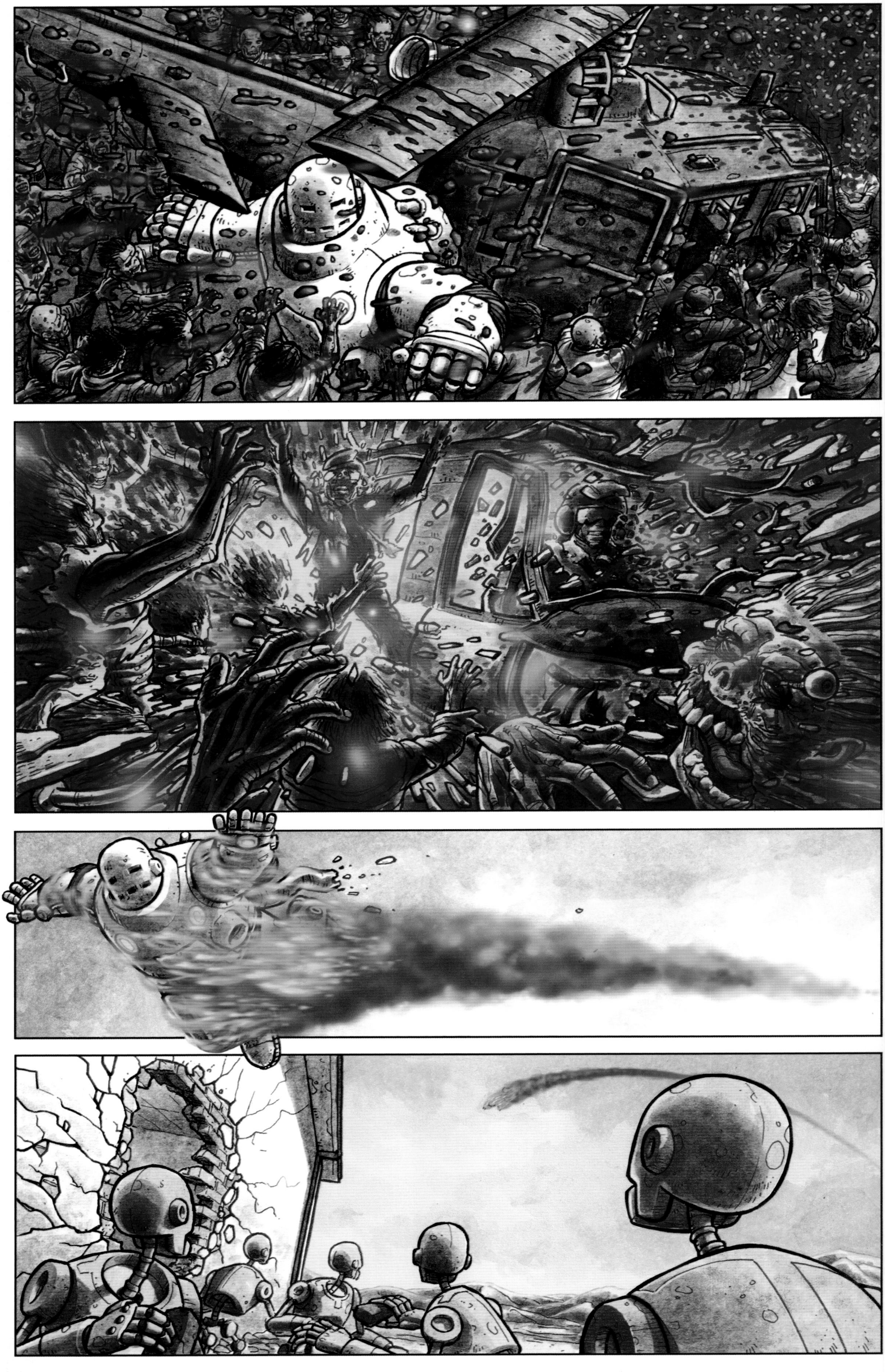

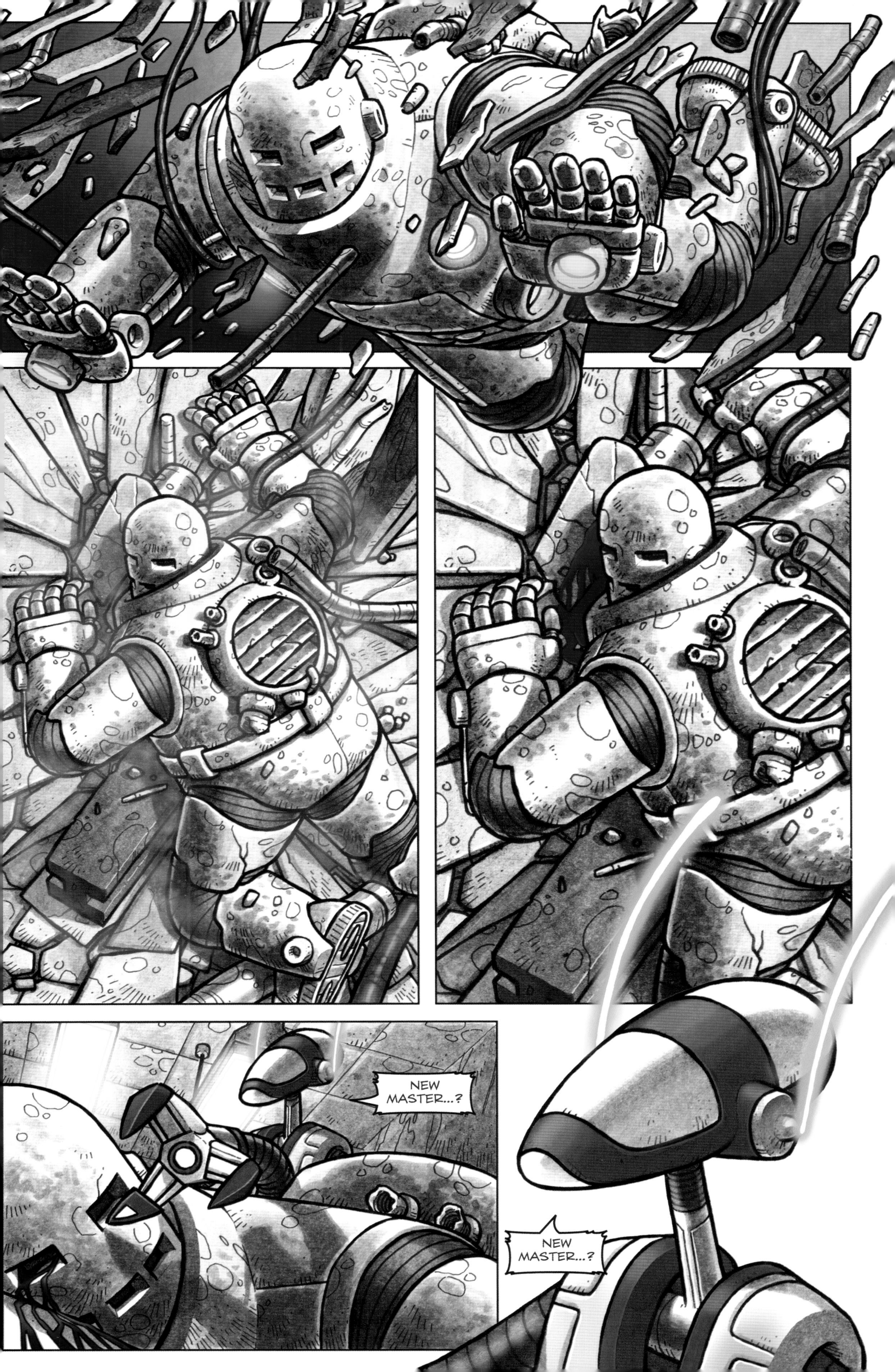
NEW MASTER...?
NEW MASTER...?

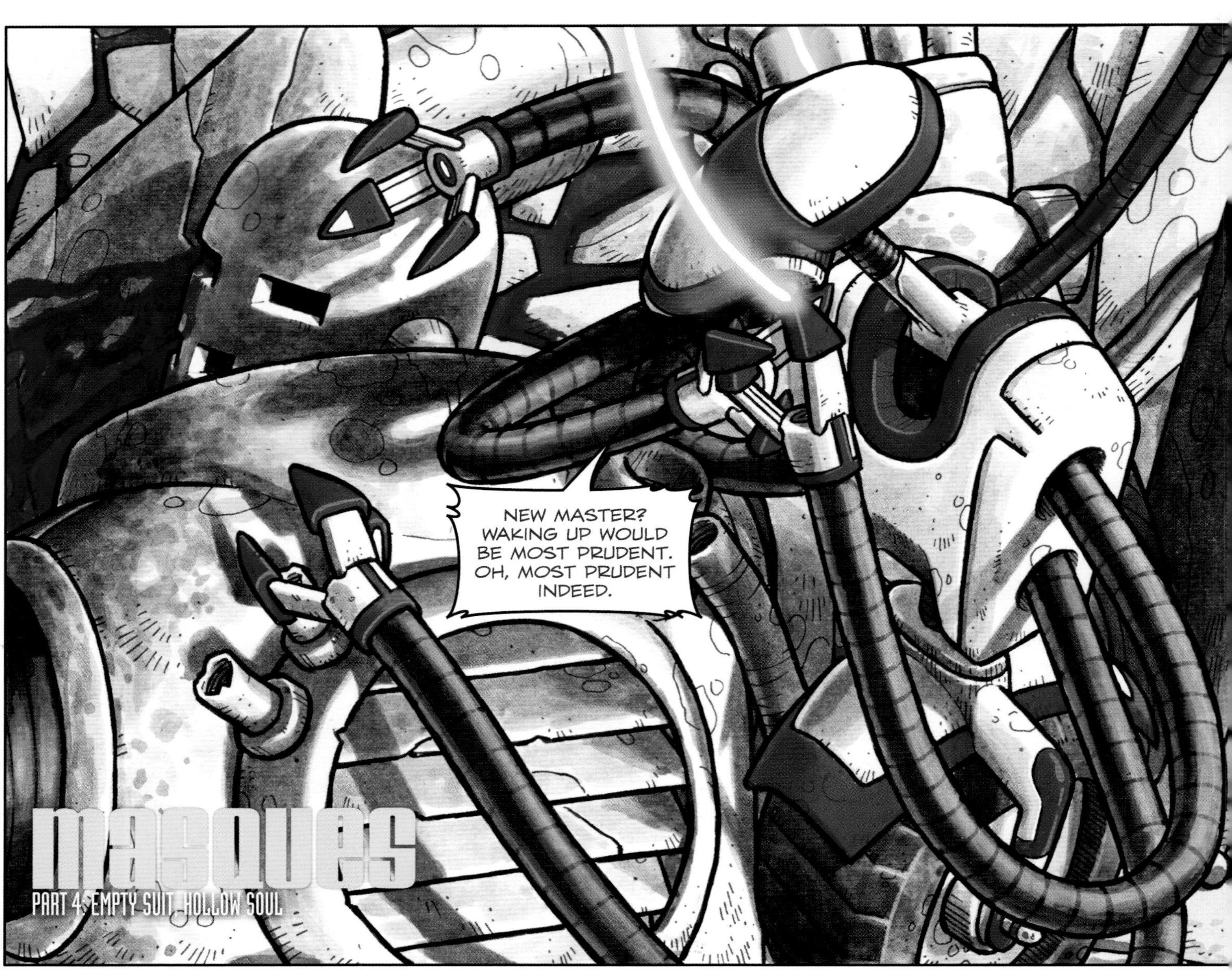
NEW MASTER? WAKING UP WOULD BE MOST PRUDENT. OH, MOST PRUDENT INDEED.
MASQUES
PART 4: EMPTY SUIT, HOLLOW SOUL

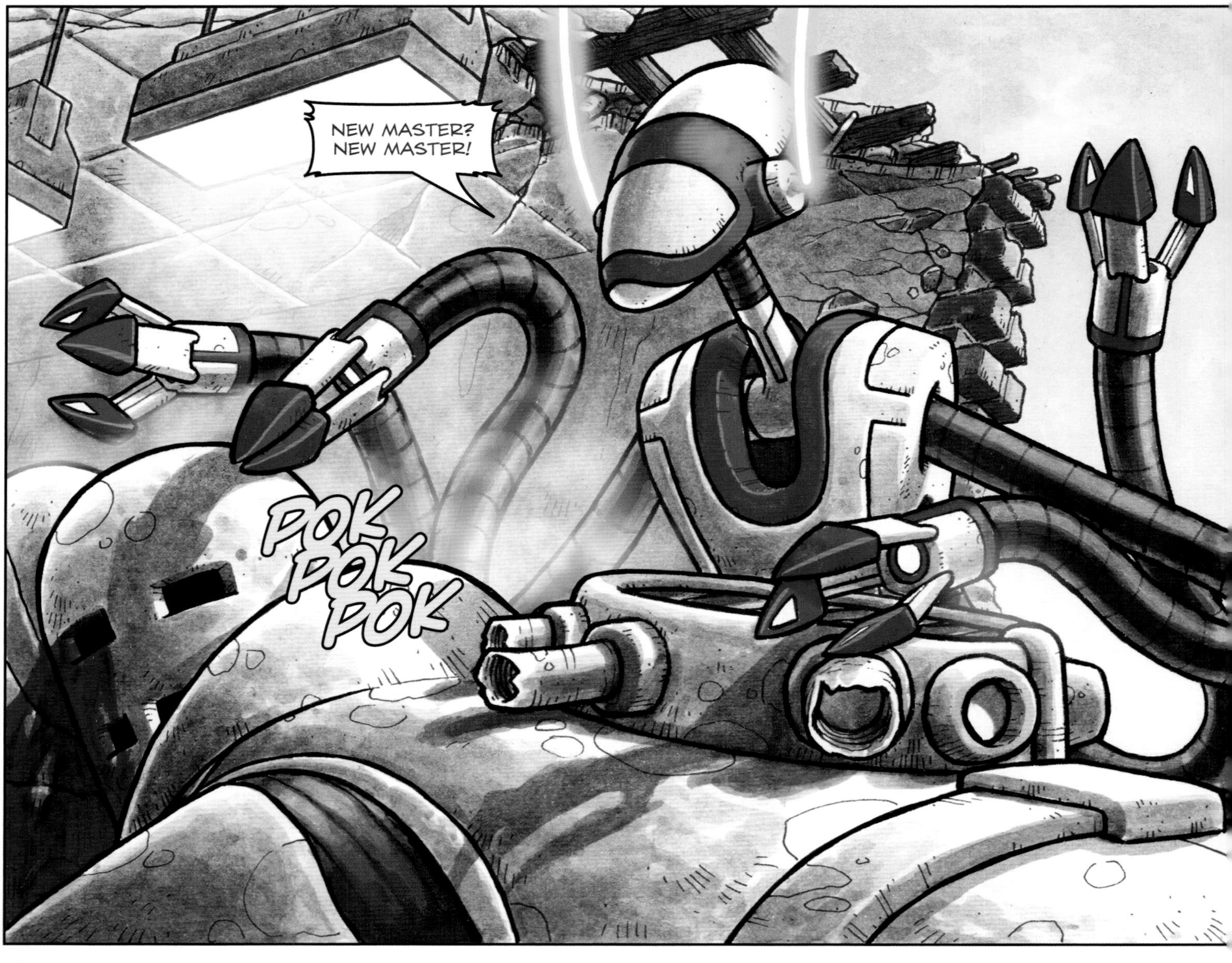
NEW MASTER? NEW MASTER!
POK POK POK

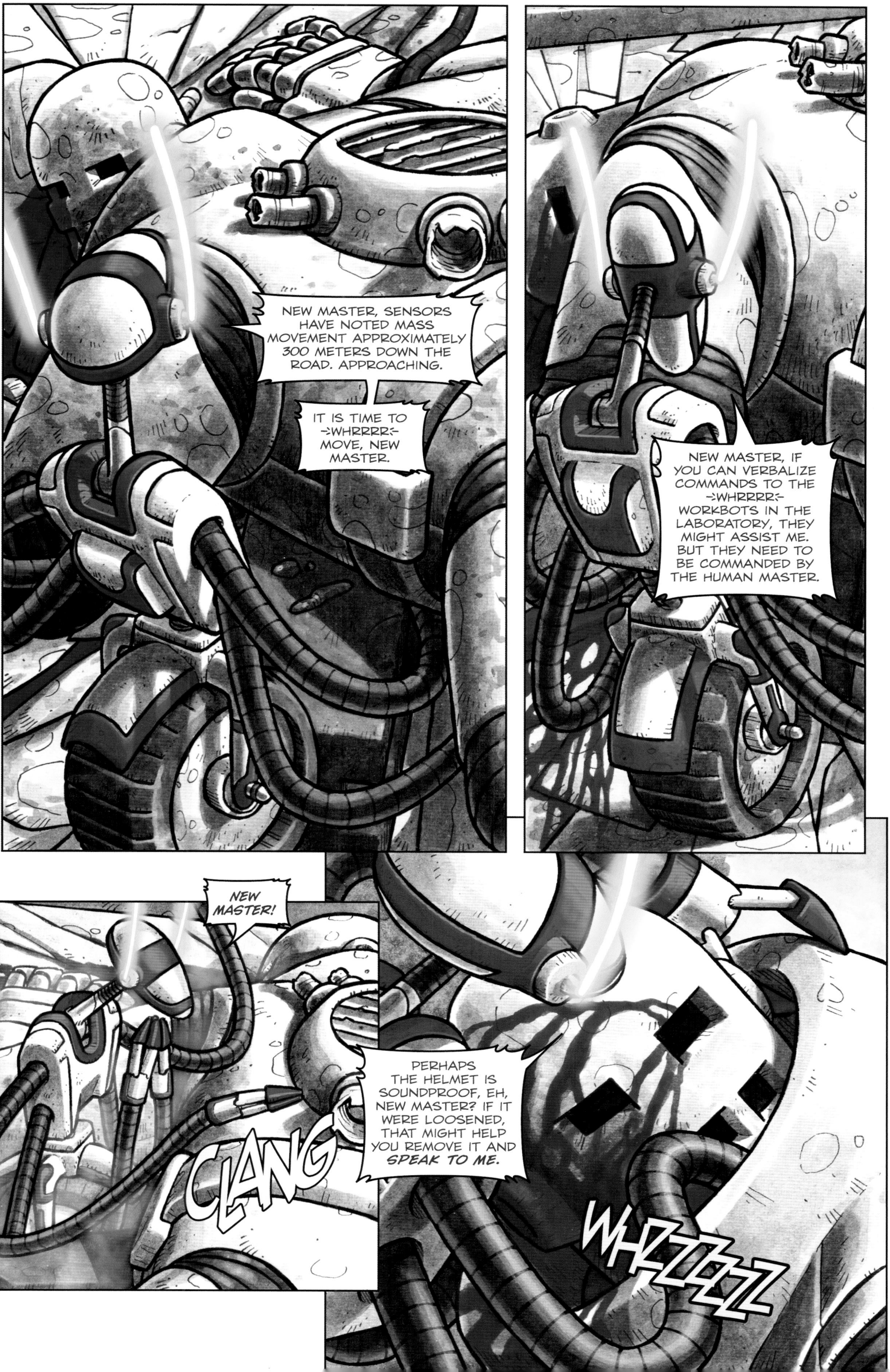

NEW MASTER, SENSORS HAVE NOTED MASS MOVEMENT APPROXIMATELY 300 METERS DOWN THE ROAD. APPROACHING.
IT IS TIME TO -WHRRRR- MOVE, NEW MASTER.
NEW MASTER, IF YOU CAN VERBALIZE COMMANDS TO THE -WHRRRR- WORKBOTS IN THE LABORATORY, THEY MIGHT ASSIST ME. BUT THEY NEED TO BE COMMANDED BY THE HUMAN MASTER.
NEW MASTER!
CLANG
PERHAPS THE HELMET IS SOUNDPROOF, EH, NEW MASTER? IF IT WERE LOOSENED, THAT MIGHT HELP YOU REMOVE IT AND SPEAK TO ME.
WHRZZZZZ

EH? NEW MASTER, SENSORS ARE SHOWING THE MOVEMENT OUTSIDE DRAWING VERY CLOSE. PERHAPS I SHOULD EXPLORE THE—
—SOURCE. OH.
NEW MASTER! APPROACHING LIFEFORMS GIVE OFF NO SIGN OF LIFE. NO LIFE SIGNS DETECTED AT ALL! BUT THEY ARE MOVING THIS WAY NONETHELESS.
OH, SENSORS DETECT NO LIFESIGNS AT ALL. OH. OH.

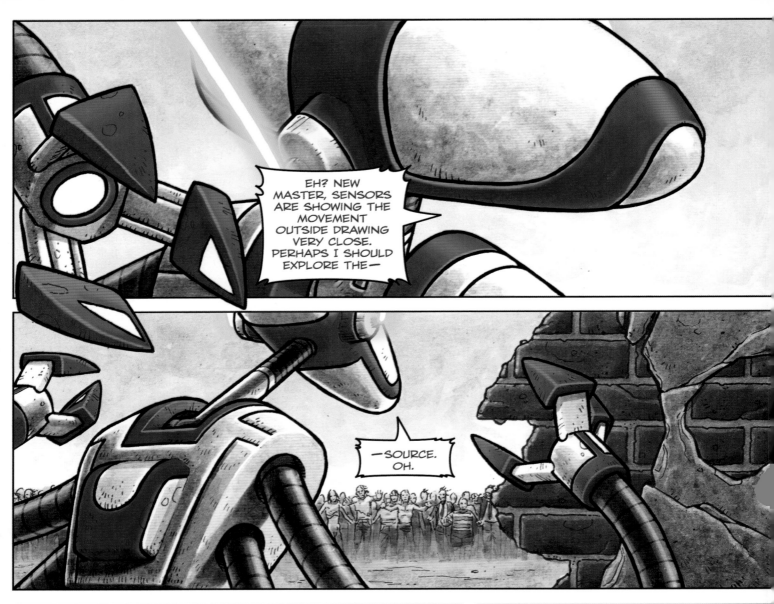

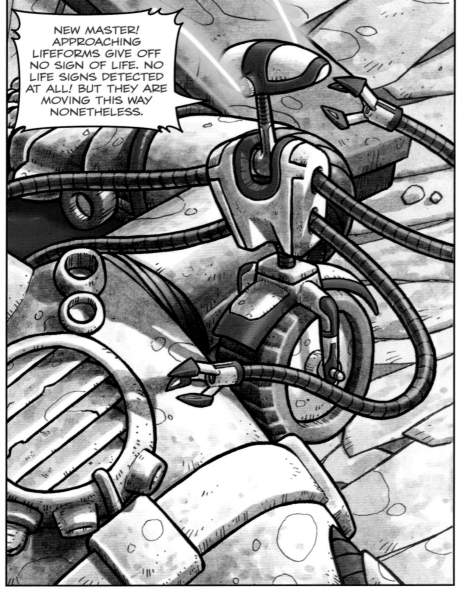

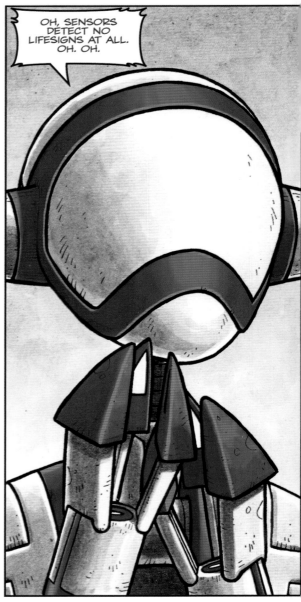

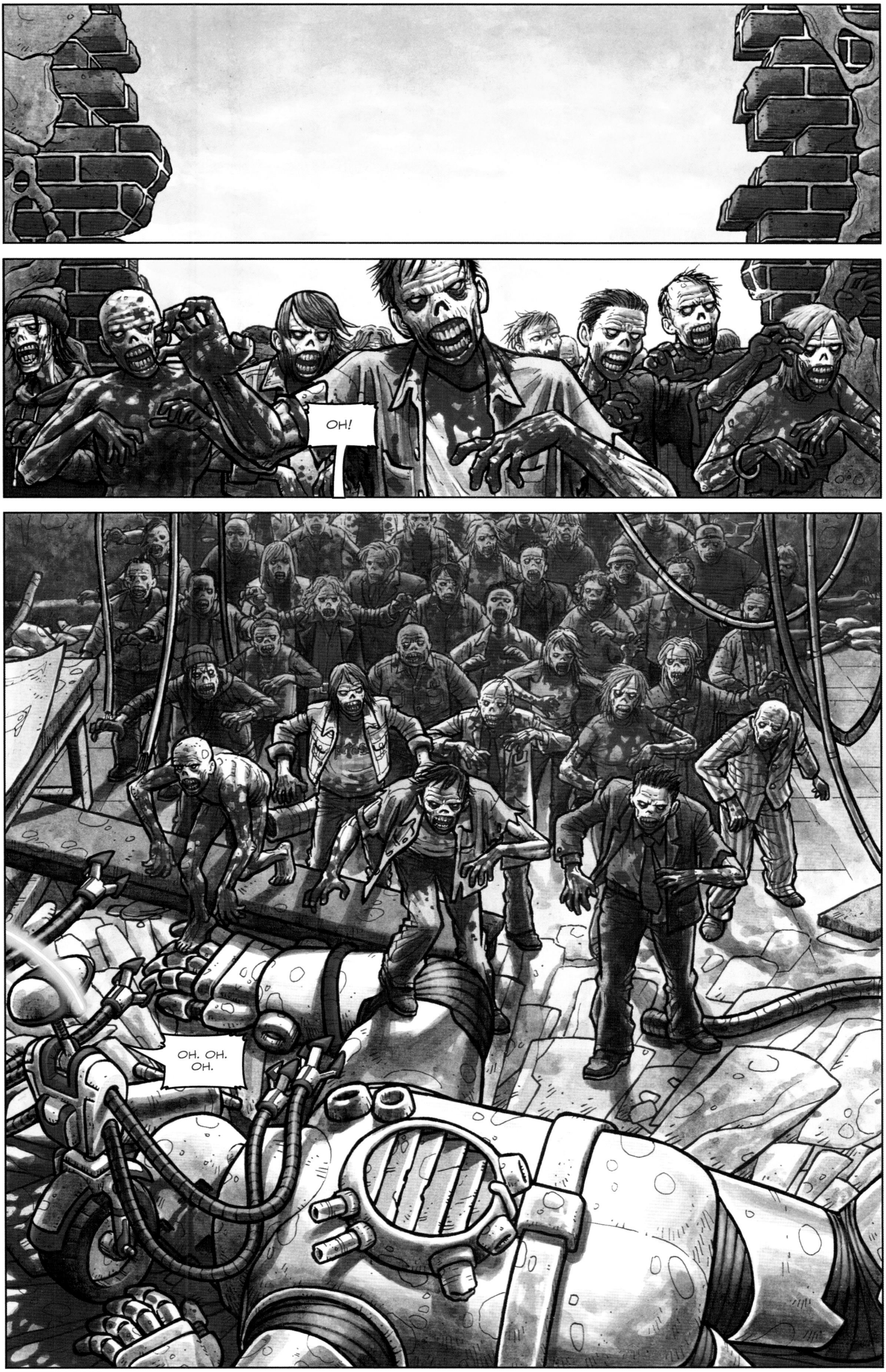
OH!
OH. OH. OH.

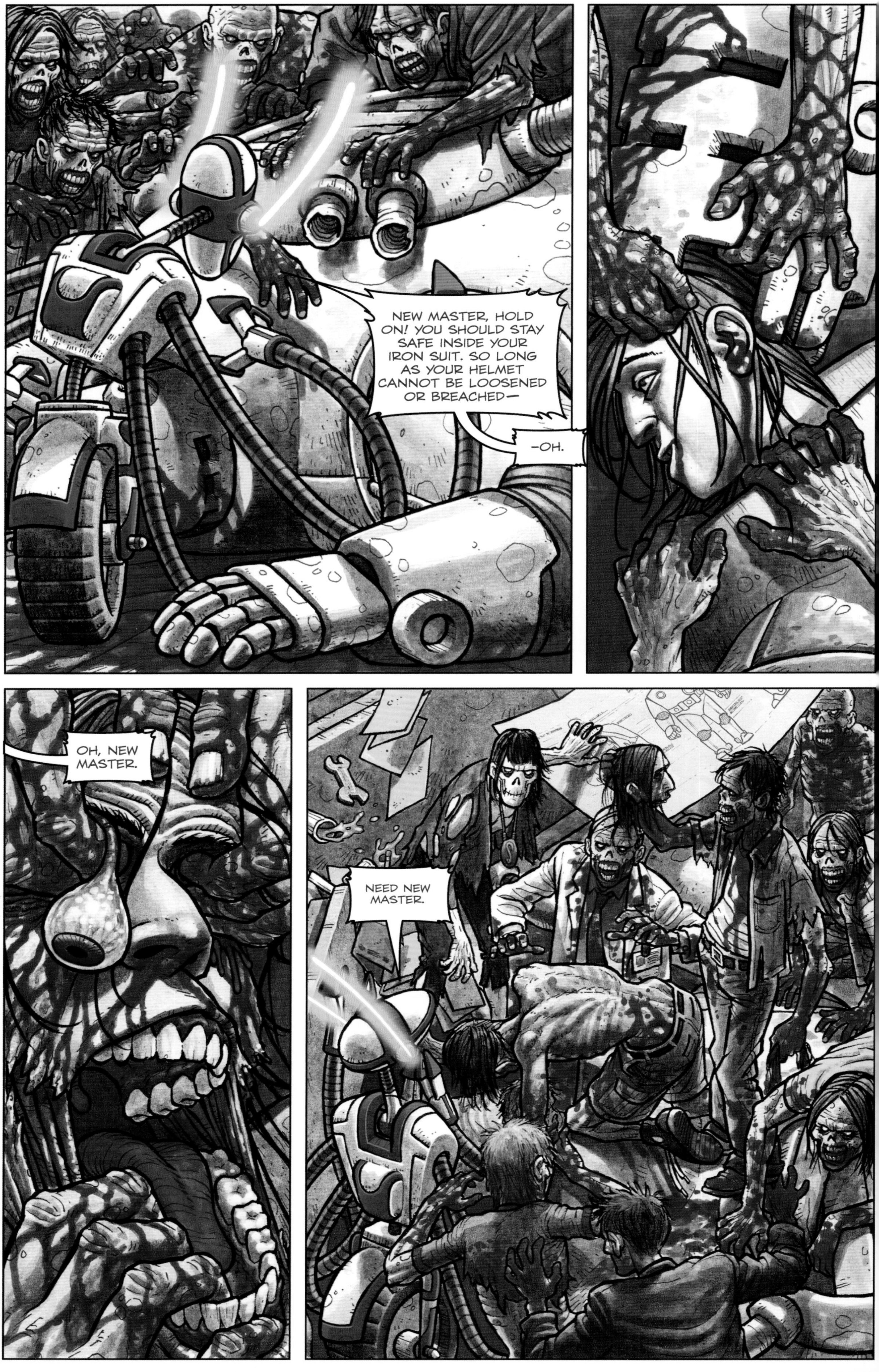
NEW MASTER, HOLD ON! YOU SHOULD STAY SAFE INSIDE YOUR IRON SUIT. SO LONG AS YOUR HELMET CANNOT BE LOOSENED OR BREACHED—
—OH.
OH, NEW MASTER.
NEED NEW MASTER.

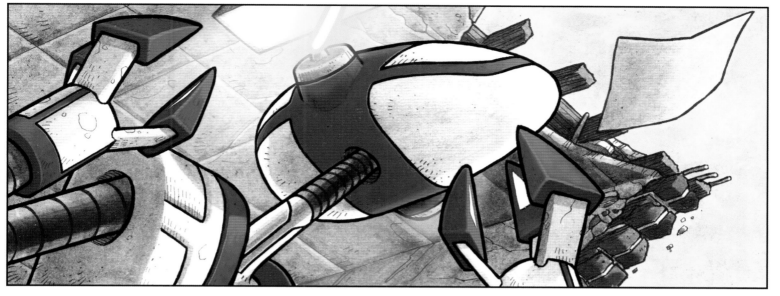

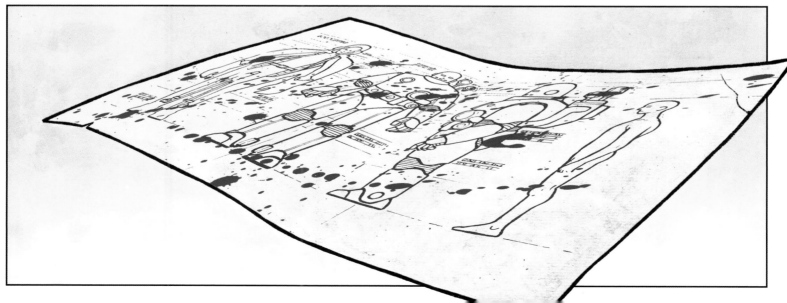

PAUL'S AUTO SALVAGE

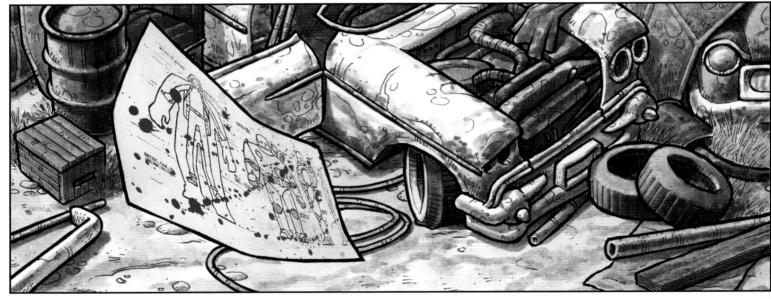

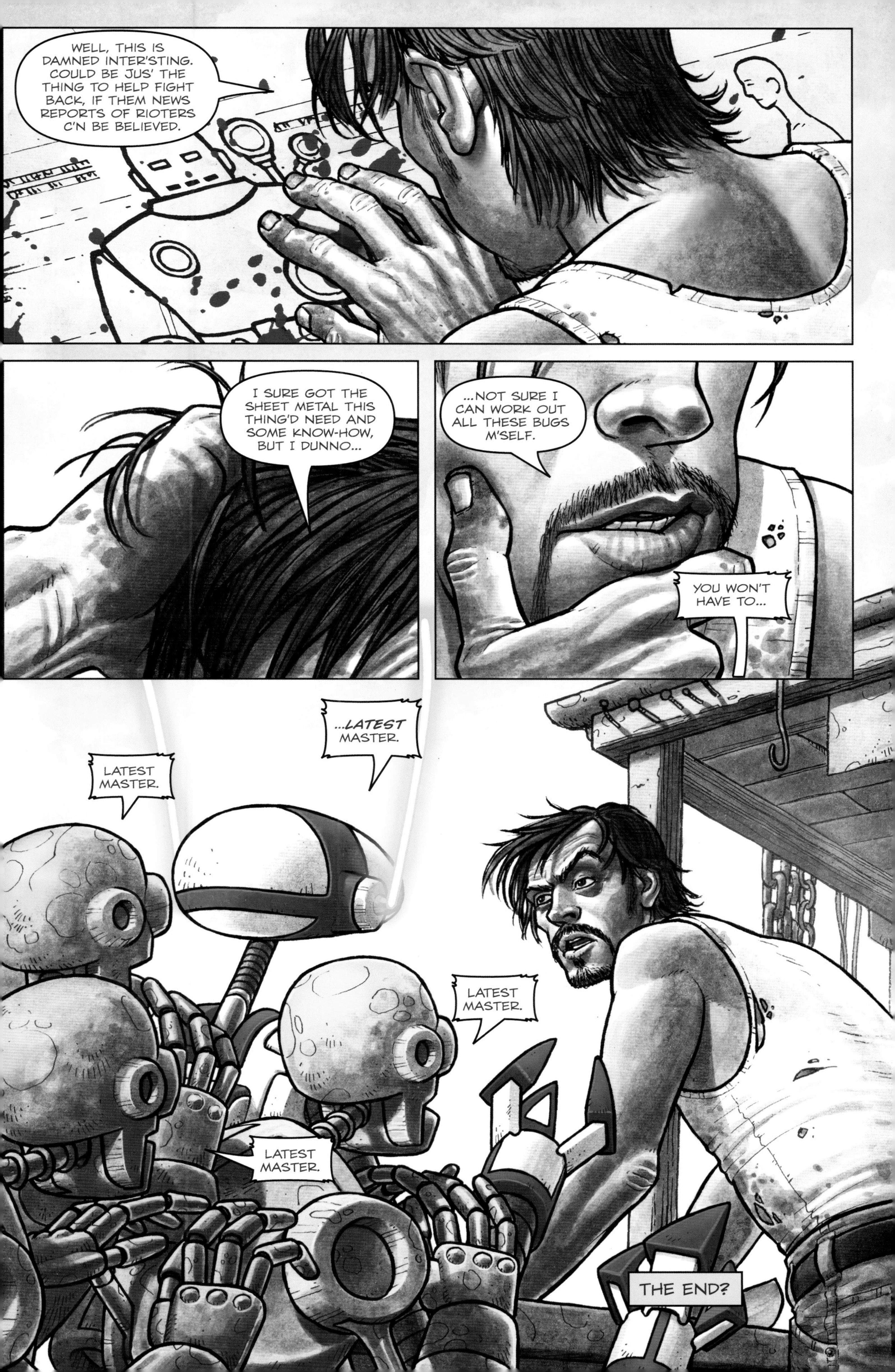
WELL, THIS IS DAMNED INTER'STING. COULD BE JUS' THE THING TO HELP FIGHT BACK, IF THEM NEWS REPORTS OF RIOTERS C'N BE BELIEVED.
I SURE GOT THE SHEET METAL THIS THING'D NEED AND SOME KNOW-HOW, BUT I DUNNO...
...NOT SURE I CAN WORK OUT ALL THESE BUGS M'SELF.
YOU WON'T HAVE TO...
...*LATEST* MASTER.
LATEST MASTER.
LATEST MASTER.
LATEST MASTER.
THE END?

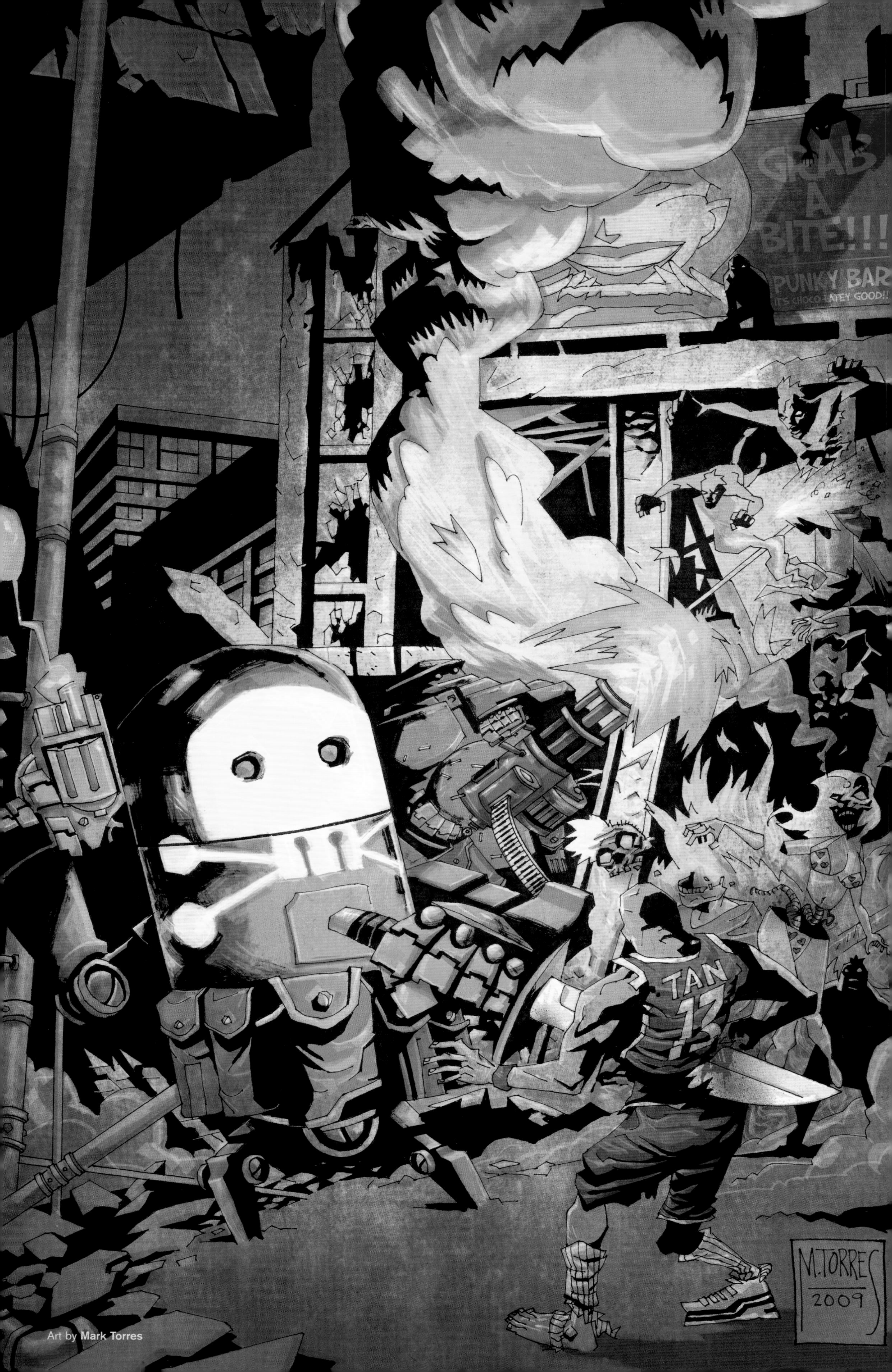
GRAB A BITE!!!
PUNKY BAR
IT'S CHOCO LATEY GOOD!!
TAN 13
M. TORRES 2009
Art by **Mark Torres**

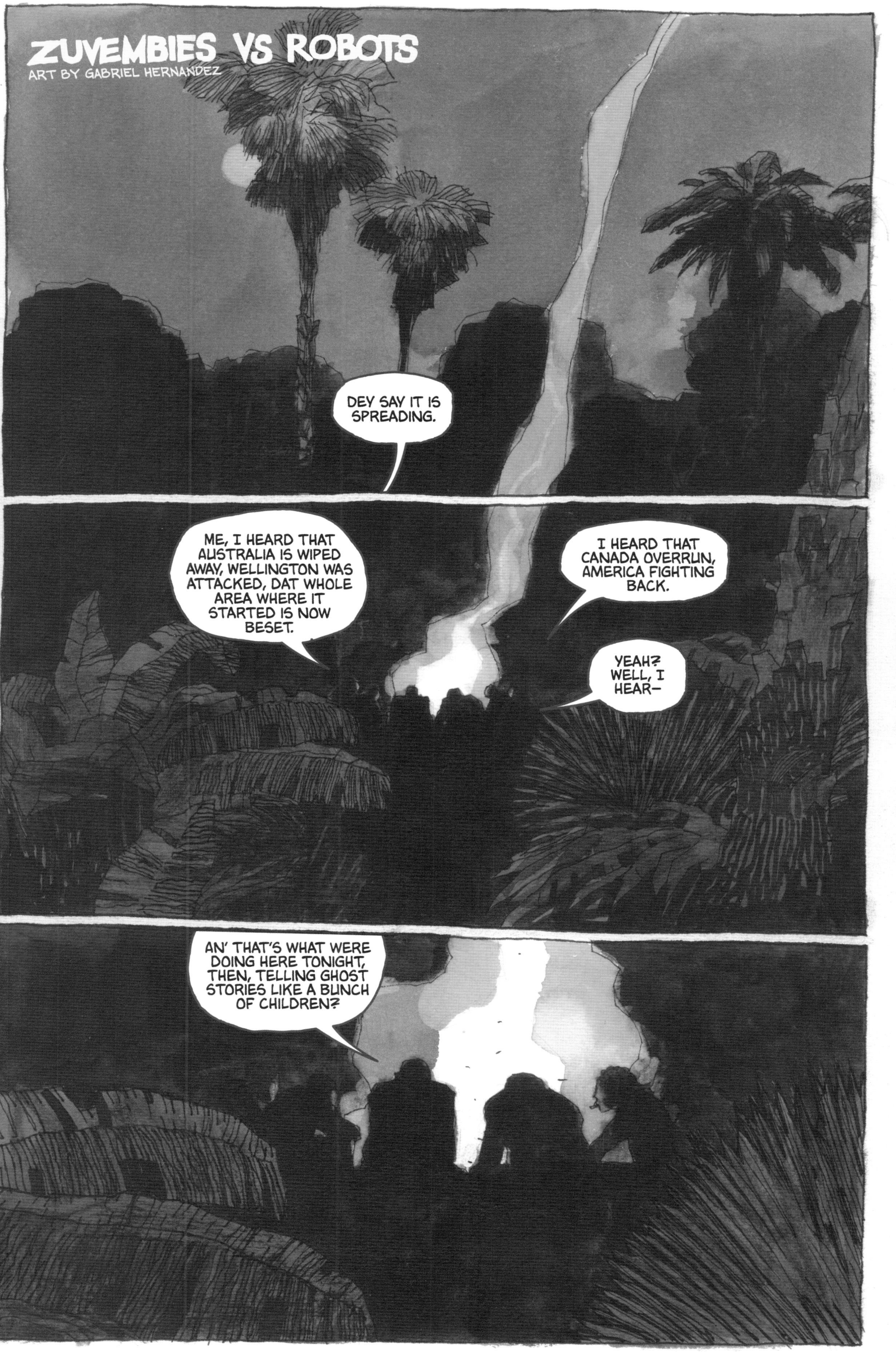
ZUVEMBIES VS ROBOTS
ART BY GABRIEL HERNANDEZ
DEY SAY IT IS SPREADING.
ME, I HEARD THAT AUSTRALIA IS WIPED AWAY, WELLINGTON WAS ATTACKED, DAT WHOLE AREA WHERE IT STARTED IS NOW BESET.
I HEARD THAT CANADA OVERRUN, AMERICA FIGHTING BACK.
YEAH? WELL, I HEAR–
AN' THAT'S WHAT WERE DOING HERE TONIGHT, THEN, TELLING GHOST STORIES LIKE A BUNCH OF CHILDREN?

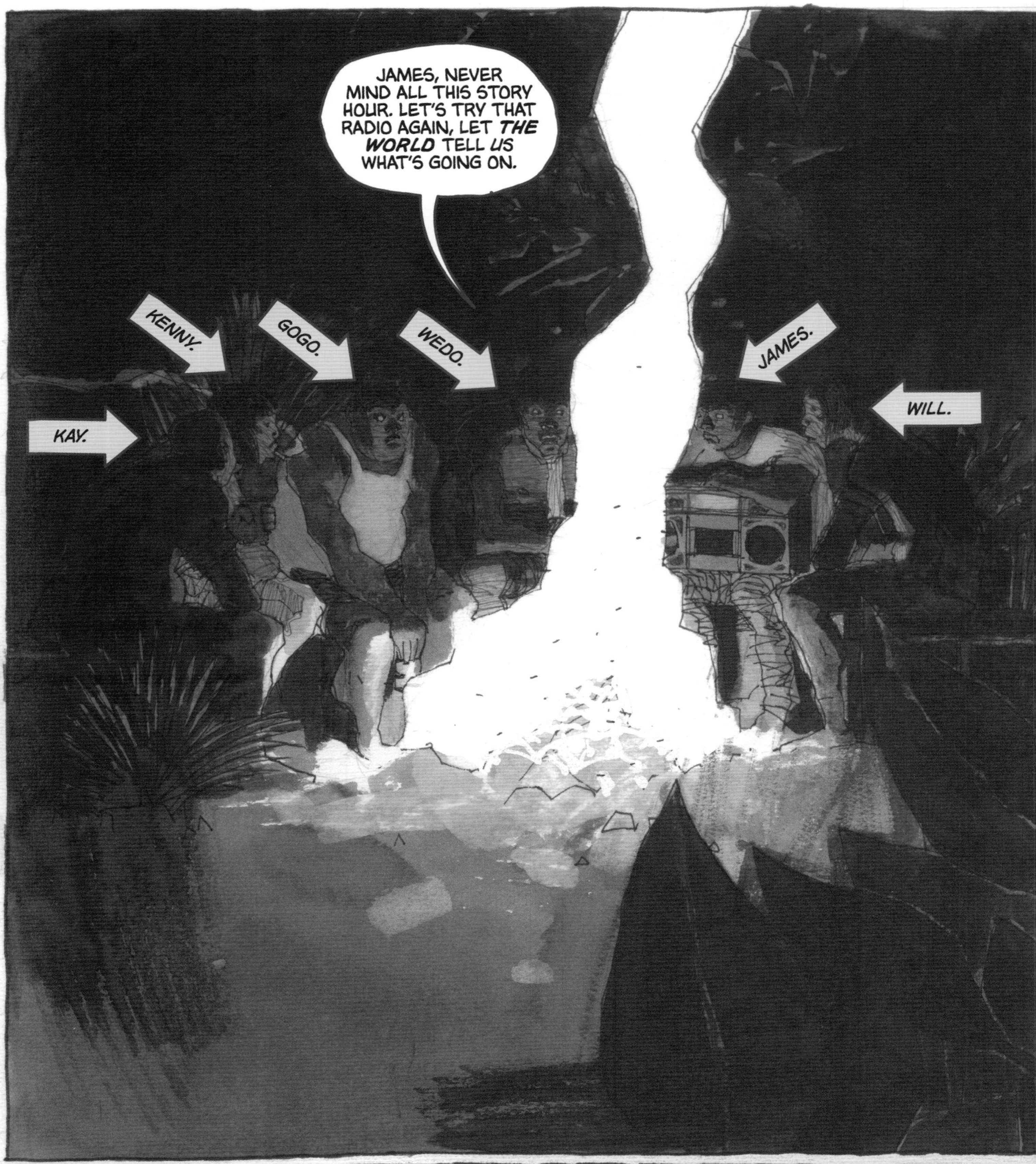
JAMES, NEVER MIND ALL THIS STORY HOUR. LET'S TRY THAT RADIO AGAIN, LET ***THE WORLD*** TELL ***US*** WHAT'S GOING ON.
KENNY.
GOGO.
WEDO.
JAMES.
KAY.
WILL.

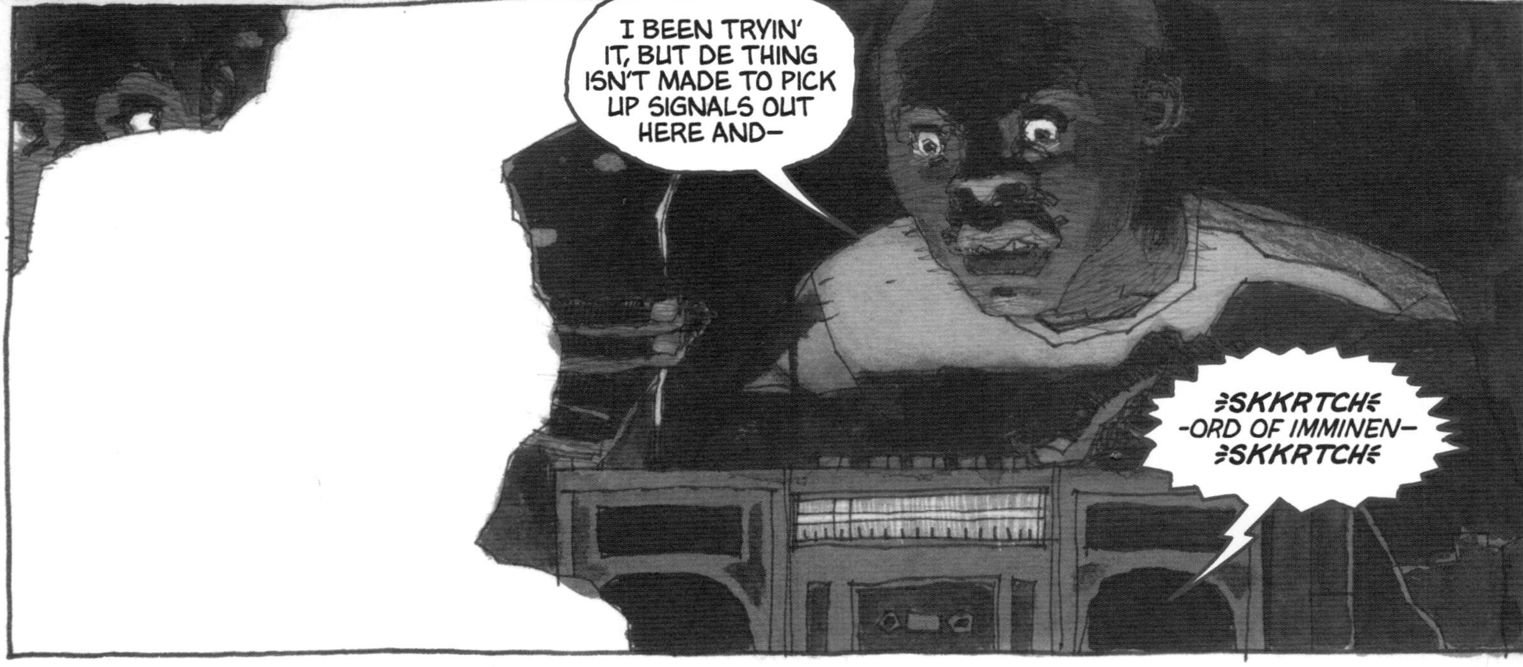
I BEEN TRYIN' IT, BUT DE THING ISN'T MADE TO PICK UP SIGNALS OUT HERE AND—
SKKRTCH -ORD OF IMMINEN- *SKKRTCH*

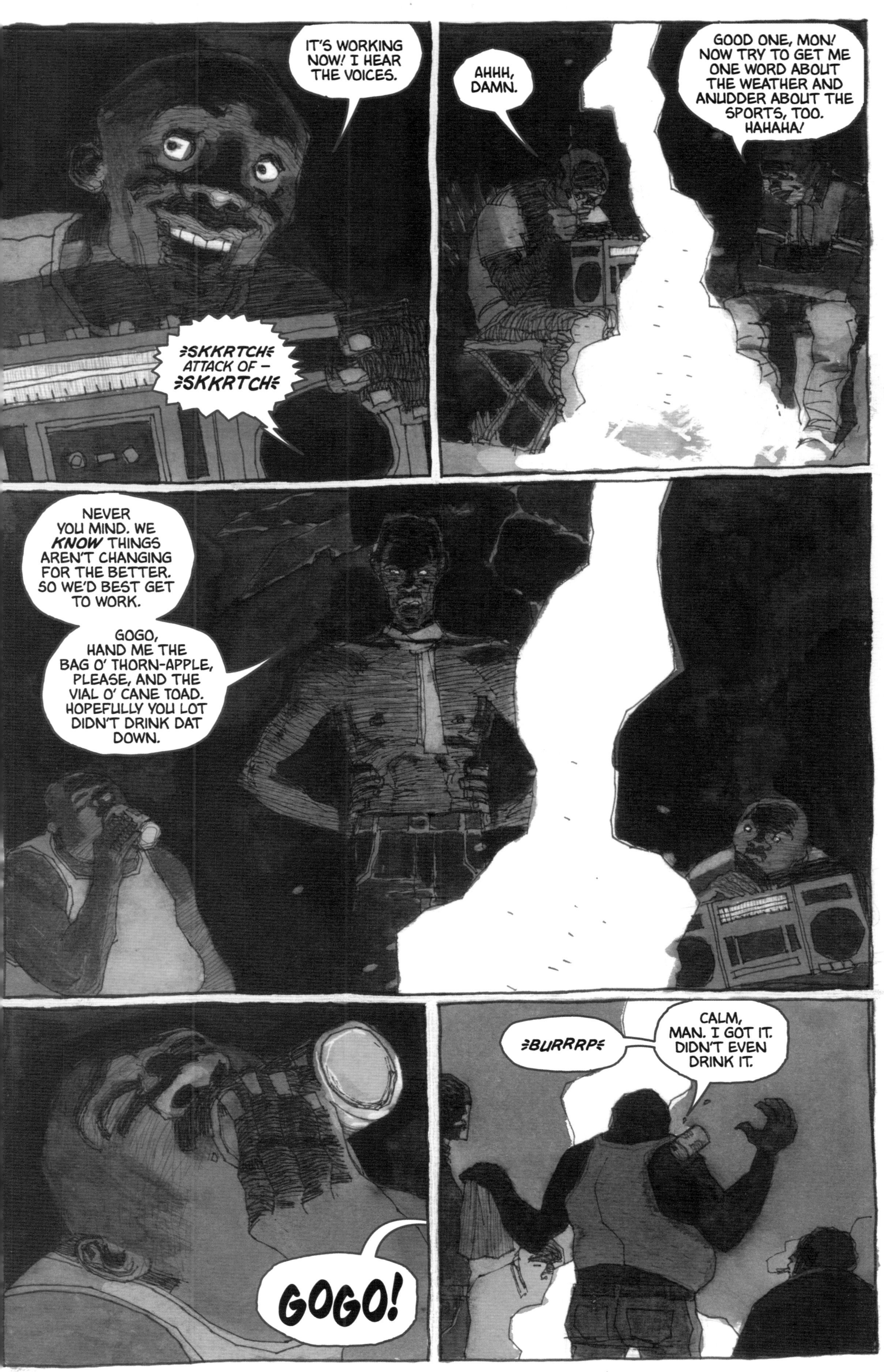
IT'S WORKING NOW! I HEAR THE VOICES.
SKKRTCH ATTACK OF— SKKRTCH
AHHH, DAMN.
GOOD ONE, MON! NOW TRY TO GET ME ONE WORD ABOUT THE WEATHER AND ANUDDER ABOUT THE SPORTS, TOO. HAHAHA!
NEVER YOU MIND. WE KNOW THINGS AREN'T CHANGING FOR THE BETTER. SO WE'D BEST GET TO WORK.
GOGO, HAND ME THE BAG O' THORN-APPLE, PLEASE, AND THE VIAL O' CANE TOAD. HOPEFULLY YOU LOT DIDN'T DRINK DAT DOWN.
GOGO!
BURRRP
CALM, MAN. I GOT IT. DIDN'T EVEN DRINK IT.

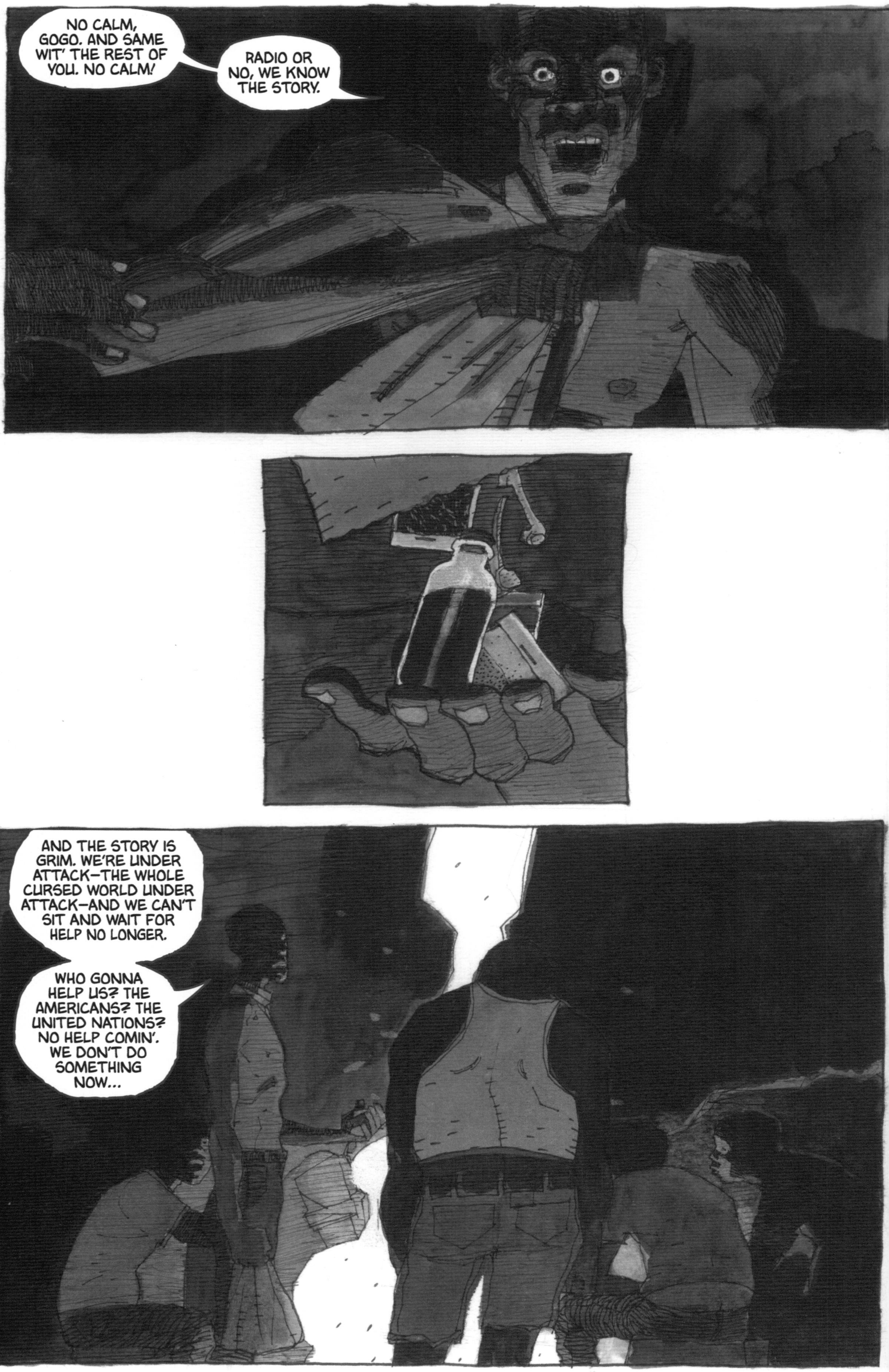
NO CALM, GOGO. AND SAME WIT' THE REST OF YOU. NO CALM!
RADIO OR NO, WE KNOW THE STORY.
AND THE STORY IS GRIM. WE'RE UNDER ATTACK—THE WHOLE CURSED WORLD UNDER ATTACK—AND WE CAN'T SIT AND WAIT FOR HELP NO LONGER.
WHO GONNA HELP US? THE AMERICANS? THE UNITED NATIONS? NO HELP COMIN'. WE DON'T DO SOMETHING NOW...

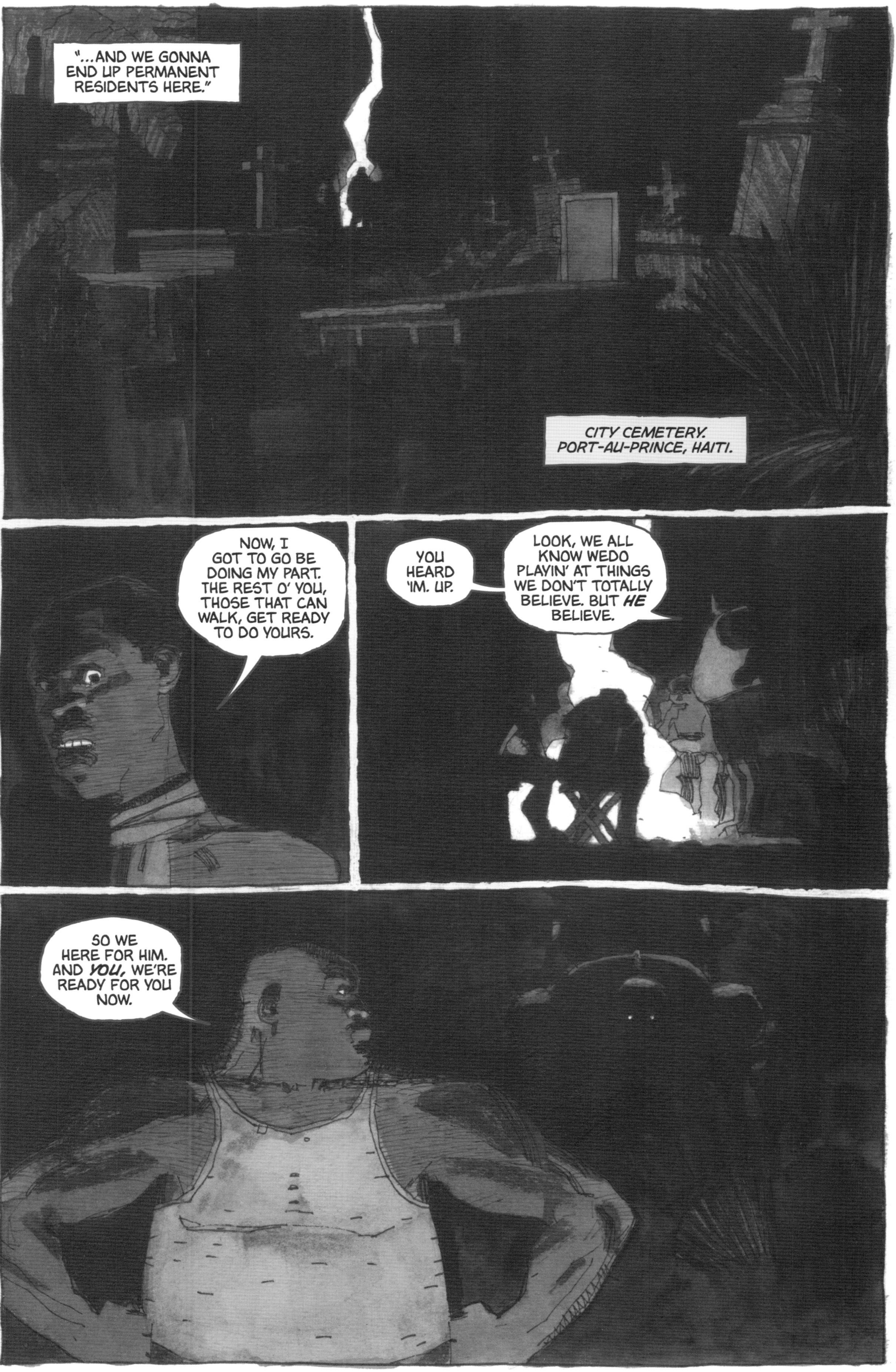
"...AND WE GONNA END UP PERMANENT RESIDENTS HERE."
CITY CEMETERY. PORT-AU-PRINCE, HAITI.
NOW, I GOT TO GO BE DOING MY PART. THE REST O' YOU, THOSE THAT CAN WALK, GET READY TO DO YOURS.
YOU HEARD 'IM. UP.
LOOK, WE ALL KNOW WEDO PLAYIN' AT THINGS WE DON'T TOTALLY BELIEVE. BUT HE BELIEVE.
SO WE HERE FOR HIM. AND YOU, WE'RE READY FOR YOU NOW.

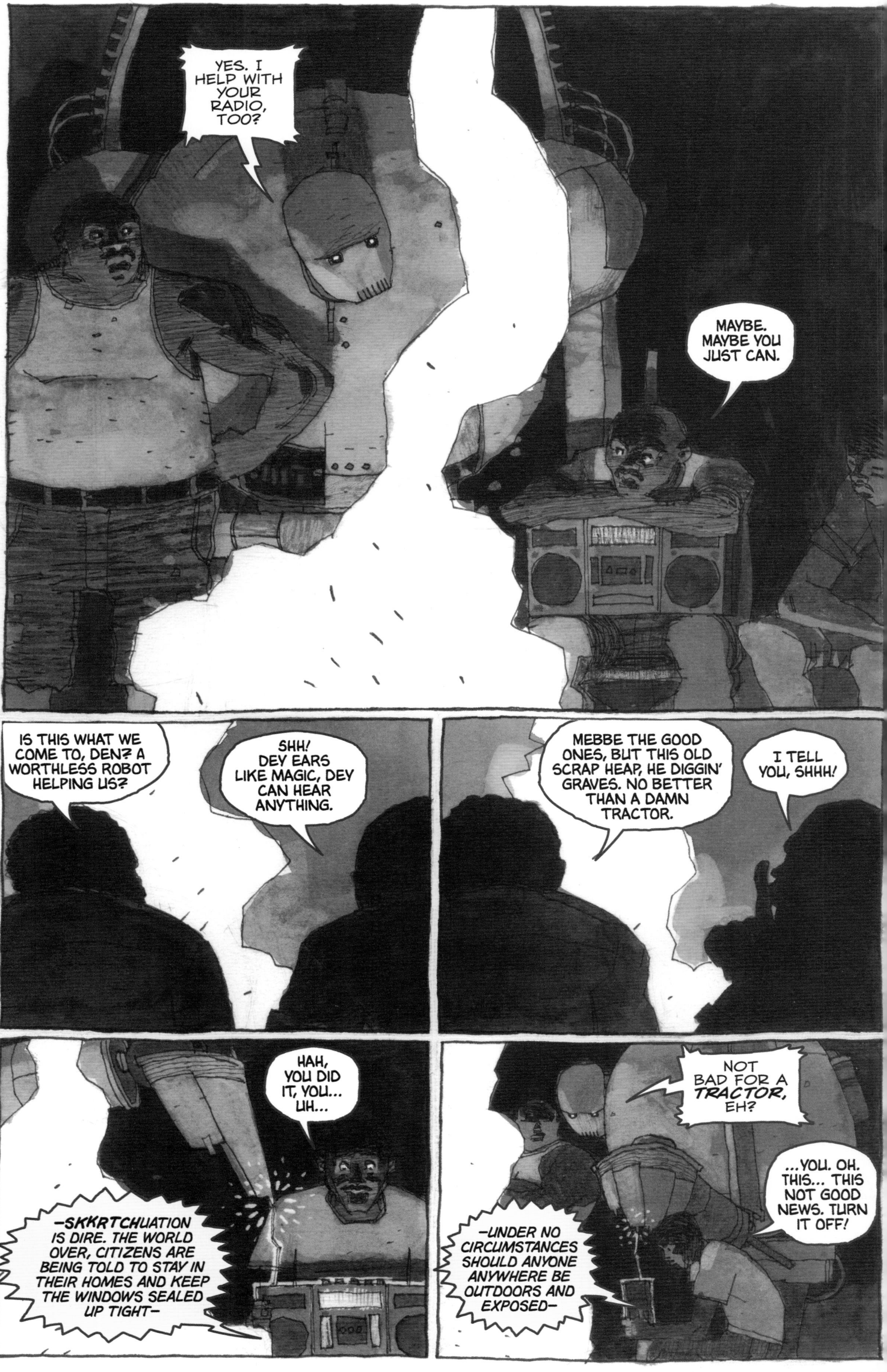
YES. I HELP WITH YOUR RADIO, TOO?
MAYBE. MAYBE YOU JUST CAN.
IS THIS WHAT WE COME TO, DEN? A WORTHLESS ROBOT HELPING US?
SHH! DEY EARS LIKE MAGIC, DEY CAN HEAR ANYTHING.
MEBBE THE GOOD ONES, BUT THIS OLD SCRAP HEAP, HE DIGGIN' GRAVES. NO BETTER THAN A DAMN TRACTOR.
I TELL YOU, SHHH!
HAH, YOU DID IT, YOU... UH...
—SKKRTCHUATION IS DIRE. THE WORLD OVER, CITIZENS ARE BEING TOLD TO STAY IN THEIR HOMES AND KEEP THE WINDOWS SEALED UP TIGHT—
NOT BAD FOR A TRACTOR, EH?
...YOU. OH. THIS... THIS NOT GOOD NEWS. TURN IT OFF!
—UNDER NO CIRCUMSTANCES SHOULD ANYONE ANYWHERE BE OUTDOORS AND EXPOSED—

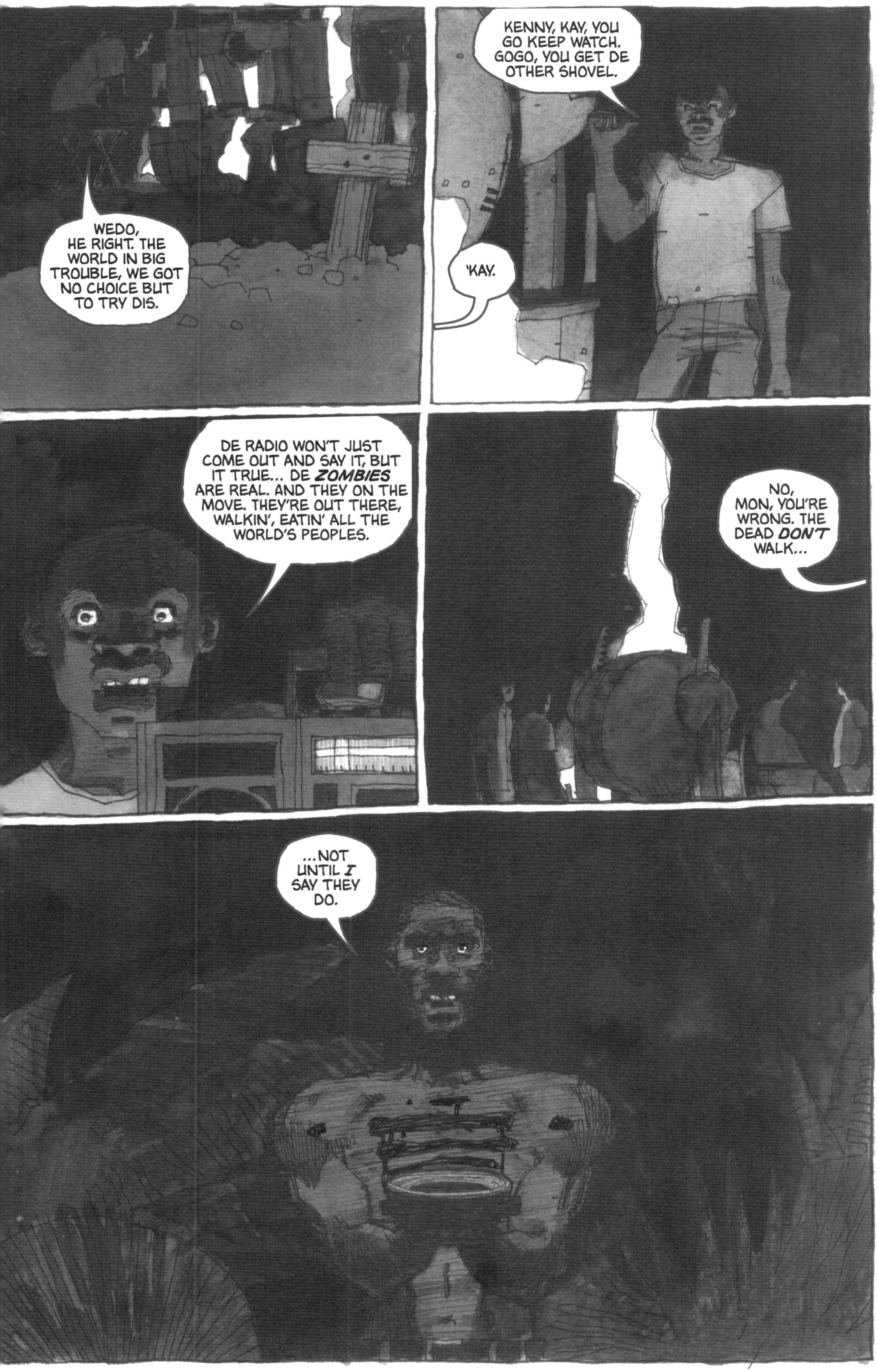
WEDO, HE RIGHT. THE WORLD IN BIG TROUBLE, WE GOT NO CHOICE BUT TO TRY DIS.
KENNY, KAY, YOU GO KEEP WATCH. GOGO, YOU GET DE OTHER SHOVEL.
'KAY.
DE RADIO WON'T JUST COME OUT AND SAY IT, BUT IT TRUE... DE *ZOMBIES* ARE REAL. AND THEY ON THE MOVE. THEY'RE OUT THERE, WALKIN', EATIN' ALL THE WORLD'S PEOPLES.
NO, MON, YOU'RE WRONG. THE DEAD *DON'T* WALK...
...NOT UNTIL *I* SAY THEY DO.

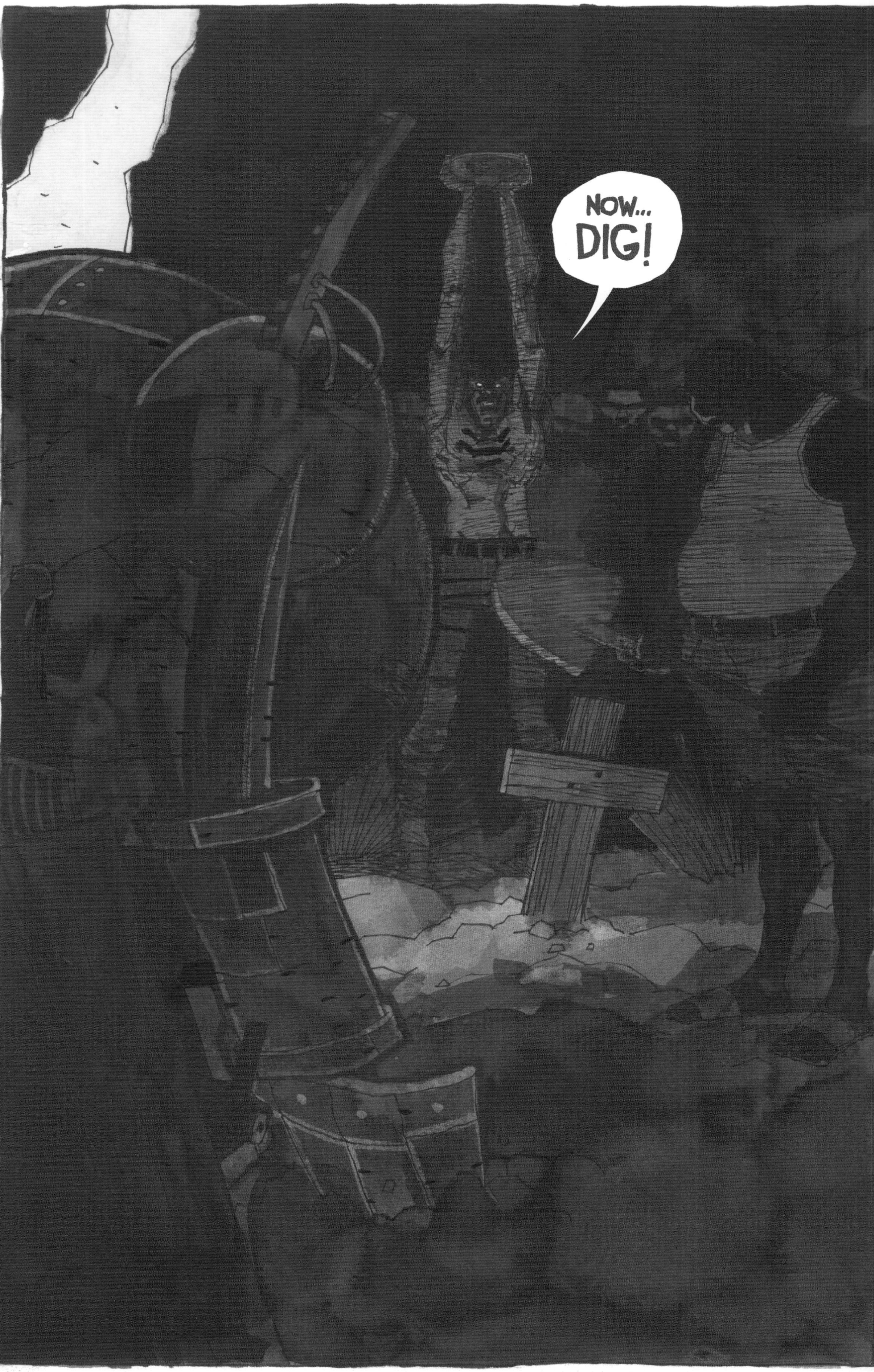
NOW... DIG!

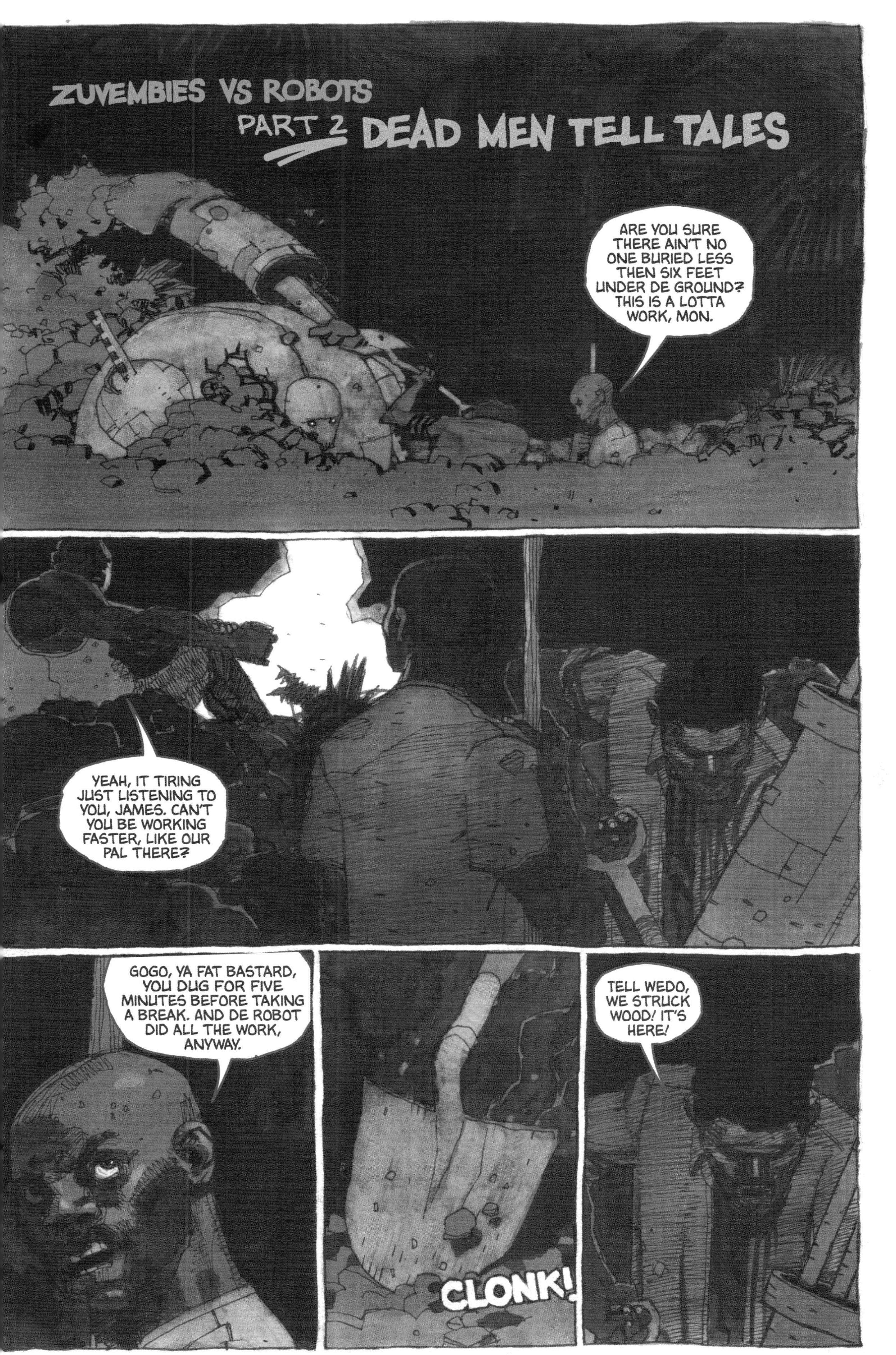
ZUVEMBIES VS ROBOTS
PART 2 DEAD MEN TELL TALES
ARE YOU SURE THERE AIN'T NO ONE BURIED LESS THEN SIX FEET UNDER DE GROUND? THIS IS A LOTTA WORK, MON.
YEAH, IT TIRING JUST LISTENING TO YOU, JAMES. CAN'T YOU BE WORKING FASTER, LIKE OUR PAL THERE?
GOGO, YA FAT BASTARD, YOU DUG FOR FIVE MINUTES BEFORE TAKING A BREAK. AND DE ROBOT DID ALL THE WORK, ANYWAY.
CLONK!
TELL WEDO, WE STRUCK WOOD! IT'S HERE!

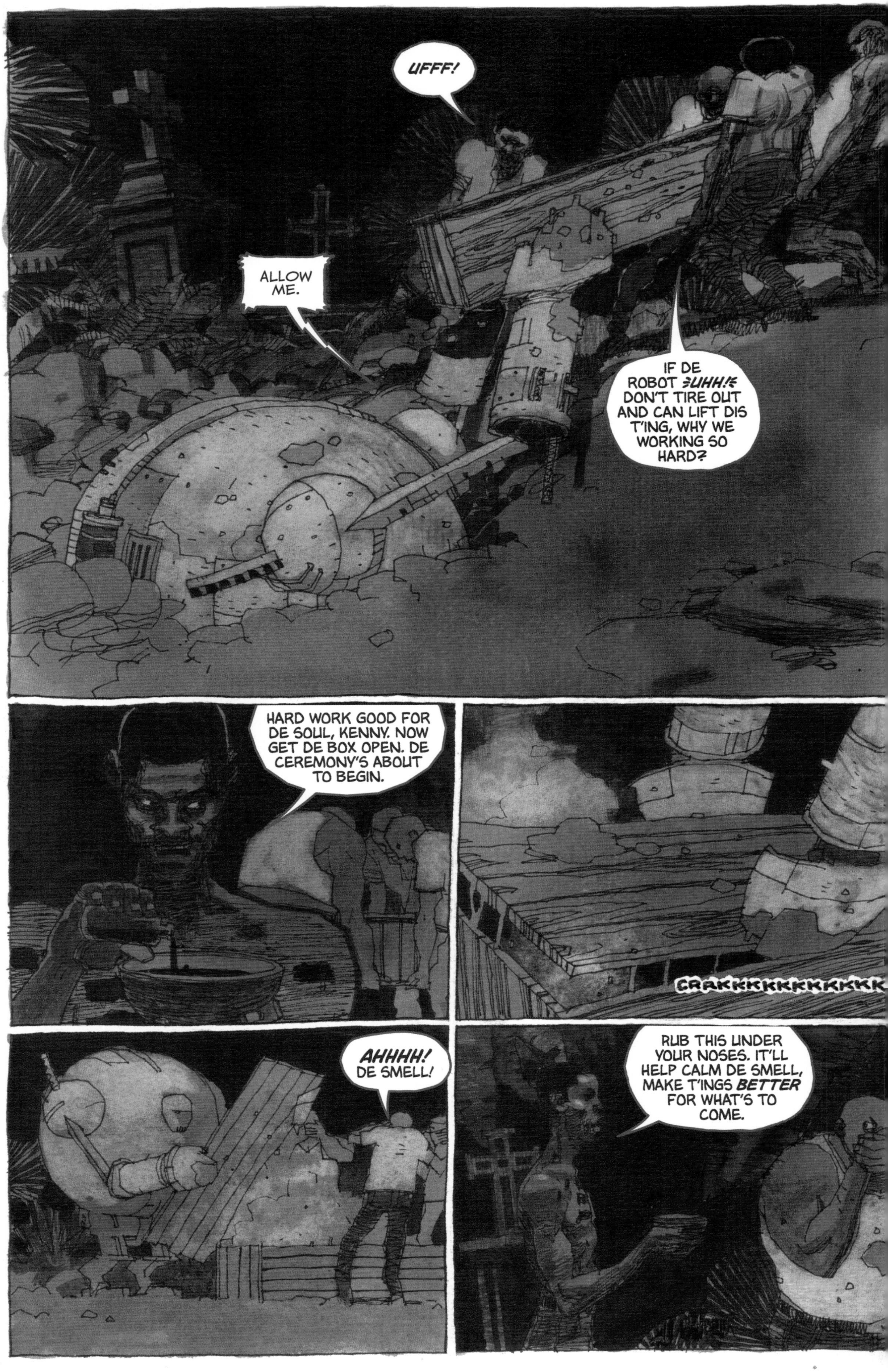
UFFF!
ALLOW ME.
IF DE ROBOT UHH! DON'T TIRE OUT AND CAN LIFT DIS T'ING, WHY WE WORKING SO HARD?
HARD WORK GOOD FOR DE SOUL, KENNY. NOW GET DE BOX OPEN. DE CEREMONY'S ABOUT TO BEGIN.
CRAKKKKKKKKKKK
AHHHH! DE SMELL!
RUB THIS UNDER YOUR NOSES. IT'LL HELP CALM DE SMELL, MAKE T'INGS BETTER FOR WHAT'S TO COME.

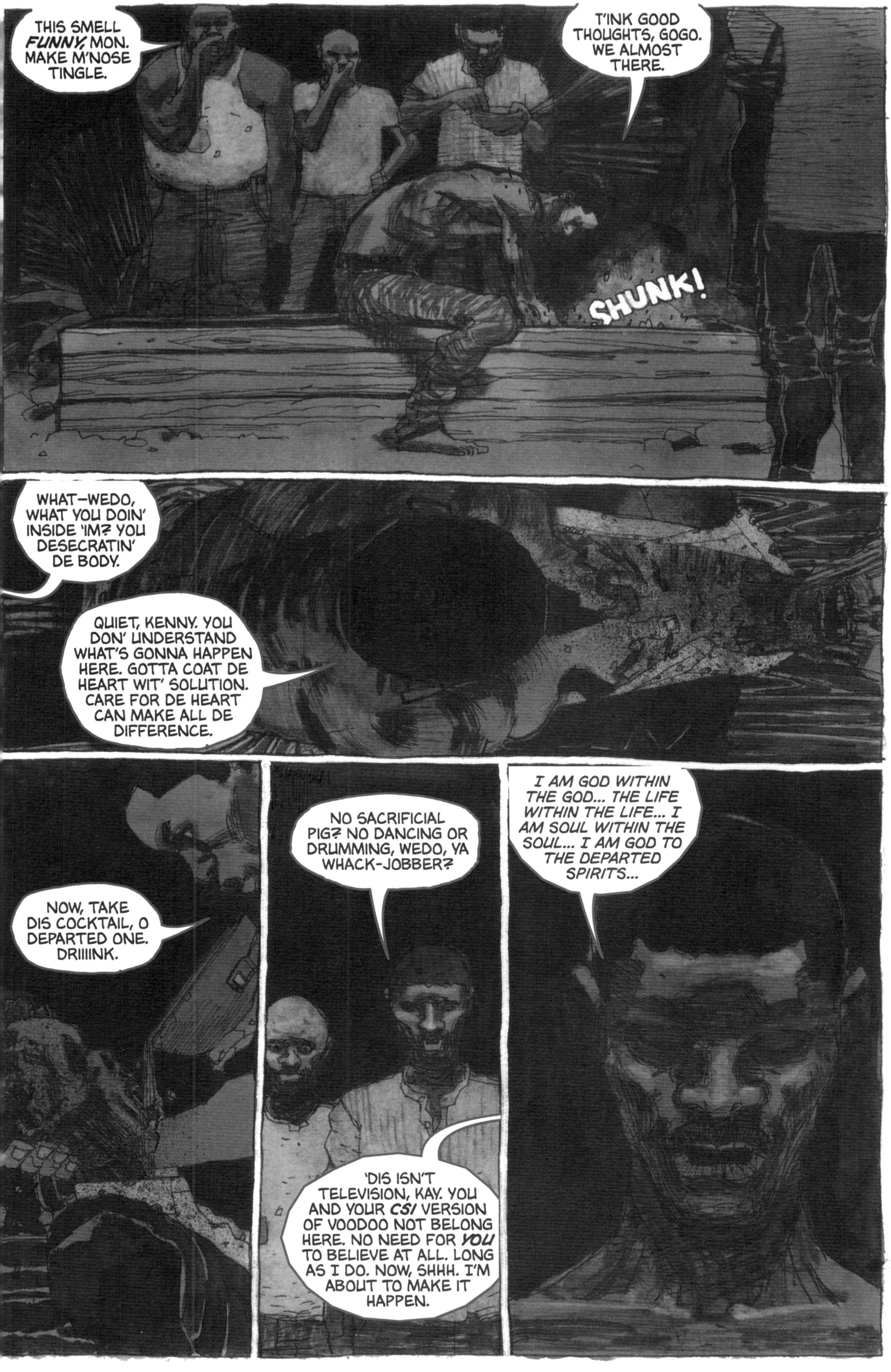
THIS SMELL FUNNY, MON. MAKE M'NOSE TINGLE.
T'INK GOOD THOUGHTS, GOGO. WE ALMOST THERE.
SHUNK!
WHAT—WEDO, WHAT YOU DOIN' INSIDE 'IM? YOU DESECRATIN' DE BODY.
QUIET, KENNY. YOU DON' UNDERSTAND WHAT'S GONNA HAPPEN HERE. GOTTA COAT DE HEART WIT' SOLUTION. CARE FOR DE HEART CAN MAKE ALL DE DIFFERENCE.
NOW, TAKE DIS COCKTAIL, O DEPARTED ONE. DRIIIINK.
NO SACRIFICIAL PIG? NO DANCING OR DRUMMING, WEDO, YA WHACK-JOBBER?
'DIS ISN'T TELEVISION, KAY. YOU AND YOUR CSI VERSION OF VOODOO NOT BELONG HERE. NO NEED FOR YOU TO BELIEVE AT ALL. LONG AS I DO. NOW, SHHH. I'M ABOUT TO MAKE IT HAPPEN.
I AM GOD WITHIN THE GOD... THE LIFE WITHIN THE LIFE... I AM SOUL WITHIN THE SOUL... I AM GOD TO THE DEPARTED SPIRITS...

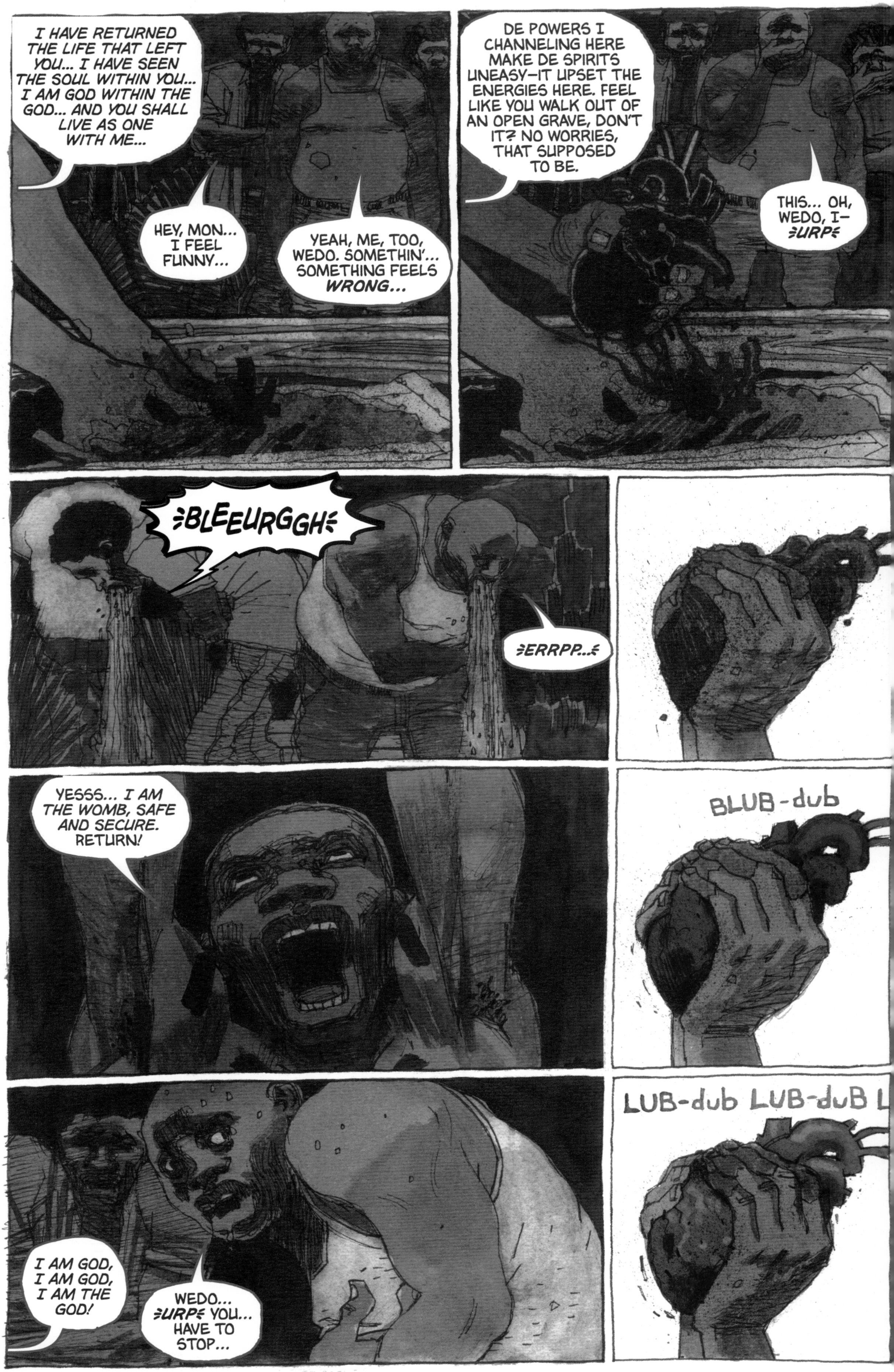
I HAVE RETURNED THE LIFE THAT LEFT YOU... I HAVE SEEN THE SOUL WITHIN YOU... I AM GOD WITHIN THE GOD... AND YOU SHALL LIVE AS ONE WITH ME...
HEY, MON... I FEEL FUNNY...
YEAH, ME, TOO, WEDO. SOMETHIN'... SOMETHING FEELS WRONG...
DE POWERS I CHANNELING HERE MAKE DE SPIRITS UNEASY—IT UPSET THE ENERGIES HERE. FEEL LIKE YOU WALK OUT OF AN OPEN GRAVE, DON'T IT? NO WORRIES, THAT SUPPOSED TO BE.
THIS... OH, WEDO, I— URP
BLEEURGGH
ERRPP...
YESSS... I AM THE WOMB, SAFE AND SECURE. RETURN!
BLUB-dub
I AM GOD, I AM GOD, I AM THE GOD!
WEDO... URP YOU... HAVE TO STOP...
LUB-dub LUB-duB L

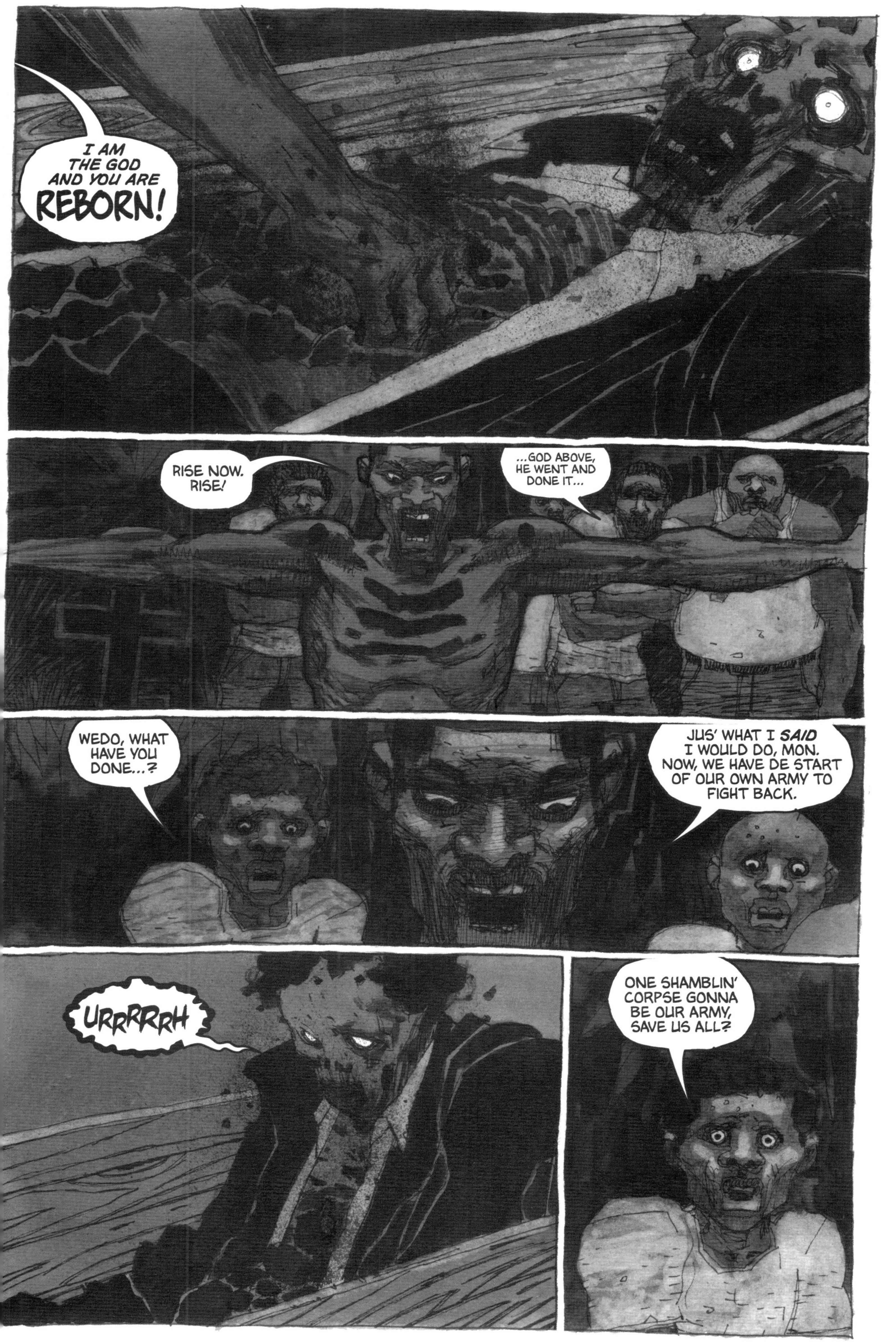
I AM THE GOD AND YOU ARE REBORN!
RISE NOW. RISE!
...GOD ABOVE, HE WENT AND DONE IT...
WEDO, WHAT HAVE YOU DONE...?
JUS' WHAT I *SAID* I WOULD DO, MON. NOW, WE HAVE DE START OF OUR OWN ARMY TO FIGHT BACK.
URRRRRH
ONE SHAMBLIN' CORPSE GONNA BE OUR ARMY, SAVE US ALL?

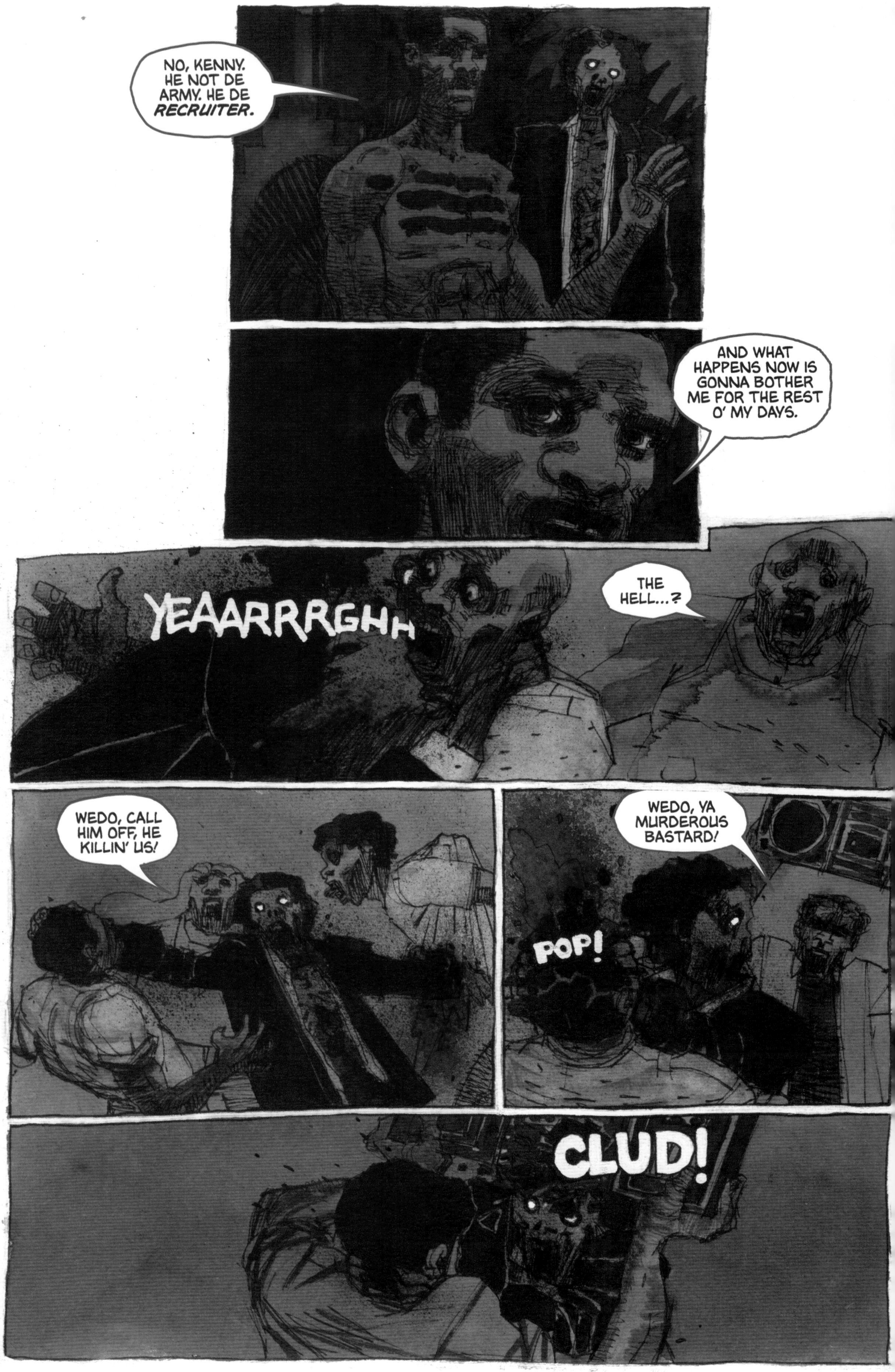
NO, KENNY. HE NOT DE ARMY. HE DE *RECRUITER*.
AND WHAT HAPPENS NOW IS GONNA BOTHER ME FOR THE REST O' MY DAYS.
YEAARRRGHH
THE HELL...?
WEDO, CALL HIM OFF, HE KILLIN' US!
WEDO, YA MURDEROUS BASTARD!
POP!
CLUD!

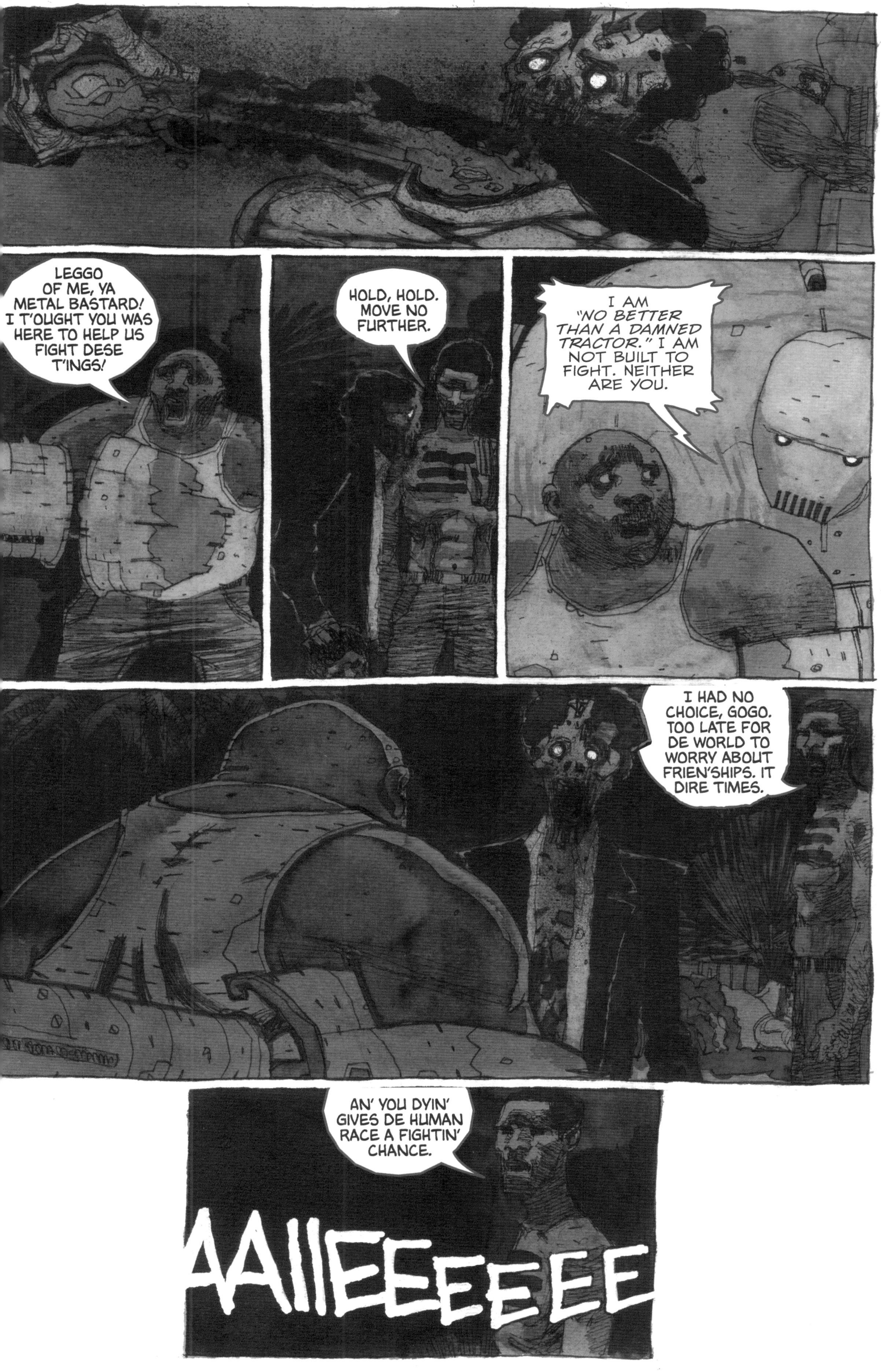
LEGGO OF ME, YA METAL BASTARD! I T'OUGHT YOU WAS HERE TO HELP US FIGHT DESE T'INGS!
HOLD, HOLD. MOVE NO FURTHER.
I AM *"NO BETTER THAN A DAMNED TRACTOR."* I AM NOT BUILT TO FIGHT. NEITHER ARE YOU.
I HAD NO CHOICE, GOGO. TOO LATE FOR DE WORLD TO WORRY ABOUT FRIEN'SHIPS. IT DIRE TIMES.
AN' YOU DYIN' GIVES DE HUMAN RACE A FIGHTIN' CHANCE.
AAIIEEEEEEE

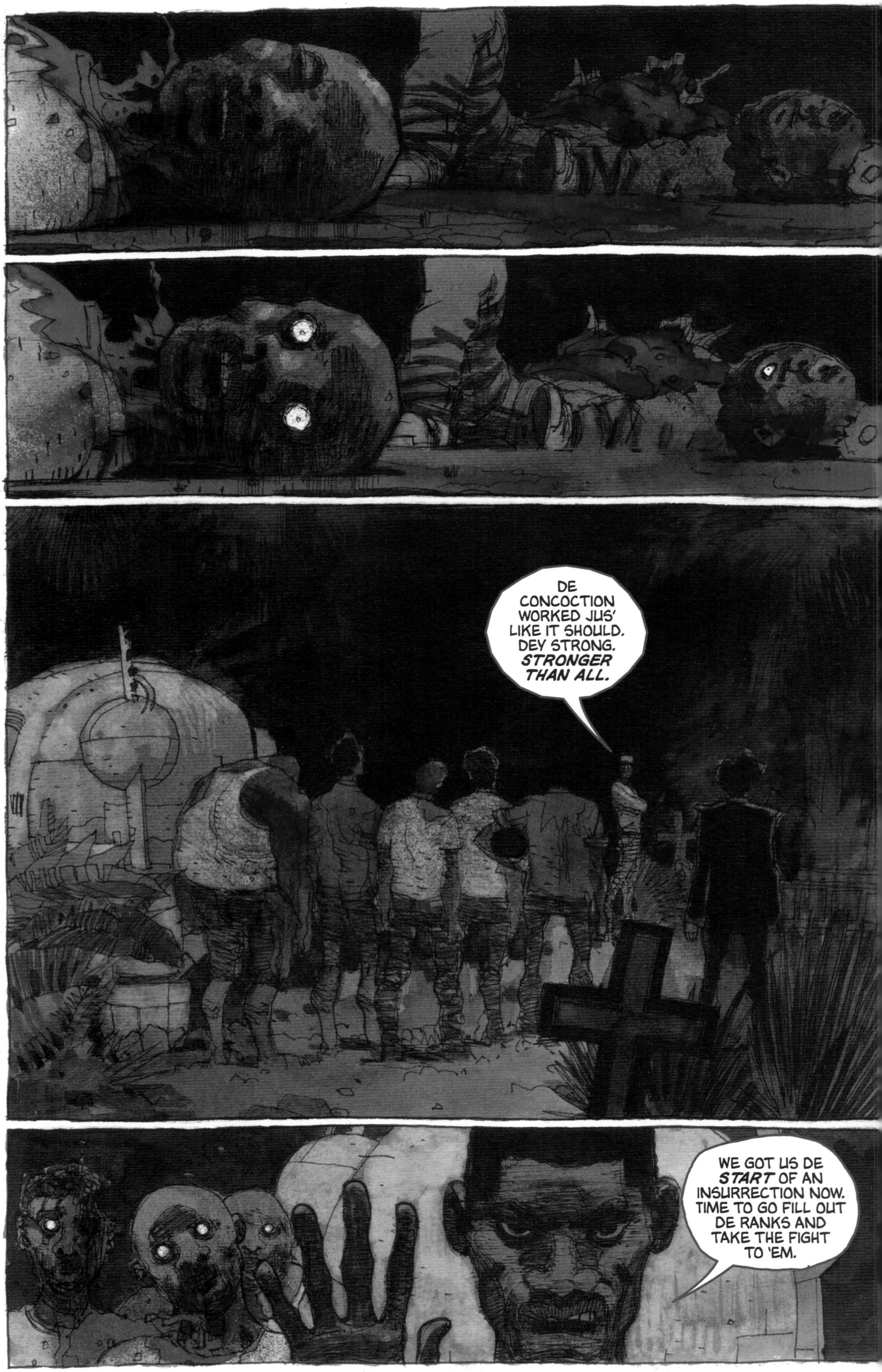

DE CONCOCTION WORKED JUS' LIKE IT SHOULD. DEY STRONG. *STRONGER THAN ALL.*
WE GOT US DE *START* OF AN INSURRECTION NOW. TIME TO GO FILL OUT DE RANKS AND TAKE THE FIGHT TO 'EM.

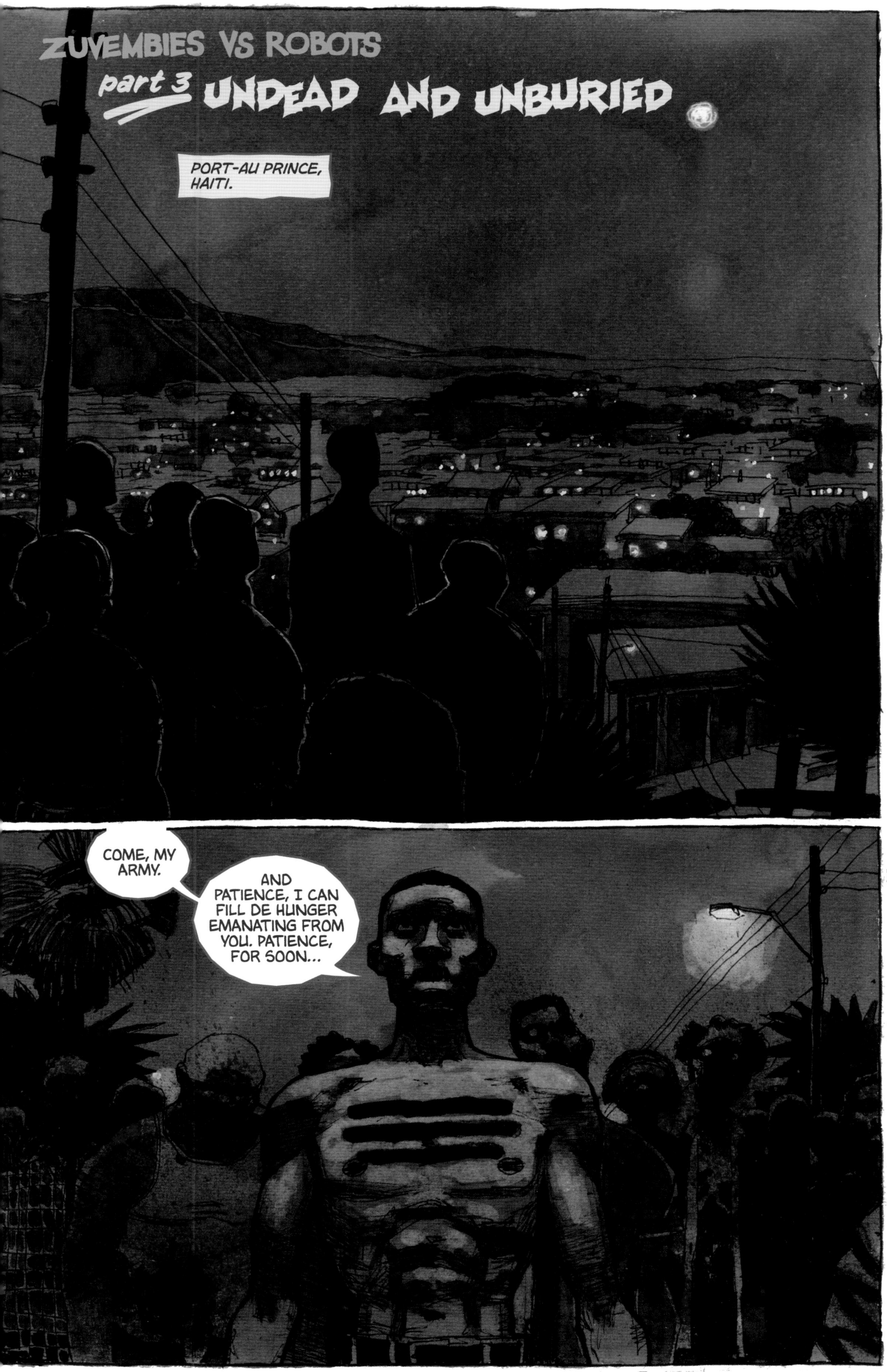
ZUVEMBIES VS ROBOTS
part 3 UNDEAD AND UNBURIED
PORT-AU PRINCE, HAITI.
COME, MY ARMY.
AND PATIENCE, I CAN FILL DE HUNGER EMANATING FROM YOU. PATIENCE, FOR SOON...

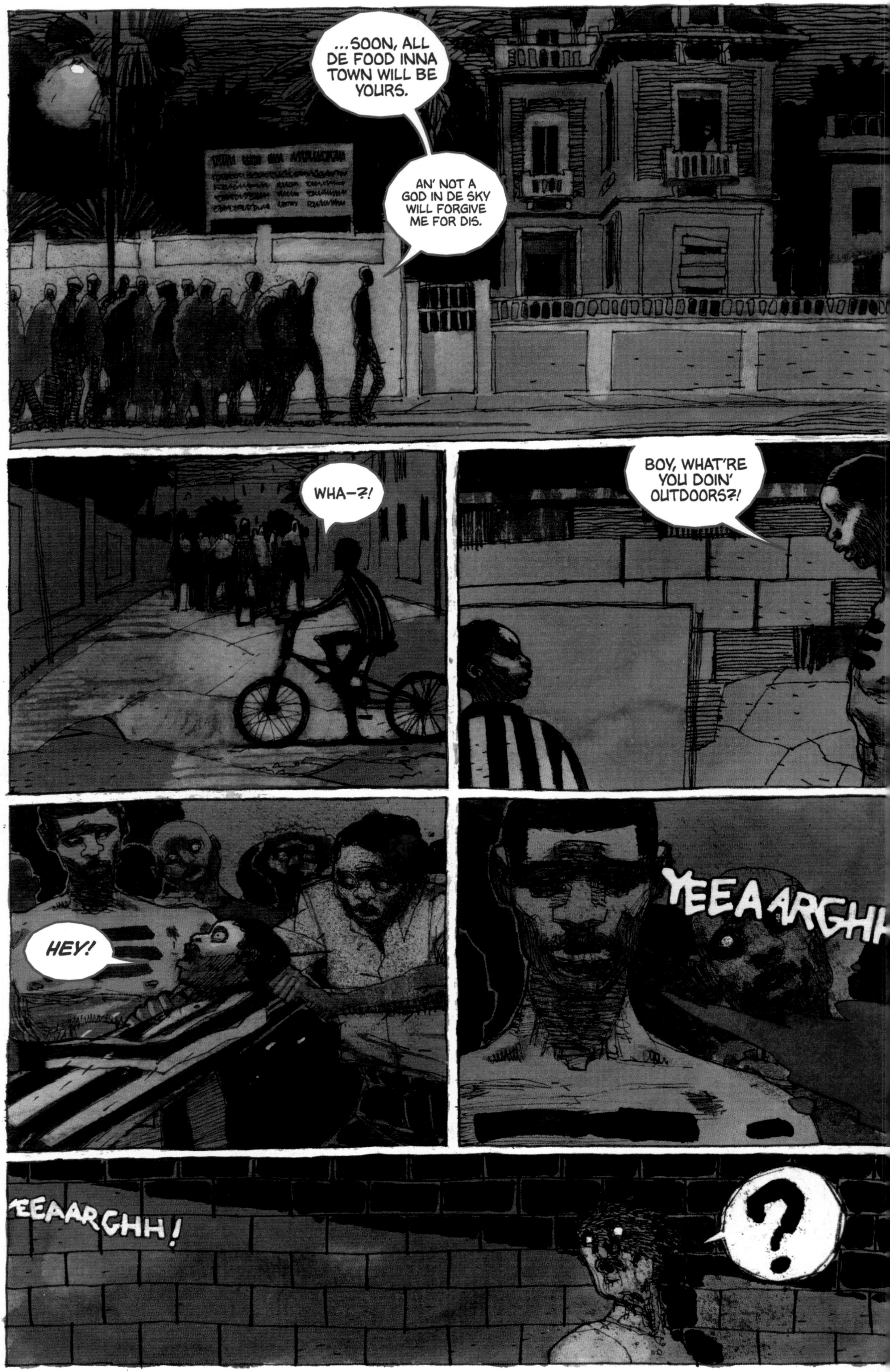
...SOON, ALL DE FOOD INNA TOWN WILL BE YOURS.
AN' NOT A GOD IN DE SKY WILL FORGIVE ME FOR DIS.
WHA–?!
BOY, WHAT'RE YOU DOIN' OUTDOORS?!
HEY!
YEEAARGHH
EEAARGHH!
?

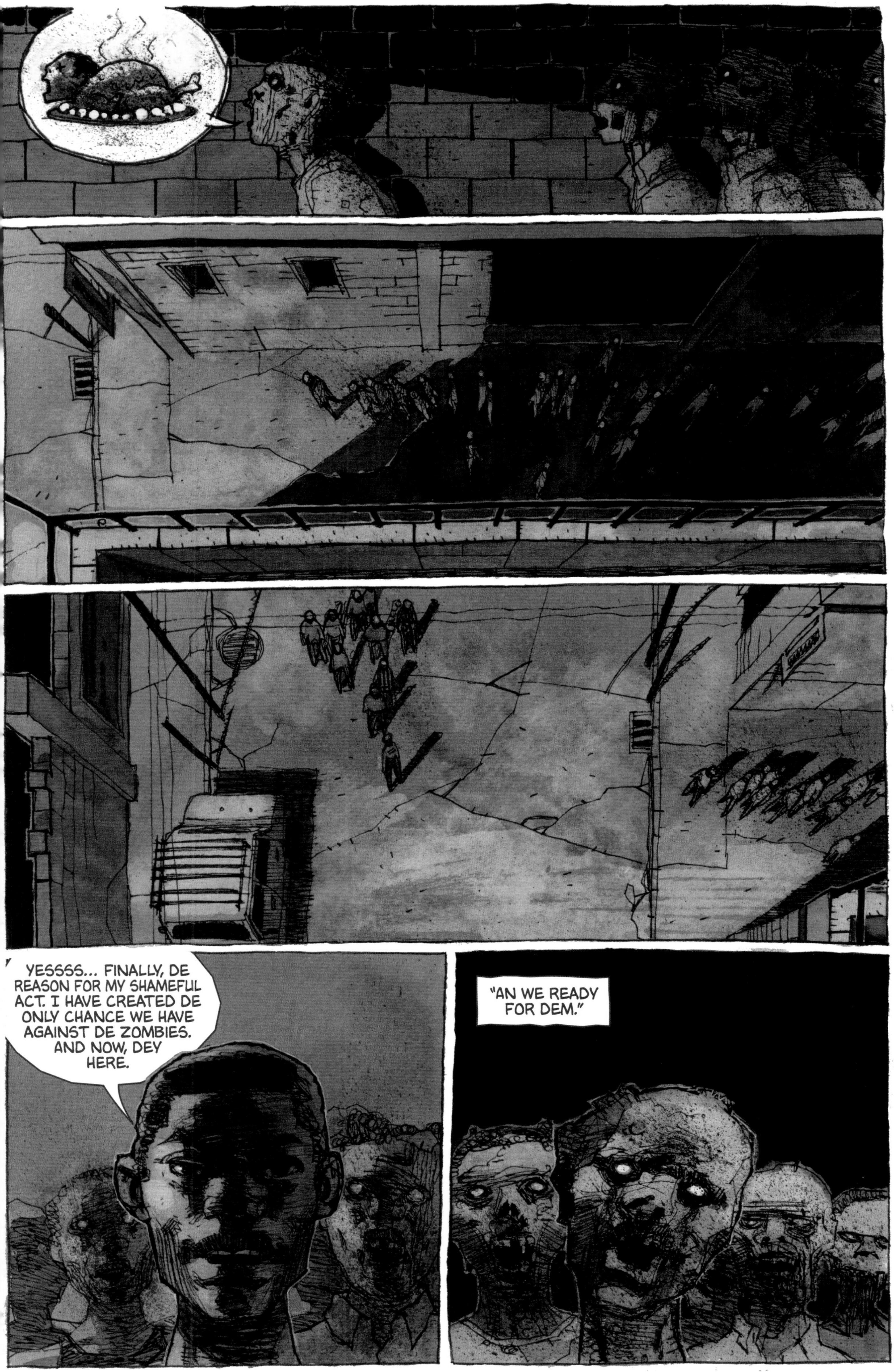
YESSSS... FINALLY, DE REASON FOR MY SHAMEFUL ACT. I HAVE CREATED DE ONLY CHANCE WE HAVE AGAINST DE ZOMBIES. AND NOW, DEY HERE.
"AN WE READY FOR DEM."

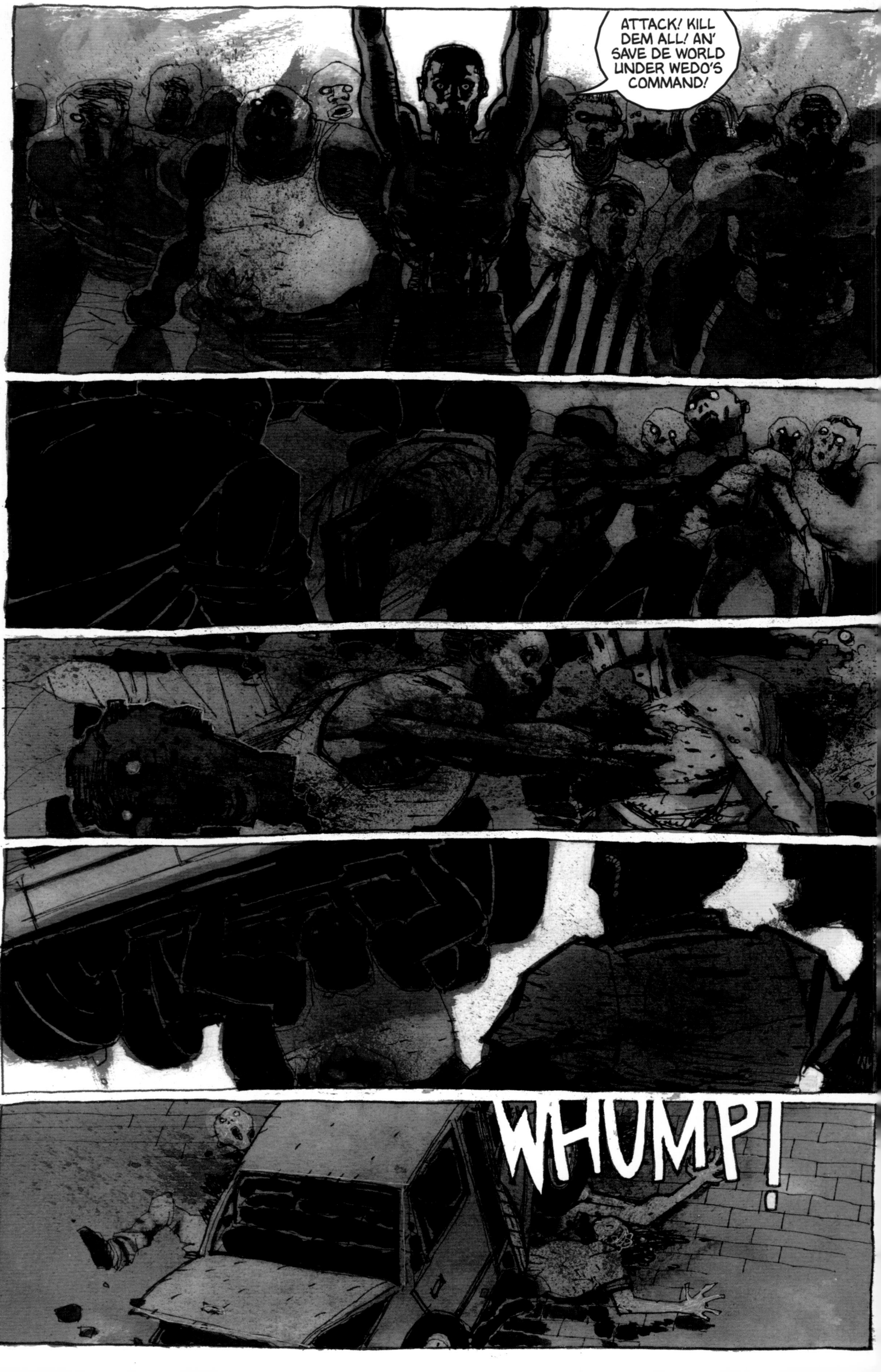
ATTACK! KILL DEM ALL! AN' SAVE DE WORLD UNDER WEDO'S COMMAND!
WHUMP!

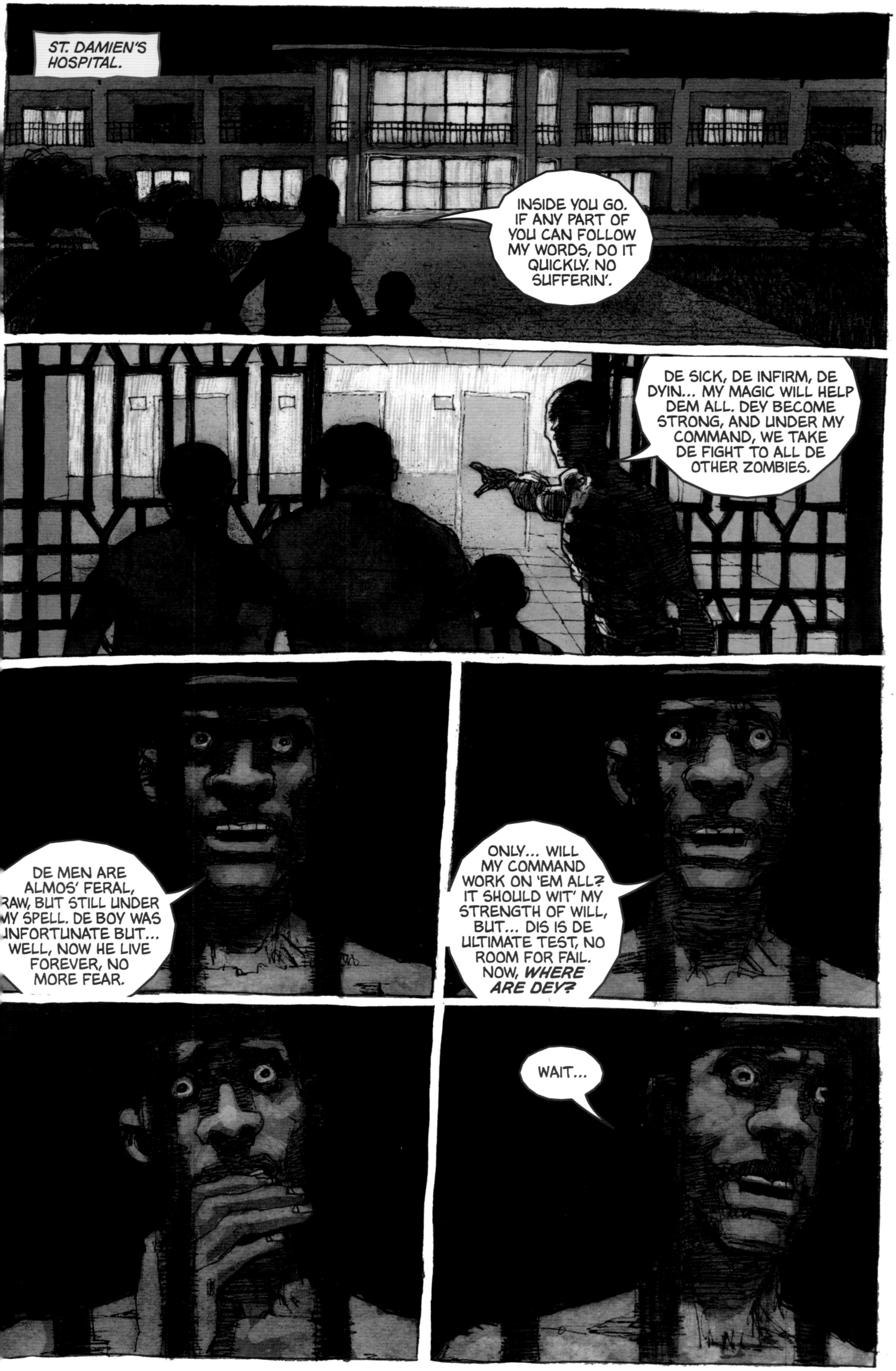
ST. DAMIEN'S HOSPITAL.
INSIDE YOU GO. IF ANY PART OF YOU CAN FOLLOW MY WORDS, DO IT QUICKLY. NO SUFFERIN'.
DE SICK, DE INFIRM, DE DYIN... MY MAGIC WILL HELP DEM ALL. DEY BECOME STRONG, AND UNDER MY COMMAND, WE TAKE DE FIGHT TO ALL DE OTHER ZOMBIES.
DE MEN ARE ALMOS' FERAL, RAW, BUT STILL UNDER MY SPELL. DE BOY WAS UNFORTUNATE BUT... WELL, NOW HE LIVE FOREVER, NO MORE FEAR.
ONLY... WILL MY COMMAND WORK ON 'EM ALL? IT SHOULD WIT' MY STRENGTH OF WILL, BUT... DIS IS DE ULTIMATE TEST, NO ROOM FOR FAIL. NOW, *WHERE ARE DEY?*
WAIT...

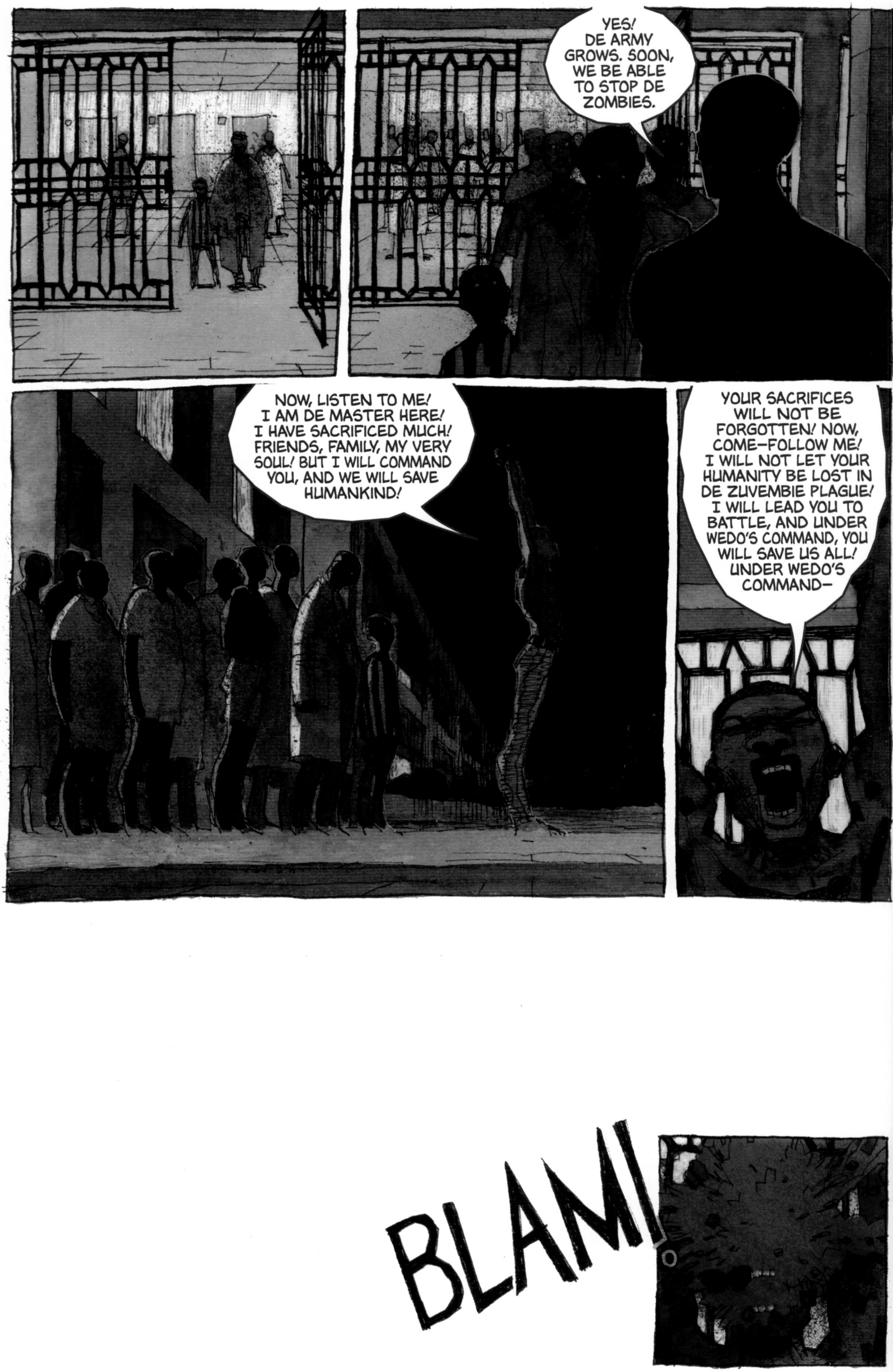
YES! DE ARMY GROWS. SOON, WE BE ABLE TO STOP DE ZOMBIES.
NOW, LISTEN TO ME! I AM DE MASTER HERE! I HAVE SACRIFICED MUCH! FRIENDS, FAMILY, MY VERY SOUL! BUT I WILL COMMAND YOU, AND WE WILL SAVE HUMANKIND!
YOUR SACRIFICES WILL NOT BE FORGOTTEN! NOW, COME—FOLLOW ME! I WILL NOT LET YOUR HUMANITY BE LOST IN DE ZUVEMBIE PLAGUE! I WILL LEAD YOU TO BATTLE, AND UNDER WEDO'S COMMAND, YOU WILL SAVE US ALL! UNDER WEDO'S COMMAND—
BLAM!

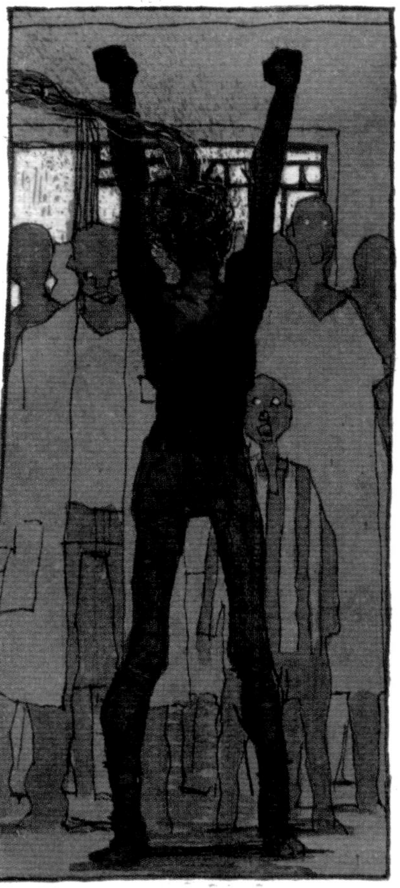

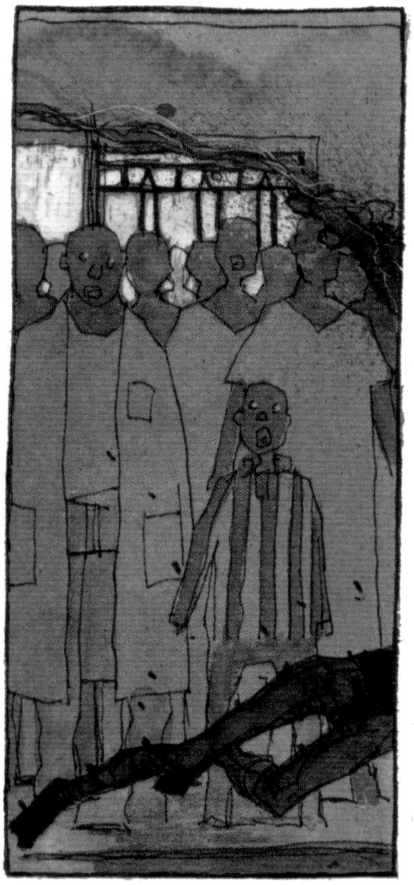

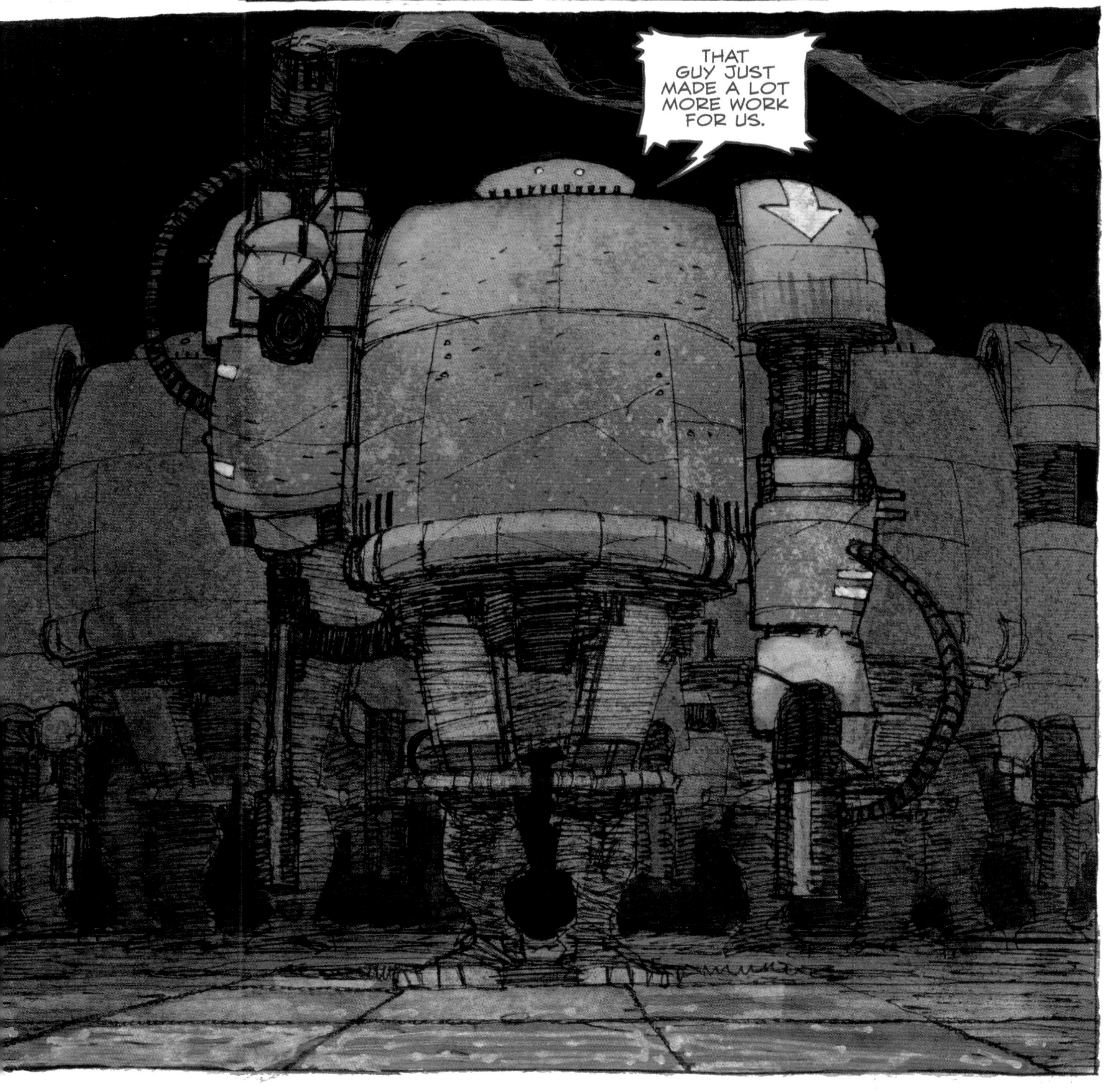
THAT GUY JUST MADE A LOT MORE WORK FOR US.

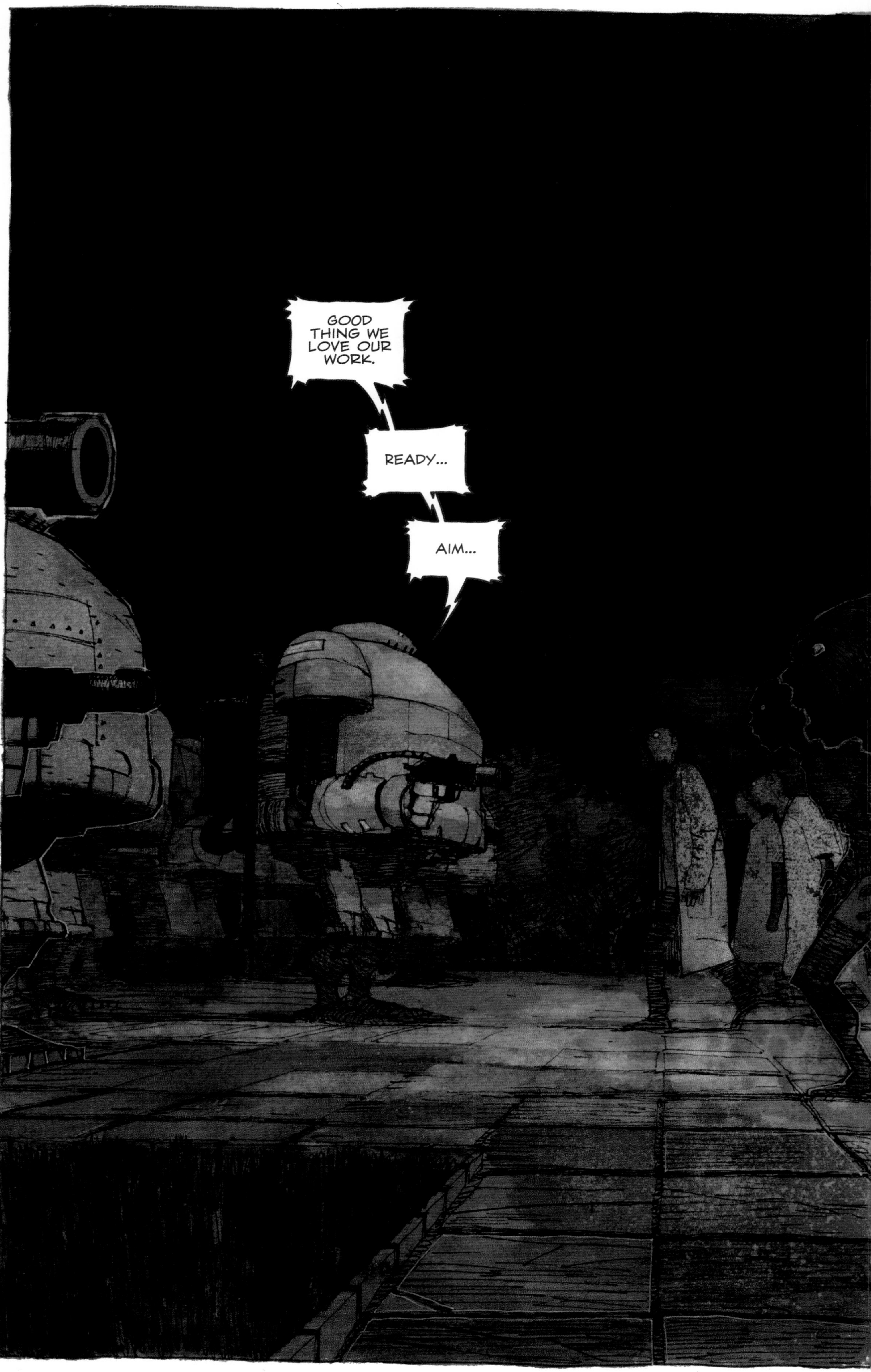
GOOD THING WE LOVE OUR WORK.
READY...
AIM...

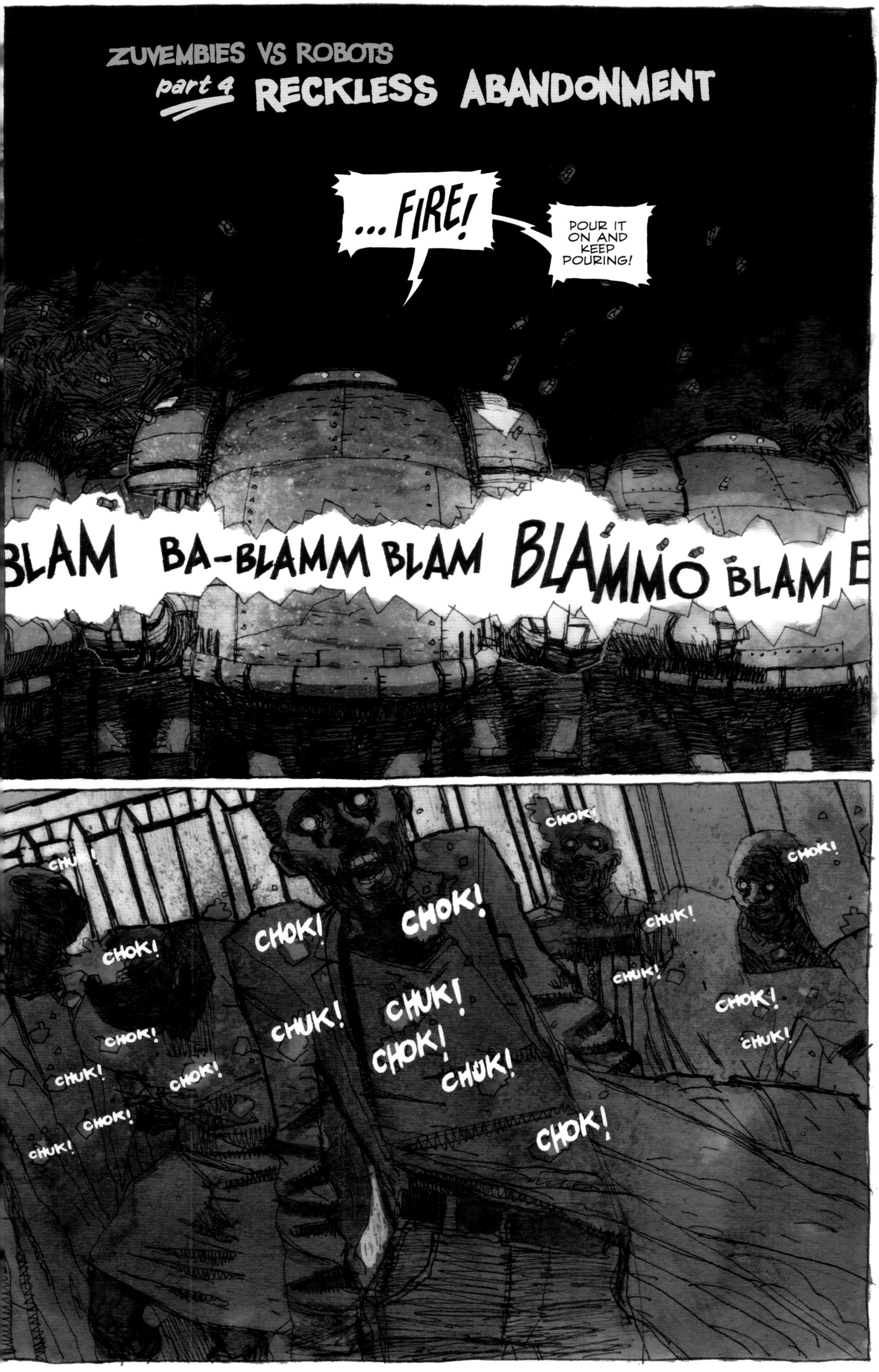
ZUVEMBIES VS ROBOTS
part 4 RECKLESS ABANDONMENT
...FIRE!
POUR IT ON AND KEEP POURING!
BLAM BA-BLAMM BLAM BLAMMO BLAM
CHUK! CHOK! CHOK! CHOK! CHOK! CHUK! CHOK!
CHUK! CHUK! CHUK! CHOK! CHOK! CHUK! CHOK! CHUK!
CHUK! CHOK! CHUK! CHOK! CHOK!

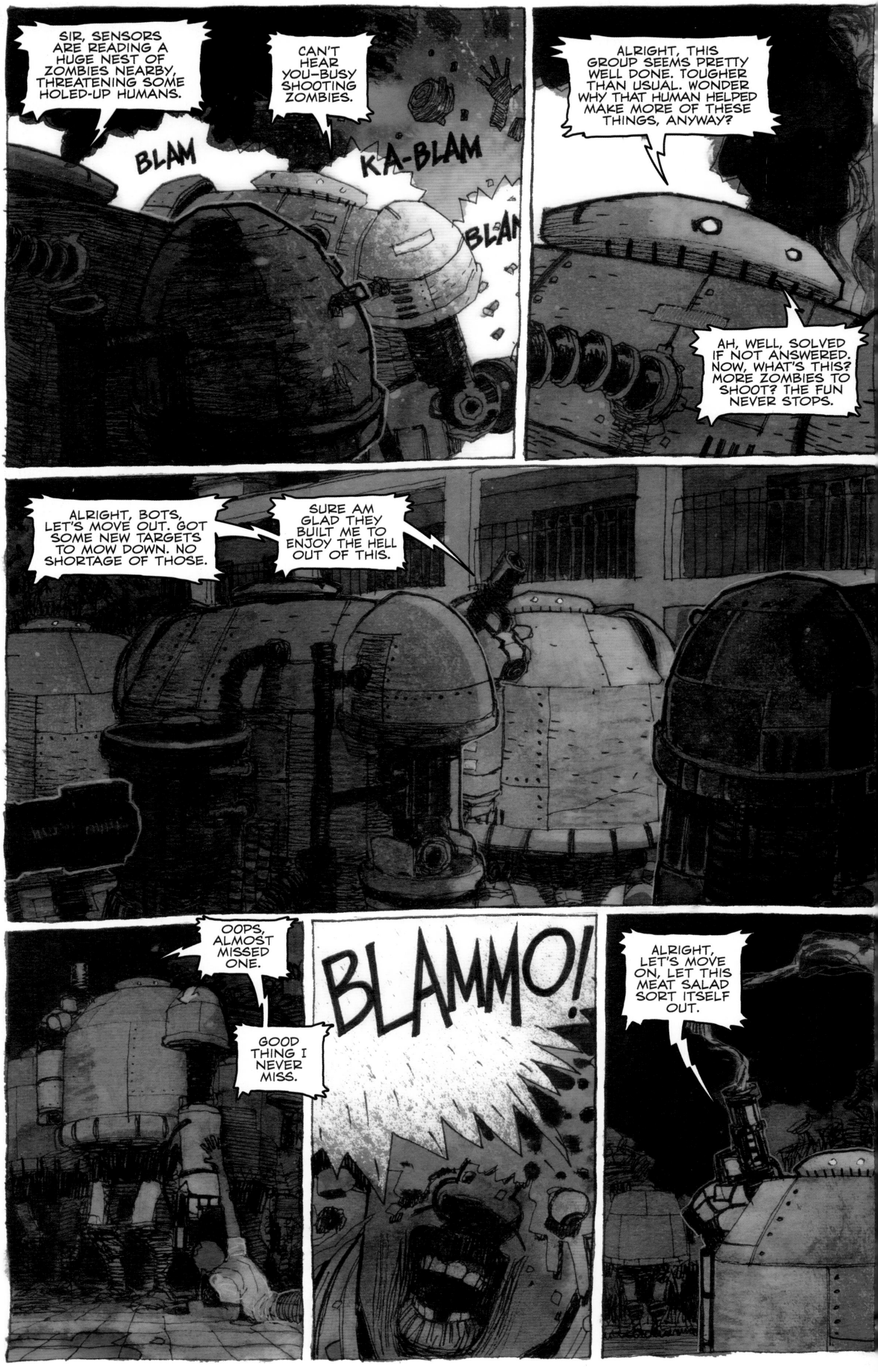
SIR, SENSORS ARE READING A HUGE NEST OF ZOMBIES NEARBY, THREATENING SOME HOLED-UP HUMANS.
BLAM
CAN'T HEAR YOU–BUSY SHOOTING ZOMBIES.
KA-BLAM
BLAM
ALRIGHT, THIS GROUP SEEMS PRETTY WELL DONE. TOUGHER THAN USUAL. WONDER WHY THAT HUMAN HELPED MAKE MORE OF THESE THINGS, ANYWAY?
AH, WELL, SOLVED IF NOT ANSWERED. NOW, WHAT'S THIS? MORE ZOMBIES TO SHOOT? THE FUN NEVER STOPS.
ALRIGHT, BOTS, LET'S MOVE OUT. GOT SOME NEW TARGETS TO MOW DOWN. NO SHORTAGE OF THOSE.
SURE AM GLAD THEY BUILT ME TO ENJOY THE HELL OUT OF THIS.
OOPS, ALMOST MISSED ONE.
GOOD THING I NEVER MISS.
BLAMMO!
ALRIGHT, LET'S MOVE ON, LET THIS MEAT SALAD SORT ITSELF OUT.

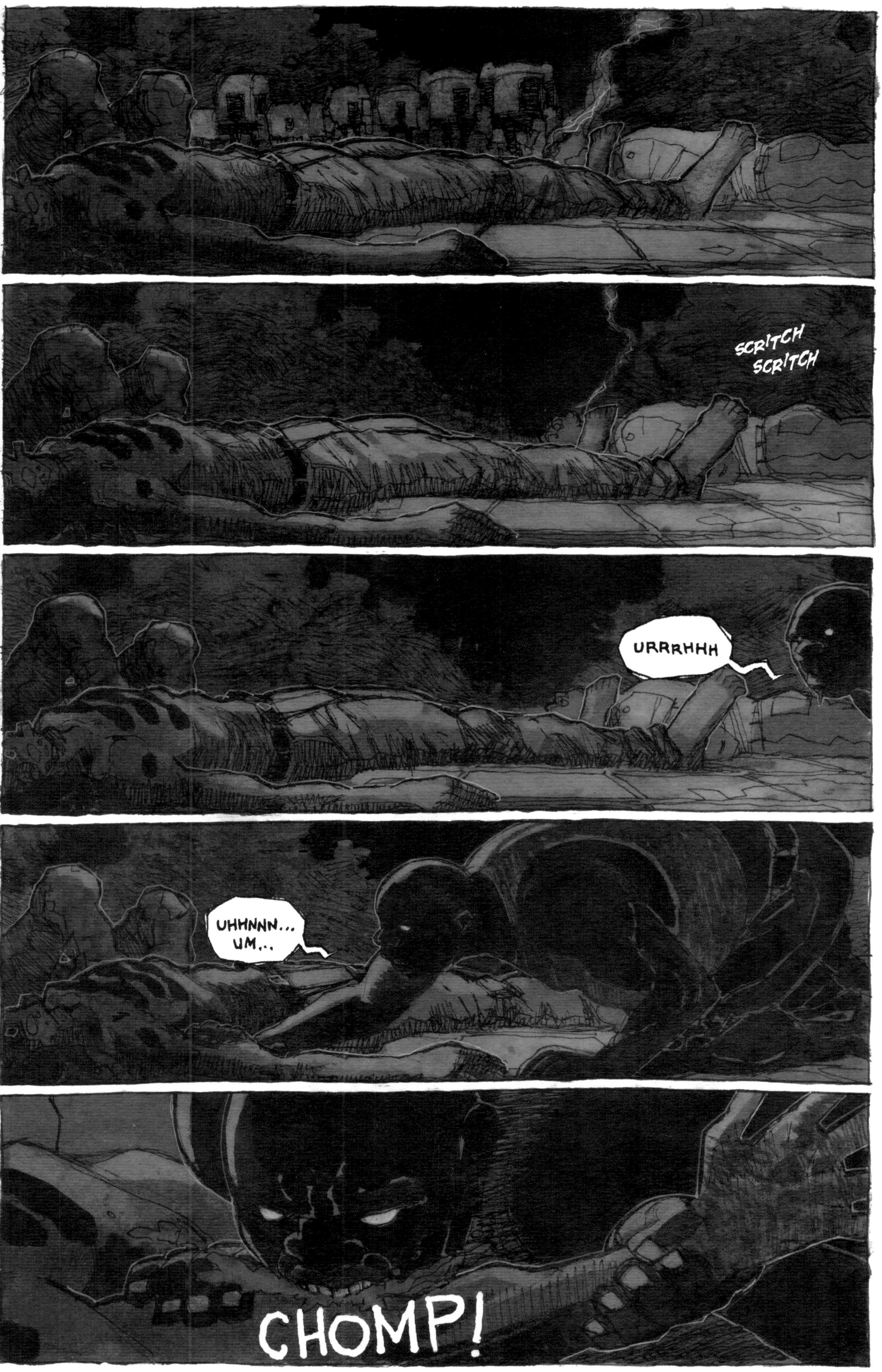
SCRITCH
SCRITCH
URRRHHH
UHHNNN...
UM...
CHOMP!

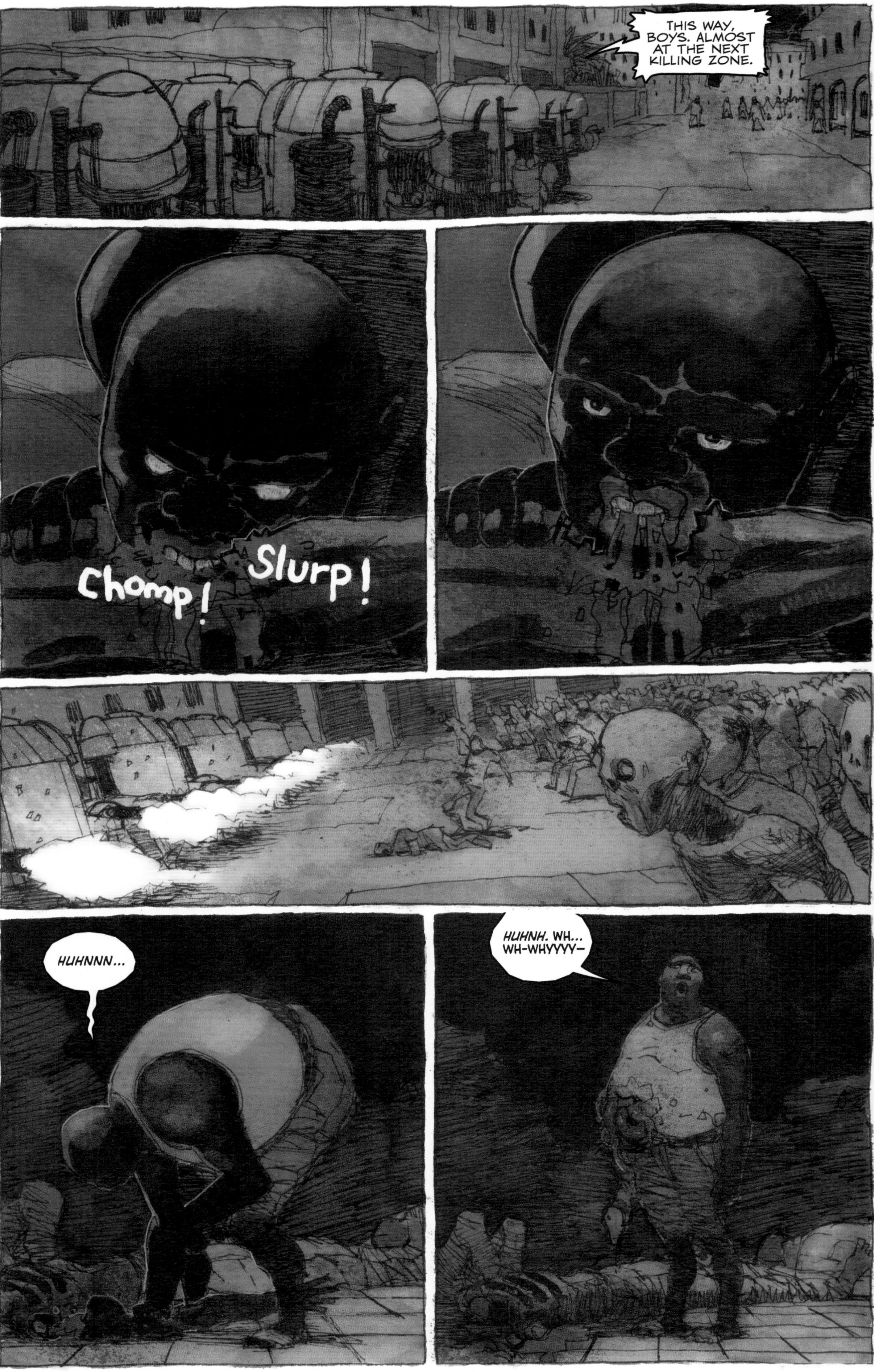
THIS WAY, BOYS. ALMOST AT THE NEXT KILLING ZONE.
Chomp!
Slurp!
HUHNNN...
HUHNH. WH... WH-WHYYYY-

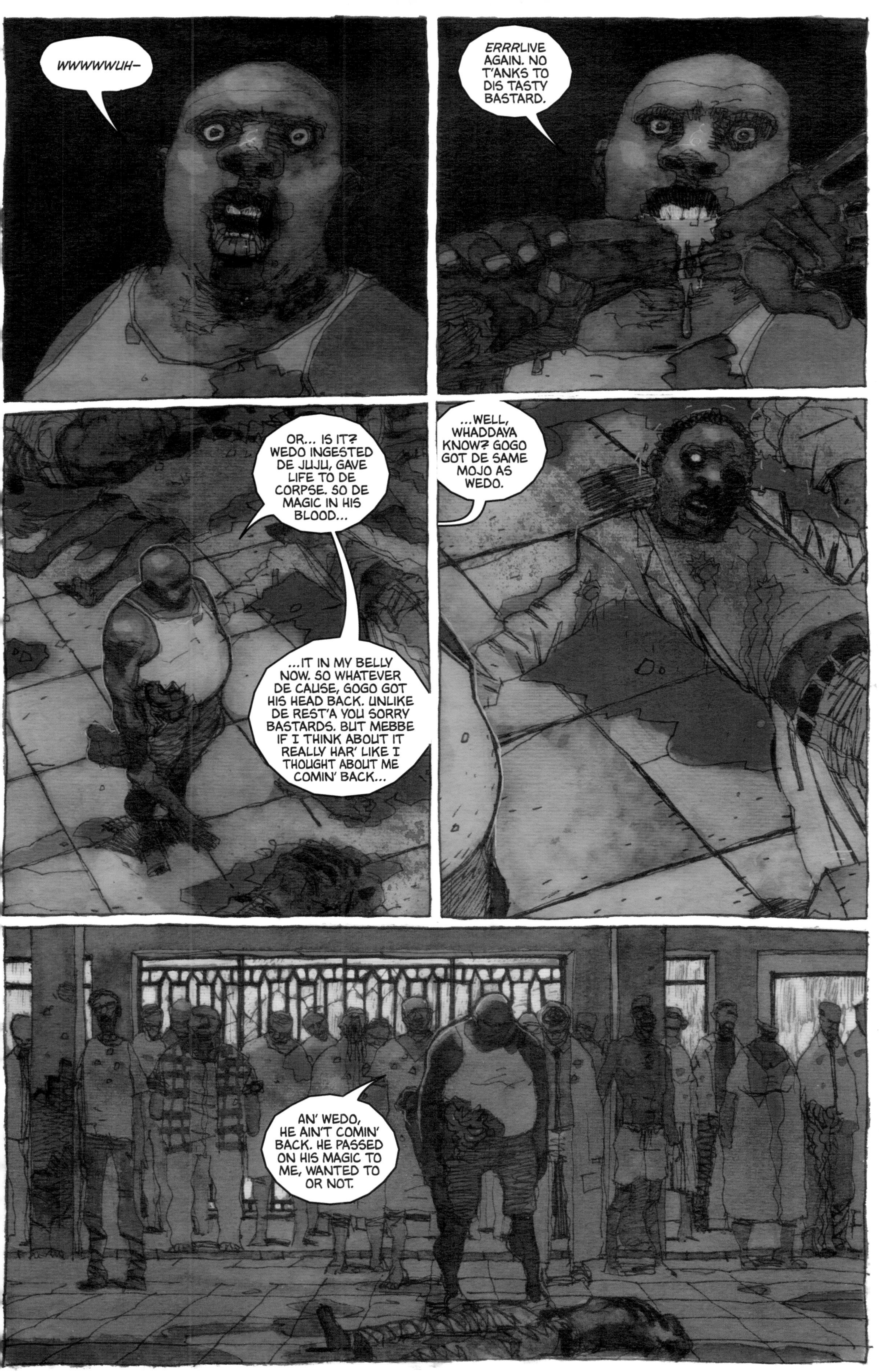
WWWWWUH–
ERRRLIVE AGAIN. NO T'ANKS TO DIS TASTY BASTARD.
OR... IS IT? WEDO INGESTED DE JUJU, GAVE LIFE TO DE CORPSE. SO DE MAGIC IN HIS BLOOD...
...IT IN MY BELLY NOW. SO WHATEVER DE CAUSE, GOGO GOT HIS HEAD BACK. UNLIKE DE REST'A YOU SORRY BASTARDS. BUT MEBBE IF I THINK ABOUT IT REALLY HAR' LIKE I THOUGHT ABOUT ME COMIN' BACK...
...WELL, WHADDAYA KNOW? GOGO GOT DE SAME MOJO AS WEDO.
AN' WEDO, HE AIN'T COMIN' BACK. HE PASSED ON HIS MAGIC TO ME, WANTED TO OR NOT.

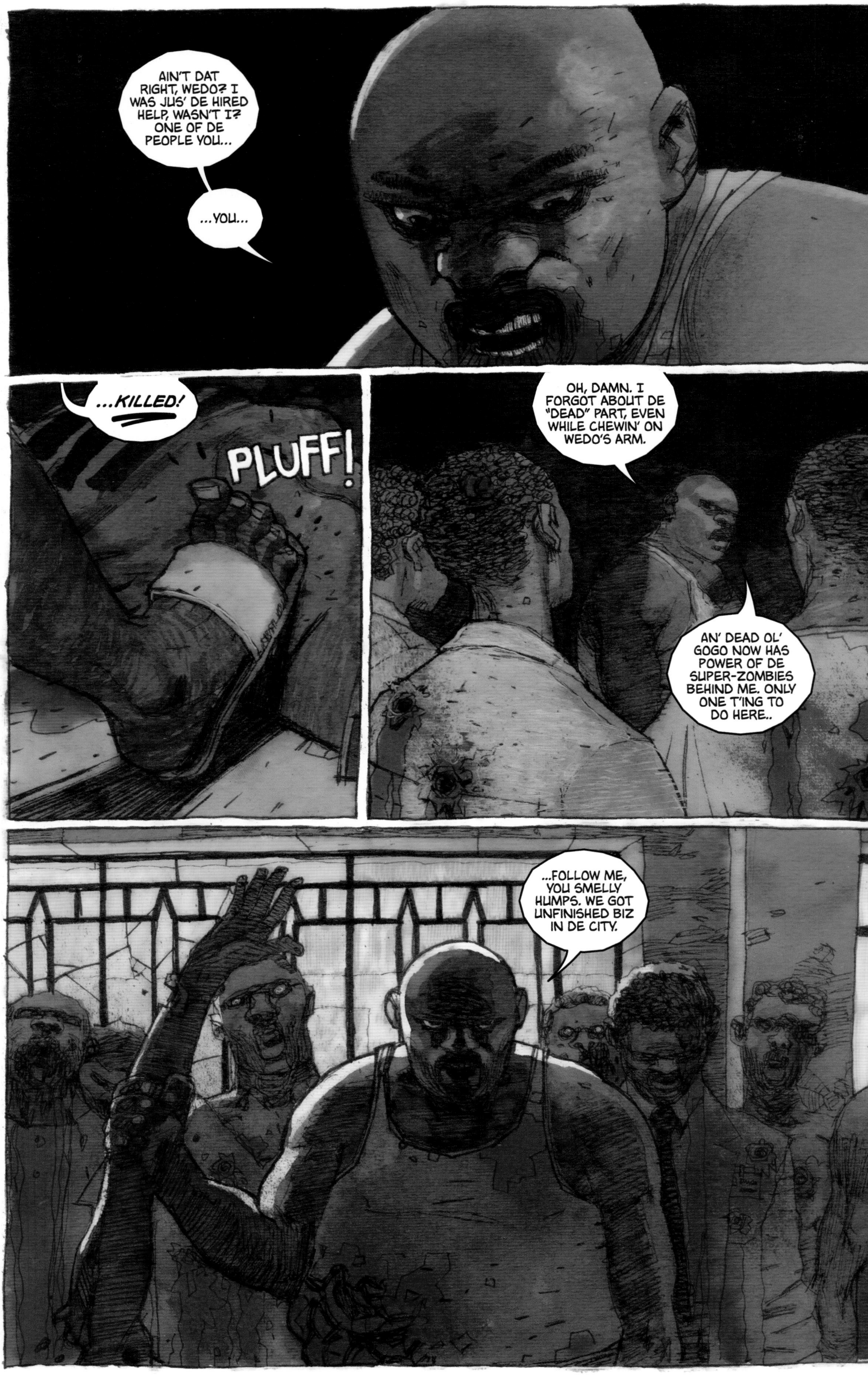
AIN'T DAT RIGHT, WEDO? I WAS JUS' DE HIRED HELP, WASN'T I? ONE OF DE PEOPLE YOU...
...YOU...
...KILLED!
PLUFF!
OH, DAMN. I FORGOT ABOUT DE "DEAD" PART, EVEN WHILE CHEWIN' ON WEDO'S ARM.
AN' DEAD OL' GOGO NOW HAS POWER OF DE SUPER-ZOMBIES BEHIND ME. ONLY ONE T'ING TO DO HERE..
...FOLLOW ME, YOU SMELLY HUMPS. WE GOT UNFINISHED BIZ IN DE CITY.

MAKING THE MESS IS SO MUCH MORE FUN THAN CLEANING IT UP. THE SWEEPER-BOTS MUST HATE US.

BLAM

BLAM

BLAM

BLAM

BLAM

BLAM

BLAM

BLAM

BLAM

THE SWEEPER-BOTS CAN GO UNSCREW.

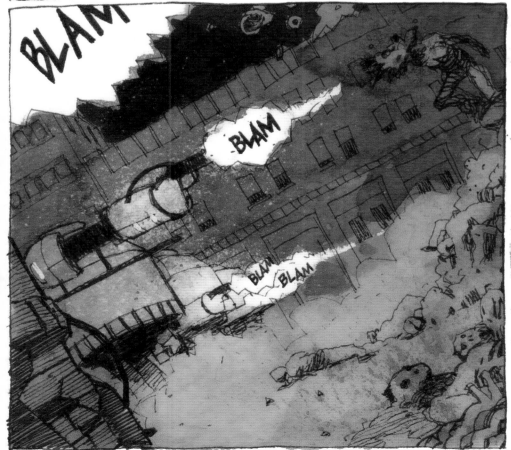

BLAM

BLAM

BLAM

BLAM

CEASE FIRE! I THINK THIS POD'S DONE FOR, TOO. WHERE WE HEADED NEXT?

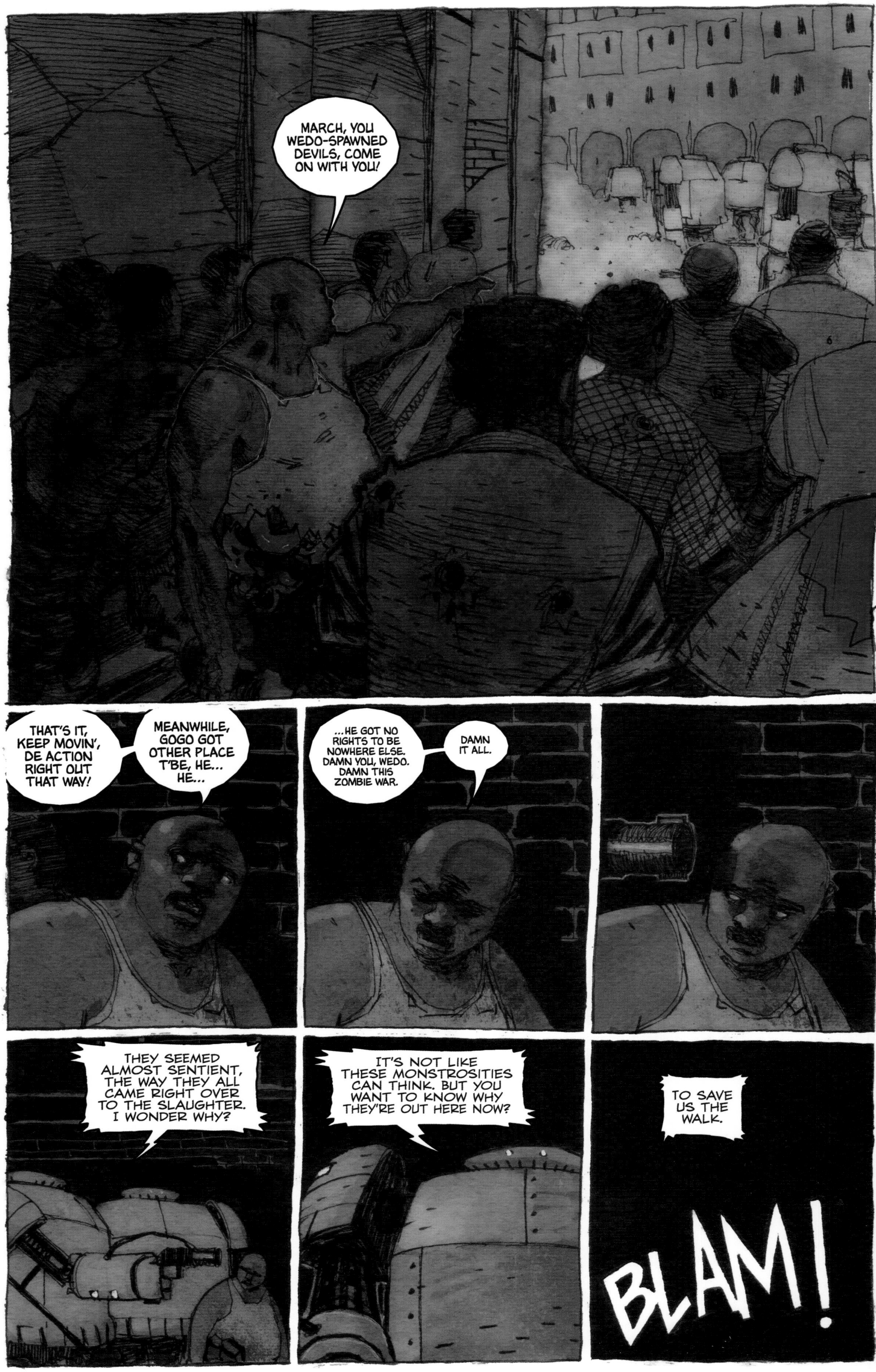
MARCH, YOU WEDO-SPAWNED DEVILS, COME ON WITH YOU!
THAT'S IT, KEEP MOVIN', DE ACTION RIGHT OUT THAT WAY!
MEANWHILE, GOGO GOT OTHER PLACE T'BE, HE... HE...
...HE GOT NO RIGHTS TO BE NOWHERE ELSE. DAMN YOU, WEDO. DAMN THIS ZOMBIE WAR.
DAMN IT ALL.
THEY SEEMED ALMOST SENTIENT, THE WAY THEY ALL CAME RIGHT OVER TO THE SLAUGHTER. I WONDER WHY?
IT'S NOT LIKE THESE MONSTROSITIES CAN THINK. BUT YOU WANT TO KNOW WHY THEY'RE OUT HERE NOW?
TO SAVE US THE WALK.
BLAM!

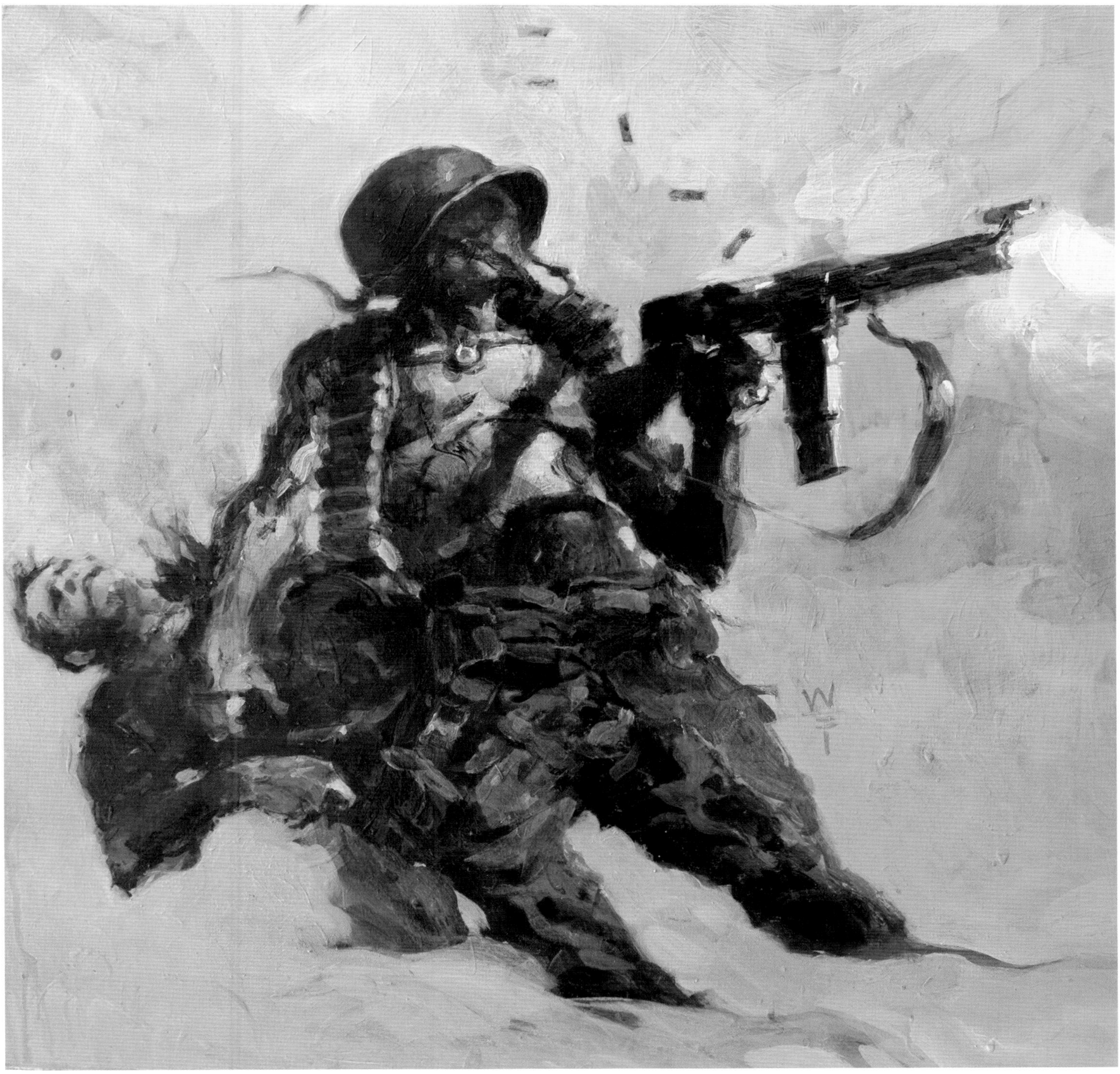

Art Gallary by **Ashley Wood**

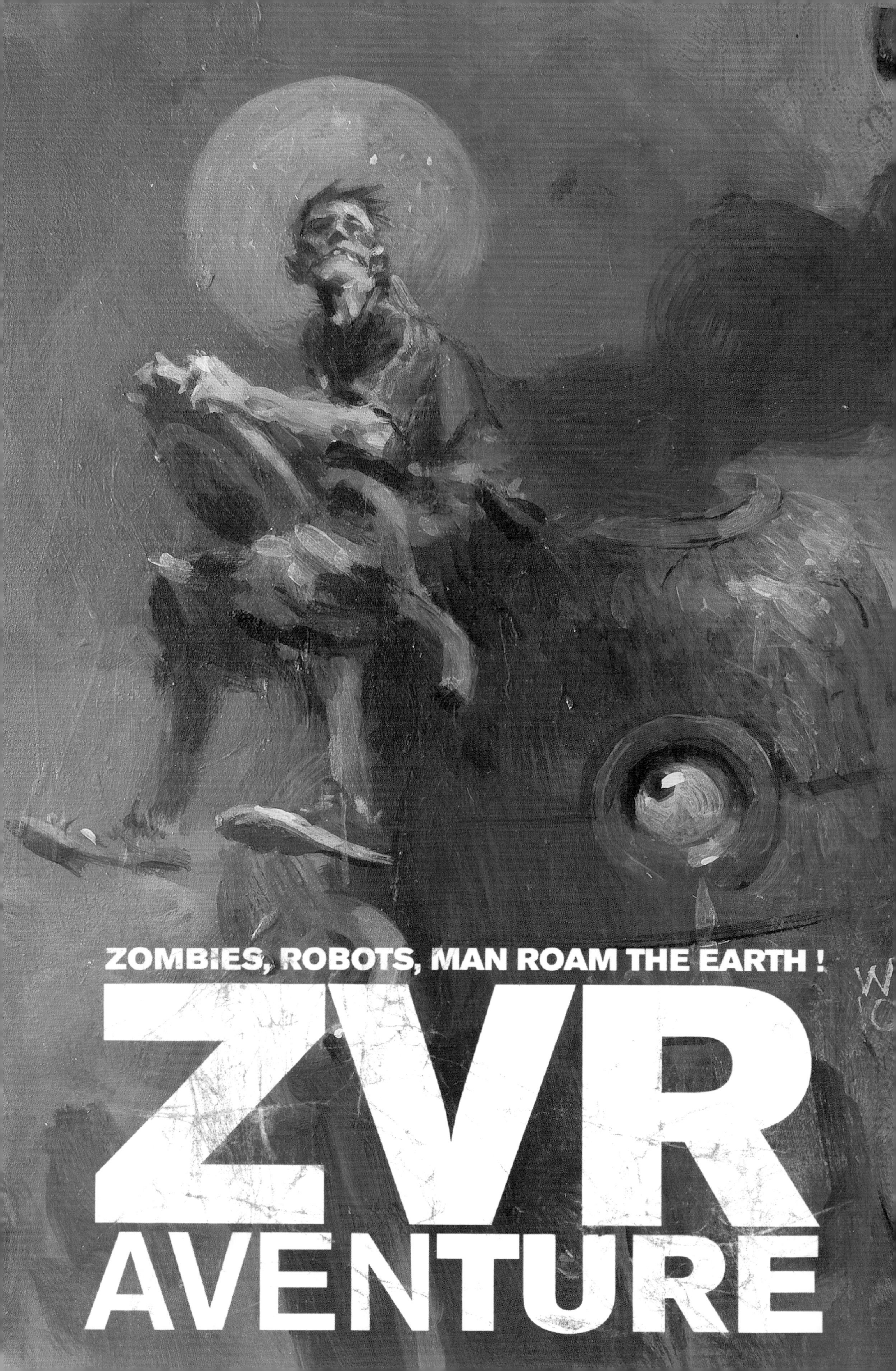
ZOMBIES, ROBOTS, MAN ROAM THE EARTH !
ZVR
AVENTURE

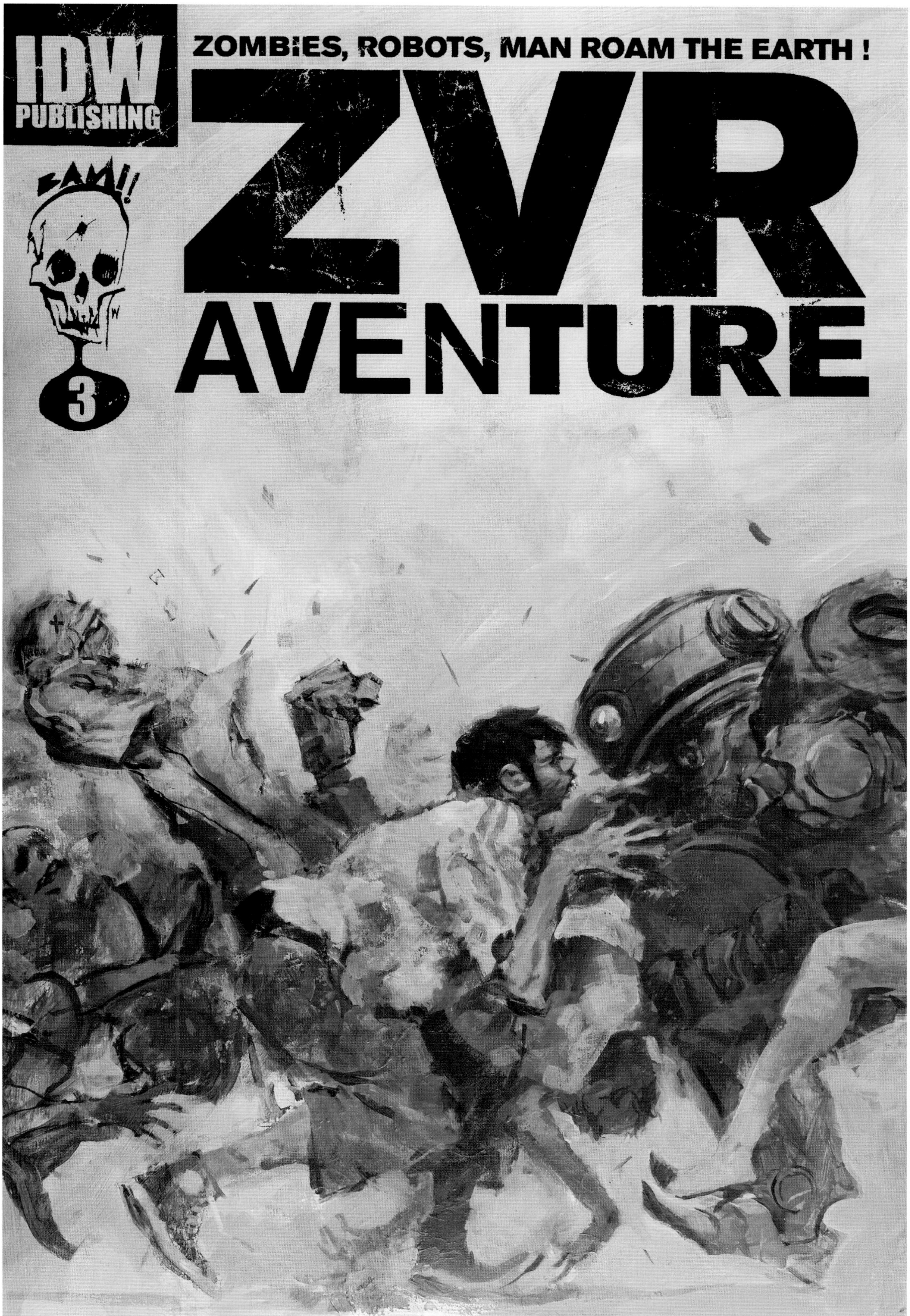

IDW PUBLISHING
ZOMBIES, ROBOTS, MAN ROAM THE EARTH !
ZVR
AVENTURE
BAM!!
3

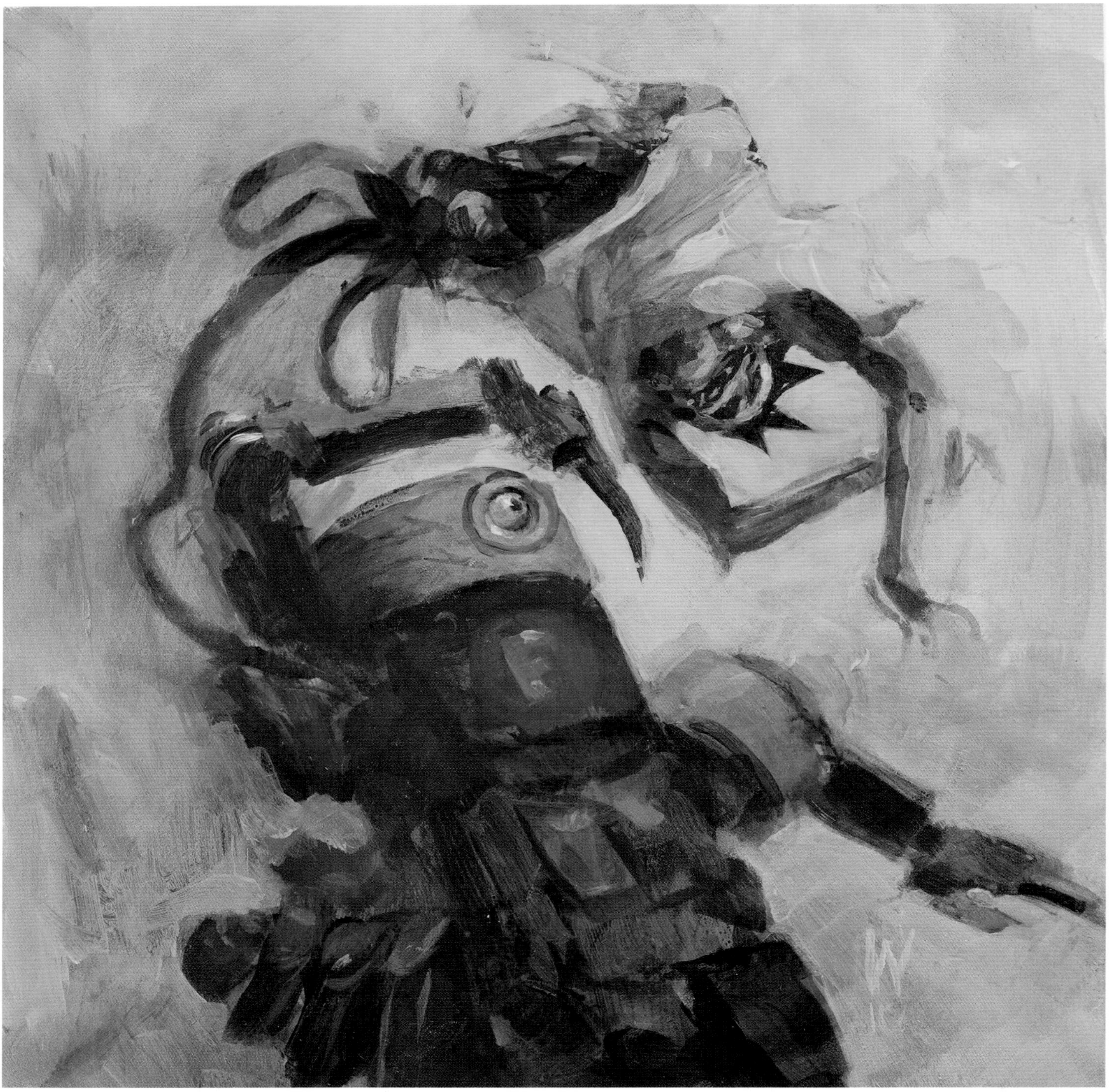

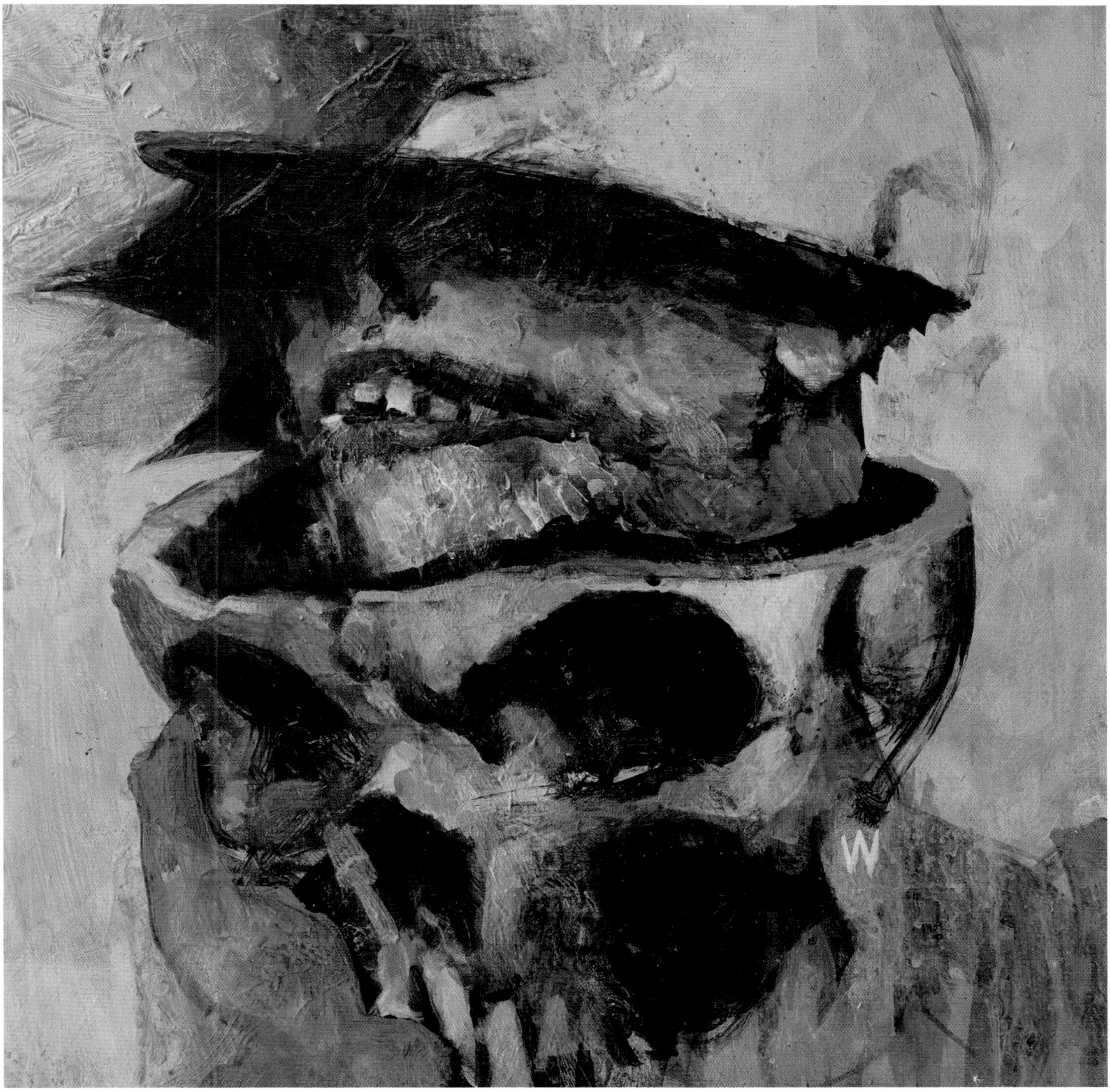

ZOMBIES, ROBOTS, MAN ROAM THE EARTH !

ZVR AVENTURE

4